Sallie Martin

MOTHER OF GOSPEL MUSIC

MUSIC IN AMERICAN LIFE

The Music in American Life series documents and celebrates the dynamic and multifaceted relationship between music and American culture. From its first publication in 1972 through its half-century mark and beyond, the series has embraced a wide variety of methodologies, from biography and memoir to history and musical analysis, and spans the full range of musical forms, from classical through all types of vernacular music. The series showcases the wealth of musical practice and expression that characterizes American music, as well as the rich diversity of its stylistic, regional, racial, ethnic, and gendered contexts. Characterized by a firm grounding in material culture, whether archival or ethnographic, and by work that honors the musical activities of ordinary people and their communities, Music in American Life continually redefines and expands the very definition of what constitutes music in American culture, whose voices are heard, and how music and musical practices are understood and valued.

For a list of books in the series, please see our website at www.press.uillinois.edu.

MOTHER OF GOSPEL MUSIC

KAY NORTON

UNIVERSITY OF ILLINOIS PRESS
Urbana, Chicago, and Springfield

Publication of this book was supported in part by grants from the Judith McCulloh Endowment for American Music, the Joseph Kerman Fund, and the General Fund of the American Musicological Society.

Manufactured in the United States of America
1 2 3 4 5 C P 5 4 3 2 1
∞ This book is printed on acid-free paper.

Library of Congress Cataloging-in-Publication Data
Names: Norton, Kay author
Title: Sallie Martin, mother of gospel music / Kay Norton.
Description: Urbana: University of Illinois Press, 2025. | Series: Music in American life | Includes bibliographical references and index.
Identifiers: LCCN 2025023596 (print) | LCCN 2025023597 (ebook) | ISBN 9780252046964 hardcover | ISBN 9780252089114 paperback | ISBN 9780252048616 ebook
Subjects: LCSH: Martin, Sallie, 1895–1988 | Sallie Martin Singers /no2003025502 | Gospel singers—United States—Biography | Gospel music—History and criticism | LCGFT: Biographies
Classification: LCC ML420.M27375 N67 2025 (print) | LCC ML420.M27375 (ebook) | DDC 782.25/4092—dc23/eng/20250520
LC record available at https://lccn.loc.gov/2025023596
LC ebook record available at https://lccn.loc.gov/2025023597

The manufacturer's authorized representative in the EU for product safety is Mare Nostrum Group B.V., Mauritskade 21D, 1091 GC Amsterdam, The Netherlands. Email: gpsr@mare-nostrum.co.uk

To Sallie Martin
and all the fierce women

Contents

Acknowledgments

My Sallie Martin project will have spanned ten years and generated countless inquiries and conversations by the time of its publication in book form. In this section, I hope I've mentioned a majority of all those who have informed, upheld, and inspired me.

This book and the publications leading to it have benefitted from several anonymous reviewers, one in particular to whom I'm especially grateful for holding my feet to the fire. Others were known to me and include Karen Ahlquist, Judith A. Mabary, Marva Carter, Deborah Smith Pollard, Johari Jabir, Ashon Crawley, and Robert M. Marovich, who, in addition to answering dozens of questions spanning the decade of our acquaintance to date, arranged for me to meet Kenneth Woods Jr.

I was fortunate to interview Kenneth Morris's middle son, Reginald Morris, in February of 2016, in the home where he grew up. Marcella Thomas was kind to discuss briefly the history of First Church of Deliverance with me in February of 2023. Worshipping at First Church that week, under the leadership of Rev. James R. Bryson Jr., was a profound and moving experience.

I'm thankful for the many scholars whose work has stimulated my thoughts and informed this book. They include Tammy Kernodle, Mark Burford, Birgitta Johnson, Jacqueline DjeDje, Horace Clarence Boyer, Anthony Heilbut, Michael Harris, Sandra Graham, Wallace Best, Rae Linda Brown, Judith Tick, Robert Darden, Nina Sun Eidsheim, Alicia Lola Jones, Roxanne Reed, Jonathan M. Bryant, Naomi André, Bernice Johnson Reagon, Laurraine Goreau, James Standifer, Luvenia George, and Robert Marovich.

Archivists who attended to my repeated requests include Kay Peterson at the Archives Center of the National Museum of American History, Jena Jones at the Atlanta History Center, and Amy Sherwood at Columbia College Chicago.

I received travel funding, a book subvention, and sabbatical leaves from the School of Music, Dance, and Theatre and the Herberger Institute for Design and the Arts at Arizona State University. In the musicology/ethnomusicology area, we cover for each other and I'm thankful that my colleagues did that for me in fall of 2016 and again in spring of 2023. I am also indebted to the Director of Music, Dance, and Theatre at ASU, Heather Landes, for her continuing support.

My other friends don't realize just how much I appreciate their support. I'm looking at you, Helen Johnston, Catherine J. Nichols, Kim Holmes, Kim Simonis, and colleague-friends Marg Schmidt, Ted Solís, and Julie Codell. Jeannie Dawson and Randy Dawson drove me around the area of Penfield, Georgia, and my cousin, Lisa Vaughan Smith, gave me a tour of Scull Shoals, all of which helped me write chapter 1. Jan Vartzikos and Walt Shoemaker allowed me to stay in their home on Capitol Hill more than once, but especially during an eleven-day research trip to the National Museum of American History. In that fall of 2015, I decided on the topic for my next book.

Laurie Matheson, former head of acquisitions of the Music in American Life Series, University of Illinois Press, made it clear in our first conversation that she would love to see a book on Sallie Martin. Thanks for your confidence in me and the topic. Her successor, Mariah Mendes Schaefer, stepped confidently into the editor position and guided me through final stages of submission and publication. I have been extremely lucky to work with these women as my advocates.

I am thankful for almost daily gestures of support, and for the Sallie Martin Lego set, from Charlie Norton Hill, my most excellent son. Your integrity, creativity, and thoughtfulness never fail to move me.

Once I understood how I wanted to approach Sallie Martin, I became weighed down with the enormity of this goal, worrying for the obvious reason: I am not Black. I worked my way out of that insecurity by spending mental time with several Black Americans I've known and who indirectly invited me to observe their worlds. Mrs. Wilhelmina Bowles, my high school teacher, is my model of Sallie Martin's authority, dignity, and expertise. Catherine Cooper found a way to thrive as the only Black cheerleader on our high school squad; she let us form a white shell around her as we entered away team gyms, allowing us to believe that it made a difference in her safety. I remembered a rainy Sunday on a European choir tour when Wendy Washington explained the intricacies of caring for Black hair. Vanita Moon helped me understand how it is to be the first Black woman to win a historically white award. Floanche Thompson and I navigated hilarious and unexpected times in a small French hotel. Howard Gant showed me how it works to negotiate without accommodating. Stephen Marc taught my son and me why Black men in Phoenix still put their hands on the dashboard, rather than reaching for their driver's license, at traffic stops. Jennie Allen trusted me enough to share struggle, frustration, and joy. Sharon Dryer-Jones engaged me in a big talk about faith. Many students who cannot be named have educated me in endless ways. This a partial list, but if I've struck a note that's true about Sallie Martin's Black experience, it's because these and other people trusted me to understand, just a little. Thank you.

Introduction

I teach a graduate seminar called "Writing the History of Women in Music"—a 1980s title, to be sure. If I hadn't already been convinced that it still belongs in a twenty-first-century music curriculum, trying to write definitively about Sallie Martin these past ten years would have convinced me of that fact. Agreeing with Leo Treitler that music history is a "discourse of myth through which 'Western civilization' contemplates and presents itself," I was still struck by strange tidbits in early Sallie Martin accounts, given that she was steering the bus, so to speak, when gospel gained traction in the 1930s and spread rapidly afterwards.[1] Anthony Heilbut, a gospel enthusiast whose book Martin recommended to an interviewer, offers praise ("Sallie Martin is real, and everyone trusts her to be herself"), but occasionally turns patronizing ("Once again, it's Sallie Martin against the world").[2] Michael W. Harris, informed by multiple interviews with Thomas A. Dorsey and a conversation with Martin, followed a similar pattern. He confirmed her centrality to Dorsey's first business, but editorialized that she was "characteristically brusque," a woman possessing a zeal "all too customary." He labeled one of her greatest accomplishments "guerrilla tactics," referring to her long track record of establishing new Gospel Choral Unions as regional chapters of the National Convention of Gospel Choirs and Choruses (NCGCC), then keeping them motivated about traveling to the annual Convention.[3] In *The Golden Age of Gospel*, the respected practitioner and scholar Horace Clarence Boyer reiterated what others had written; she was "argumentative and adversarial by nature and constantly on the attack."[4] Small wonder that Roxanne Reed perpetuated the tone of these writings in the twenty-first century, when she interviewed Chicago gospel informants for her 2003 dissertation. About Roberta Martin, Reed asked, "What was her personality like?"; but about Sallie Martin, Reed asked, "Was she very demanding? Intimidating?"[5] Some early writers knew Martin and may have expressed their own impressions of her, but Thomas A. Dorsey's own ambivalence toward Martin ("Sallie can't sing a lick, but she can get over anywhere in the world"; "It was a great loss to me for her to go") is the likely origin of this historical thread.[6] His words, as well as their persistent echoes, have left a lasting impression that receives due attention in this book.

Previous writers also foregrounded Sallie Martin's innate flair for building and running a music publishing company.[7] Those qualities, her combative nature and business acumen, were the two sides of the Sallie Martin coin that had been transmitted when I began this book. Henry Louis Gates Jr.'s important documentary entitled *GOSPEL* (2024) is but the latest installment in a popular history that ultimately devalues Martin's fuller legacy. I needed to understand how someone with such a difficult personality could have done business and collaborated with as many other musicians as she did. The historical record required greater granularity.

I found that Sallie Martin's singing voice, unique in many ways, provided an important window into her world. Strident and warm in turns, sometimes rugged overall, her upper range could be unpredictable, but her open-throated bass notes could also thrill the listener. Her intonation and sense of meter and syncopation were usually spot on in recordings. As she aged, her voice developed a waver, but it's almost impossible to find an instance of her singing without energetic intention. Martin cultivated a wide range of vocal intensities and timbres and fully utilized them as she filled roles of gospel narrator, soloist, ensemble singer, or source of the fundamental pitch in a harmonic structure. However, despite being named alongside Marion Williams, Willie Mae Ford Smith, and Mahalia Jackson as one of the "majestic soloists" of gospel in a 1997 *Rolling Stone* article, Martin's voice was not beautiful in the ways of those divas.[8] Her vocality was more closely wedded to her purpose, and her performativity better suited to demonstrating songs before an audience than recording in a studio.

The more I read, listened, and considered how best to approach the career of such a performer, the more convinced I became that, in common perception, Sallie Martin's reportedly combative personality had become indistinguishable from her vocal sound. Nina Eidsheim describes this phenomenon: "What we conceive of as a single voice . . . is a manifestation of a given culture's understanding of the vocalizer and [their] role within that culture," and further, "vocal timbre is often used to make truth claims about voice and the person emitting the vocal sound."[9] I suspected that reports of Martin's prickly nature had been exaggerated and that her voice had been wrongly aligned with a partial fiction. Gospel historians before me had replicated an incomplete picture and that image had become canonic.

Martin's very particular singing voice was perfectly suited for the cultural work in which she engaged. At the outset of her career in the late 1920s, she heard about Thomas A. Dorsey and auditioned for him. Formerly a blues piano player for Ma Rainey, Dorsey had not been successful in introducing his gospel blues to mainline churches. In 1929, Dorsey recognized in Sallie Martin's voice a partial solution to his problem. Not only was she capable of supplying the lowest notes in his female Quartette, but she had mastered the highly inflected rhythms and timbres of an evangelical "shouter" during her years in the Holiness church. She was a true force of personality and a dynamic front woman, and could as easily ignite an audience for Dorsey's songs as she could for the Lord. When she sang, people got excited.

Martin's natural timbre was further roughened by the hard usage she and Dorsey required of it in the 1930s, before microphones were readily available, as she remembered:

> [When] I started to traveling as a soloist for Mr. Dorsey, . . . there was nobody, that . . . I could say, . . . maybe they can relieve me. . . . We used to go to Vermont Avenue Baptist Church in Washington, DC. It seats 2,000 people. They would have their place packed at twenty-five cents admission, no kind of a microphone, but it was just as easy as using a microphone, because the Lord prepares you for that age, whatever you go through with seems like the Lord makes it possible . . . (Now I couldn't really . . . work today without a microphone, see), . . . [but back then] I would have to . . . run sixteen or seventeen numbers. . . . Nobody was there that I could say, "will you do a number for me."[10]

This explanation was but one in an arsenal of defenses Martin kept at the ready in later life. She also liked to quip, "If Mahalia [Jackson] is a Cadillac and Roberta [Martin] is a Buick, I'm just a Motel T Ford, but I make it over the hill without shifting gears, and that is what counts, church, I make it over the hill." That was her measure of success; during her ten years' professional association with Dorsey, her durable voice had allowed them to keep going. Alongside a handful of Chicago composers and performers, the Dorsey and Martin team eventually created a place for the new gospel in mainline denominational worship. The success had unanticipated consequences for Martin, however. New audiences drew Dorsey into a new aesthetic. Having accomplished his initial goal and, it must be said, likely fatigued by her overbearing nature, Dorsey came to regard everything about Sallie Martin as unrefined and difficult.

The termination of her business relationship with Thomas A. Dorsey in 1939 was a watershed in Martin's life. Well-informed people have insisted, off the record, that Martin had wanted a romantic relationship with Dorsey after his first wife passed away. Dorsey had married Nettie Harper, a sweetheart from his days in Ma Rainey's band, in 1925. Sallie Martin began work as Dorsey's song demonstrator in 1929 and her own unhappy marriage soon dissolved. Nettie did not survive the birth of the Dorseys' first child in 1932, and their newborn son died shortly after she did.[11] Dorsey remained a widower between that time and 1941, when he married Kathryn Mosley (1915–2011). For seven years, from Nettie's death until 1939, years that saw the founding of the NCGCC in 1933, Sallie Martin poured her formidable energy into building an empire alongside a tall, handsome, creative, and increasingly powerful musician: one clearly poised to change the world of Black religious music. It seems reasonable that Martin may have fallen for Dorsey, hoping that her personal and professional lives might align and her sweat equity might pay off. In some ways, it would have been surprising had Sallie Martin *not* hoped for a personal relationship with Thomas A. Dorsey. Yet, it was not to be. In her accounts of the split, Martin cites his failure to defend her against her critics—a justifiable sentiment, given her contributions to his early success. Free with a sharp word, she probably had accrued her share of detractors by 1939. In fact, Dorsey may have felt the need to disengage himself from a singer whose shout style—essential to the early years of his gospel career—had fallen out of fashion, and whose emotions presented him with an inconvenient personal situation.

Whatever caused the rift with Dorsey, the result must have felt like a public shaming to Sallie Martin. Their lucrative collaboration was well known and admired, then suddenly, it was over. She never lived down that moment, judging by the relish with which the tale of her unrequited love continues to be recounted. Still, their work in the NCGCC and elsewhere demanded that the two maintain a cordial working relationship, which they did until her death. In payment for his lack of faith in her, Martin frequently reminded Dorsey that she had been the one most responsible for building his business.[12]

Never one to be deterred for long, Martin proved in short order that a business association with Thomas A. Dorsey was not a requirement for her success. Snappish though she was, her personal traits were well matched to the negotiation of her sexist, class-biased, and racist world. She established herself as a singer, a Christian celebrity, and a musical matriarch. Martin could be expected to put her words to action and thus, she effectively modeled Black female entrepreneurship. Not all her relationships were negatively affected by her brittle nature. In the NCGCC, as well as in performances, Martin successfully cooperated within a powerful sisterhood (and neighborhood) of equally strong personalities. Had Martin been afforded the deference naturally extended to male gospel stars such as Thomas A. Dorsey or Thurston Frazier, for example, or the powerful ministers of her day such as Clarence H. Cobbs, Junius C. Austin, or John L. Branham, she might have adopted a more approachable demeanor. In her real world, however, she maintained a siege mentality, well-honed through experience. Martin felt no need to overhaul her personality; as she was fond of saying, her gifts had taken her everywhere she wanted to go in life.

In the following chapters, I document the rapidly changing worlds of a woman propelled by extraordinary business intuition and self-knowledge ("I always really thought myself *somebody*. I've been somebody all my life").[13] I've sought to understand the meaning of her presence in gospel history by viewing Sallie Martin through several different lenses in the following chapters. Together, these perspectives bring a singular heroine in the history of American music into sharper focus.

Naively, I expected to find records that would reveal what had not previously been known: Sallie Martin's maiden name and information about her family of origin. In fact, despite a highly publicized life, she buried that information too well. I was left to learn about the young Sallie Martin through her birthplace and a handful of her memories shared in two important interviews. I looked for cultural and environmental origins of her capacity to aim high and her boldness to strike out for new environments from Penfield and Greene County, as well as Atlanta, Georgia. The result is my portrait of a racist world that could not suppress Martin's native gifts (chapter 1).[14]

In the 1930s, Sallie Martin worked as an unacknowledged partner in Thomas A. Dorsey's fledgling Chicago business and labored as diligently as he to define herself in light of the new phenomenon of gospel music. I spent some time imagining the Chicago of 1923 that met Martin as a newcomer. In the decade between 1923 and 1933, Martin made a place for herself in an exciting new musical movement. With Magnolia Lewis-Butts, Dorsey, Theodore Frye, and a handful of others, she developed the concept of a national gospel convention and was named its secretary for a year. To insure its orderly growth, she became the NCGCC's National Organizer of Gospel Choral Unions, initiating the work she continued for decades (chapter 2).

The intuitive Sallie Martin knew that self-naming would be the foundation of her professional reputation. She strategically built a personal brand beginning in the mid-1930s by controlling how her work in the NCGCC and the National Baptist Convention, performances, and tours were reported in the Black press. Song covers boosted her renown with phrases like, "as sung by Sallie Martin, Queen of Contraltos," or "as sung by Sallie Martin, evangelist."[15] The foundation of her co-owned business, Martin and Morris Music Studio (MMMS), gave her additional opportunities to develop as a professional and to shape public perception (chapter 3).

Martin's navigation of the ship of gospel professionalism in a racist, classist, and sexist world intersected often with the professional journeys of other women gospel pioneers. Shared biographical elements, together with fruitful collaborations on everything from joint tours to Convention committee work draw a fresh frame around more paternalistic accounts of Martin's personality. Summarizing the career ways of eight colleagues clarifies the role of women like Sallie Martin in the early history of gospel (chapter 4).

Martin struck out purposefully to Los Angeles soon after cofounding the MMMS, driven to expand her business to a new market. With the Sallie Martin Singers, she began her recording career, all the while maintaining the national touring crucial to the success of her business back in Chicago. She and her daughter, Cora, found belonging in the flourishing music department of LA's Saint Paul Baptist Church, whose Sunday evening worship services, broadcast on the radio, were frequented by Hollywood stars (chapter 5).

Martin's professional maturity is marked by the addition of international tours and a heightened focus on Christian fundraising: in particular, efforts to support a missionary cause in Nigeria. She also rebooted the Sallie Martin Singers after a hiatus caused by Cora Martin's retirement. The new version was trained by the young pianist and established composer Kenneth Woods Jr., whose engaging new songs and arrangements Martin took in stride, performing with characteristic enthusiasm on two albums on the Vee Jay label (chapter 6).

Retirement from national touring and the sale of her business interests in 1973 did not signal an end to Sallie Martin's active musical life. An appearance at the Newport Jazz Festival in 1975, an album recorded and dedicated to her at an Edwin Hawkins Seminar in Philadelphia in 1979, a European tour with the cantata *Gospel Caravan* the same year, and a cameo in the 1982 documentary *Say Amen, Somebody!* kept her name, voice, and image before the public.[16] Concluding paragraphs in this chapter weave together the primary threads of Sallie Martin's remarkable legacy first, through some of those she mentored, and finally, in a summary of her accomplishments (chapter 7).

A Note about Sexual Orientation

Some church folk prefer no mention at all to an affirming portrayal of a non-heterosexual historical figure. This is changing in some areas, but not in all.[17] Ashon Crawley shared with me his primary research concern:

> How to speak about the AIDS crisis, the pervasiveness of queer antagonism, the unkindness not only so many of the musicians, singers, and choir directors were made to carry, a shame that was not theirs to hold though they were still treated as such; but also how to speak about the ongoing queer antagonism that remains, the continued silence, the way silence about public health crises are internalized as personal, moral, ethical failures and, thus, theological demonstrations of individual sinfulness.[18]

Though this book mentions AIDS only in passing, Crawley's words resonate strongly with my perspective, that the long-held loyalty to guarding the open secret persisting in some circles reifies the notion that there is something wrong with non-heterosexual existence. That position has no place in this book. While it is undoubtedly true that Clarence Cobbs, James Cleveland, Arthur Atlas Peters, and a host of others who have been described as homosexual did not officially out themselves during their lifetimes, it is equally true that the coyness or omission required to maintain a decades-old fiction about these deceased musicians does violence to their legacies.

For what it's worth, a lone informant offered the possibility that Sallie Martin may not have been strictly heterosexual. If so, she kept that fact extremely well hidden. In the context of her entire life and in complete absence of any corroborating evidence, I have found her sexual identity inconsequential to her life story. Biographers of women are wise to avoid the perennial tropes about females who assume authority, assumptions that equate power and ambition with masculinity, and descriptions of such masculinity in women as lesbianism. Religious women of Martin's era negotiated this talk in creative ways. Minister Mary G. Evans adopted an overtly maternal persona, perhaps to desexualize her own body—so often on display—and neutralize the speculation that she was gay. Married preacher Lucy Smith cultivated the image of "Mother," together with "Overseer," a masculine-gendered term.[19] In this book, I honor the whole persons I discuss, and therefore will, when relevant and when established by more than a single source, treat their sexualities as I would any other aspect of personalities, as they relate to the career of Sallie Martin.

CHAPTER 1

Elusive Origins and the Power of Place

Penfield, Atlanta, and Cleveland

> I was born in Greene County, Georgia. That's out from Atlanta. Of course, I lived there with my mother, my grandmother, and my grandfather. Now, that was the family. . . . I've never known anything about my father.
> —Sallie Martin

If Sallie Martin (1895–1988) revealed the name of either biological parent or the family name by which she was known before she married Wallace Martin in 1915, it was never documented.[1] She did confirm that she was born in the small, northeastern Georgia town of Penfield.[2] Her ancestry will likely remain a mystery; still, there is more to know than that she was born in the Deep South, scarcely two generations removed from legal enslavement.[3] Penfield was in many ways a singular place for its location and era, and the consequences of its unusual history affected young Sallie Martin in several interconnected ways. First, prior to the Civil War, the average Black person living in rural Georgia would have had little experience traveling outside the plantations and farms they inhabited. Penfield, in contrast, was close to two vital arteries connecting it to the outside world, one natural and the other humanmade. The town stood eight miles east of the turbulent Oconee River, which since white settlement had facilitated both farming and the transfer of crops—managed mainly by the enslaved—to coastal Georgia and beyond. Further, after 1838, Penfield stood only eight miles west of a railroad that connected to the larger town of Athens in one direction, and in the other to Atlanta.

Second, Penfield was exceptional for one laxity practiced there before 1850. Though enslaved people in upland Georgia experienced all the cruelty and violence their coastal counterparts did, Greene County's comparatively small plantation owners chose not to enforce slave patrols, thereby opening a small window for the enslaved to visit neighboring farms. In brief moments of autonomy, desire and determination were given room to grow.

Also uniquely, among rural towns of its size, Sallie Martin's birthplace had been home to a Baptist university between 1838 and 1871. As she grew up in the late 1890s and 1900s, Martin could not have failed to notice the grand buildings left behind when Mercer University relocated to Macon, Georgia. These may have left her unmoved, or may have created a desire for grander things than Penfield could offer. More directly significant for Martin, planter-class Baptists in Penfield began to allow independent places of worship for their bondspeople in the 1840s. Black autonomy in worship was suspended during the Civil War, but came back with force soon after Emancipation. Independent Black worship was a given in Sallie Martin's youth.

Penfield, Georgia thus provided the opportunity to dream, for those who were so inclined. This chapter explores a historical framework for those potential imaginings as it explores what little is known of Sallie Martin's childhood. It then describes her time in Atlanta from around 1912 to 1917, a period punctuated by several momentous events—becoming a mother, getting married, and losing all her household goods to a devastating fire. Profound changes also occurred in Sallie Martin's next home, Cleveland, Ohio, where she lived with her husband and son until 1923. In retrospect, however, Atlanta and Cleveland were merely interim stops on Martin's migration toward the place of her most significant transformation, Chicago (chapter 2).

River, Rail, and the World Outside

The area where Sallie Martin began her transformation from country girl to national gospel icon has long been attractive to human inhabitants.[4] The Mississippian Ocute chiefdom occupied the region around 1200 CE. These mound-builders were especially attracted to Scull Shoals, eight miles northwest of the future site of Penfield.[5] Other, non-mound-building Indigenous peoples later established a community near the Ocute site, in what would become Greene County. Despite their diverse lineages, these newer groups were globally named Creeks by white settlers. Like those who came before and after them, the Creeks saw the wisdom in settling near the turbulent shoals of the Oconee River because game and fish were plentiful. During the late eighteenth and early nineteenth centuries,

Creeks traded deer skins for manufactured goods with Revolutionary-era white settlers who had won or paid pennies on the dollar for a piece of interior Georgia land. Competition was inevitable. In 1787, when Greene County was established in the midst of a thickly forested wilderness, the county seat of Greensboro boasted thirty houses, several businesses, and more than one hundred white inhabitants.[6] Creeks burned Greensboro to the ground that same year. Treaties dating between 1790 and 1826 resulted in the Creeks ceding their land in Georgia.[7]

Meanwhile, the Oconee River continued to draw white settlers looking to prosper from planting corn, cotton, and beans, and building grist and cotton mills next to the rapids. Soon, an expanded labor force was required to clear hundreds of acres of virgin forest land and plant, maintain, harvest, and ship goods on the river network to the Atlantic Ocean. Boosted by the invention of the cotton gin in 1793, the economy of Greene County rapidly narrowed to one predominant cash crop, marking its inclusion in Georgia's Piedmont Cotton Belt. One hundred years before her birth, the fates of Sallie Martin's ancestors were sealed.

In 1838, the Georgia Railroad was extended into Greene County, which supplemented the shipping of goods on the river. To hasten completion of this boon to commerce, Greene County plantation owners leased some of their enslaved workforce to the Georgia Railroad and Banking Company as builders.[8] They were transported to work sites on rail cars, witnessing vistas that surely sparked the imagination. The same railroad would later provide the luckier people of color with escape routes as war approached and widespread white vigilantism threatened their very existence.

Had her mother given birth in southern Georgia or in the mountainous northern part of the state, Sallie Martin's childhood experience would have been far different. By the time she and her mother took the train to Athens on one occasion and Atlanta another, Greene County had been served by rail for seventy years.[9]

Cracks in the Fortress of Greene County's Slavery System

Just thirty-five years prior to Sallie Martin's birth, Greene County was home to some fourteen plantations, and its economy largely reliant on enslaved labor (see figure 1.1). As elsewhere, the enslaved regularly suffered violent retribution for the smallest infractions. Runaways were beaten, sold, or both, and many were murdered. Bondswomen selected for house duties often contended with daily sexual violence and, if pregnant, were forced to wet-nurse the master's white as well as mixed-race children, only to be beaten senseless if a baby cried. Owners devised a range of unthinkable punishments, and though some Black people may have lived on the estates of comparatively benign masters, all were denied human rights and typically treated more poorly than livestock. Women were pressured to procreate and paternity was not tracked, complicating family cohesion in a culture already vulnerable to disruption by slave auctions. The enslaved in Penfield and Greene County existed as pawns susceptible to the "horrible arbitrariness of the slave system."[10]

When Sallie Martin recalled telling her cousins, around 1910, "I haven't ever liked any cotton picking . . . so I'm going to Atlanta," she referenced a twentieth-century livelihood directly tied to an enslaved past. Fifty years prior to her statement, two-thirds (or 8,398) of Greene County's 12,652 people lived in bondage. Of the 798 households in the county, 56 percent held at least one enslaved person. Six heads of household held more than 100 enslaved people, including Thomas Poullain of Scull Shoals, who owned the largest number, 134 humans (see the northernmost plantation in figure 1.1). "Among the slaveholding households, about half owned [fewer] than twelve [enslaved], 25 percent had five or fewer . . . and 10 percent owned one [enslaved] person."[11]

In comparison to the 500-person workforce on Pierce Butler's coastal Georgia plantation, bondspeople around Penfield lived in smaller groups and planters' administrative structures were simpler. Despite state mandates, owners of Greene County's smaller farms did not enforce slave patrol laws as energetically as coastal owners did before about 1850.[12] Some enslaved people were allowed to visit other households with relatively little risk of harassment by patrollers.[13] The occasional freedom to move about did not always translate into better living conditions, however. As Dosia Harris recalled, it seemed that Penfield overseers enjoyed beating their chattel just to hear them holler.[14] On the James H. McWhorter plantation, also near Penfield, as many bondspeople as could fit were forced into one room to sleep, producing literal breeding grounds for the polygamy whites liked to describe as Black immorality (see figure 1.1).

Though it's possible that the grandparents who helped raise Sallie Martin were free prior to emancipation, it's statistically much more likely that they were enslaved. If they were, Sallie Martin's self-determination may have been inherited from grandparents who experienced a modicum of agency to visit other plantations or saw others who did. In any case, agency over one's choices characterized the independent mind of Sallie Martin. Her one recorded memory of her grandfather alludes to his self-respect: "he didn't take no foolishness from nobody, white or colored."[15]

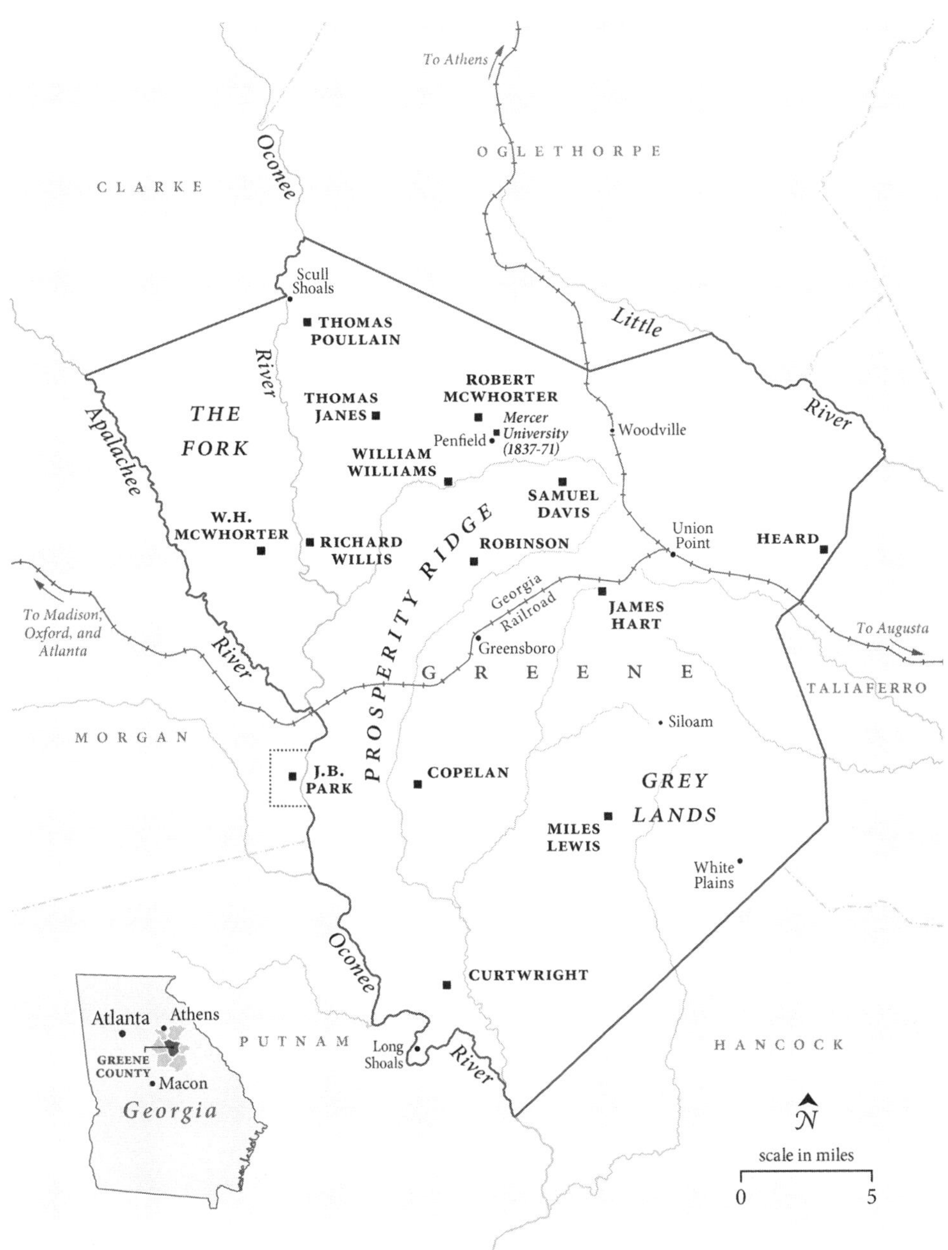

FIGURE 1.1. Jonathan M. Bryant, Greene County Plantation Map, *How Curious a Land*, 3. Map redrawn by David Deis.

Baptists, Mercer University (1837–1871), and Black Churches

Martin's birthplace was also the site of a once thriving Baptist university. In 1833, the Georgia Baptist Convention purchased a 1,000-acre plantation and began the construction of a school entitled Mercer Institute.[16] Providing white males with the chance to earn tuition through manual labor, the school's land touched as many as seven plantations (see figure 1.1).[17] In Penfield, homes of university trustees and professors of chemistry, natural science, mathematics, and astronomy, and a supervisor of manual labor were interspersed with houses of administration and faculty members of the Female Academy (est. 1838). Veterans, judges, ministers, the postmaster, and members of Congress owned homes close to student boarding houses, stores, and the office of the Baptist publication *The Christian Index and Temperance Banner*.[18] Mercer University mustered its own regiment of students (some accompanied by their Black bondsmen) during the Civil War. University buildings included an 1833 chapel, rebuilt in 1845 and extant at the time of this writing. Other campus structures included the President's House, Science Hall, Ciceronian Literary Society Hall, Phi Delta Literary Society Hall, a dormitory, and a baseball diamond. During Sallie Martin's childhood, the Mercer Chapel bore witness to Penfield's former significance; she could not have avoided seeing the imposing structure on the hill as she grew up (see figure 1.2).

Even if the historic significance of the Mercer Chapel had little effect on Sallie Martin, the dominant presence of Baptists in Greene County indirectly provided both worship and musical experiences. She remembered, "My mother used to go from place to place singing. They never had pianos, but if they sang a ballad, she could remember the tune. This gave me a great desire to travel and sing."[19] Black-only churches had history going back more than sixty years by the time Martin was born. These meeting places, along with ad hoc juke joints, may have provided her mother with places to sing for an audience.[20]

In Greene County, an early density of white Baptist and Methodist congregations set the stage for the establishment of Black-only churches.[21] Penfield Baptist Church's antebellum Black membership doubled its number of white members; the enslaved gallery in Mercer Chapel, where it met, was outgrown by 1844. White members then began to meet on Sunday mornings, while the enslaved members were allowed to congregate in the same building on Sunday afternoons. White men were supposed to attend all Black worship services, but rarely did.[22] Whites and Blacks were baptized in the same services and enslaved members attended church

FIGURE 1.2. Penfield's Mercer Chapel, built 1845–46, by David Demorest. Credit: Brian Brown/Vanishing Georgia. Used with permission.

conferences. The enslaved class took full advantage of segregated worship, fashioning their churches into sites of organization and, thus, agency.

Despite an 1845 Georgia law forbidding religious meetings for Blacks, the white minister of Penfield Baptist Church founded a completely separate congregation for the afternoon worshippers, Penfield African Church, in 1848. This right was soon withdrawn from bondspeople. Northern abolitionists were popular among the enslaved, and, in retaliation, whites denied their chattel the right to segregated worship. By 1863, a state law prohibited Black preachers. They did not know it then, but bondspeople needed wait only a few more years to continue, as freedmen, their process of redefining Christian worship to incorporate Black identity and politics.

Martin's Childhood Environment: Jim Crow vs. Black Determination in Greene County

Despite Georgia's 1868 ratification of the Fourteenth Amendment, granting citizenship to all, and the Fifteenth Amendment, which gave all men the right to vote, little appeared to change for Black Greene Countians after

1865. Whites refused to conceptualize a world absent of slavery, and most freedmen had no place to live other than their antebellum living quarters. Many stayed in place and worked the land of former masters on a contract system. Tenant farming and sharecropping agreements were engineered to keep Blacks dependent. The yearly harvests of freedmen were adequate only to cover the debt they had incurred for seed, rent, and food.

Black citizens did exercise their rights in some areas, however. Freedmen refused to work in the gang labor system, so akin to slavery, by the late 1860s.[23] Unless better conditions could be negotiated, whites' crops were not tended or harvested. Further, Black Greene Countians were elected to the state legislature in 1866, and despite immediately being expelled due to a clause in the state constitution, freedmen maintained an important caucus of voters until the election of 1876, after which their influence was again restricted.[24] That decade of participation, like so many other withdrawn freedoms, would loom large in the establishment of Georgia's Black political leadership.

The formerly enslaved also demanded access to education, founding the Georgia Educational Association of Augusta, Georgia, in 1865.[25] In Sallie Martin's home county, the Freedman's Bureau opened a school called Spring Field in 1868. Understandably, freedmen demanded Black teachers, and Spring Field School was taught by such a person.[26] In the rail junction town of Union Point in Greene County that same year were two schools, one day and one night, that were supported by the American Missionary Association. In March of 1868, one Union Point Black teacher taught 26 students; among them were 25 advanced readers. Five worked on arithmetic and 25 on writing.[27] The adults in Sallie Martin's life capitalized on these infrastructures by sending her to a segregated school from about 1902 through about 1910, when she completed the highest level of education available to her, eighth or ninth grade. In 1910, only 53 percent of the county's Black children attended school.[28]

As they watched her grow, Martin's relatives carefully instructed her in the art of coexisting without incurring white wrath. This essential precaution proscribed daily life for adults and structured their childrearing. Martin's words to Anthony Heilbut suggest that strictness and schooling set the stage for her own self-discipline later in life: "I think we had better ... lessons then because we knew the paddle would reach our hands if we failed."[29]

Tragedy befell Sallie Martin around 1910, after which time she made the first of several brave decisions in her life.

> After my Grandmother and Grandfather died, that left only my mother and myself. So, then I went to Atlanta to work for a while.... Oh, I think

> I wasn't 16 yet. I worked there for a while and went back and I just simply, after my Mother died, started to call cousins and they said, "Oh, why don't you stay here with us?" I said no, I'm going to go to Atlanta . . . because I never liked any cotton picking and no kind of working in the fields. So, therefore, I'm going back to Atlanta.[30]

Field labor was not the only work available for females, nor was it Martin's only reason to leave Greene County. She described another reality, one she encountered while living with a cousin after all three of her custodial adults had passed away: "The Smith brothers had been noted for, if Negroes would pass, they would stop them and make them dance." When one of the white brothers began to harass Martin, the head of the household where she lived confronted them: "I don't like no joking, I don't joke because one morning I might not be feeling well and you might not be feeling well, so we're just going to [go about] our business. Now you all don't give me any trouble about this girl. You all leave here." Martin remembered, "for the rest of the summer, if I'd see Mr. Smith, cause he would always ride a horse, I'd make it my business to hide in the bushes or go someplace else."[31] These reminiscences make it all the more surprising that as an adult, Martin felt safe touring extensively with her Singers throughout the Deep South. But that she did, armed with a confidence bequeathed by family members who had successfully navigated the vagaries of the slavery, reconstruction, and Jim Crow eras in Greene County.

Sallie Martin shared her Greene County origins with another prominent Black American, one who intimately knew a man who would become one of Martin's most illustrious fans. Adam Daniel Williams was born around 1861 into slavery and grew up in the Black congregations attached to Shiloh Baptist Church. In 1894, one year before Sallie Martin's birth, Williams became the pastor of Atlanta's Ebenezer Baptist Church and led the congregation, as well as that city's greater Black community, for more than thirty years. His associate pastor was Martin Luther King Sr., who married Williams's daughter, Alberta Cristine, in 1926, and assumed the lead pastorate at Ebenezer in 1931.[32] A formerly enslaved Greene County native, Williams lived to see the birth of his grandson Martin Luther King Jr. in 1929.[33] While the younger King favored the singing of Martin's friend Mahalia Jackson, Daddy King always preferred the songs of Sallie Martin.

New Family, the Great Fire, and a New Beginning

The years between her mother's death around 1910 and the birth of her son on August 25, 1915, were momentous for Sallie Martin. Though her ultimate goal in leaving Penfield was to return to Atlanta, where she and her mother had once stayed, she made a stopover of undetermined length in Athens, Georgia, presumably because she knew people with whom she could lodge. While there, the resourceful Martin met a woman who invited her to live with her Atlanta family, on the understanding that Martin, like the woman's two daughters, would not go out on the town at night or attend popular entertainments. Martin's reply to that caveat was, "Well, [that] doesn't make any difference. I've never been to a show before." The home of this unnamed woman would be Martin's domicile when she returned to Atlanta around 1912.[34]

Her Atlanta host family "went to church, and of course, they encouraged me to go. And that was when I became a Christian." Of the Holiness church where that conversion occurred, Martin remembered, "we all called it by Baptized, the Oldest Church." She was referring to the Zion Tabernacle Fire Baptized Holiness Church, which began at a tent revival in 1909 near Hogue and Irvin Streets in Atlanta.[35] About the music at Zion Tabernacle, she told Heilbut, "we didn't have no soloists. We would all sing together, or if you felt like you were going to testify, you might start out with a song, yourself."[36] Importantly for Martin and unlike the Baptists of Greene County, the Fire Baptized Holiness denomination licensed and ordained women to preach. Yet another possibility was added to Martin's conception of the world; she would be ordained as a minister in the 1970s.

Atlanta had its own set of challenges. By 1910, the Atlanta population of 150,000 included a fair number of white and Black newcomers from the rural South who had traded lives of hardscrabble farming and sharecropping for unskilled labor or trade jobs. Sallie Martin "began the long, wearying succession of typical jobs for females: babysitting ('We called it nursing'), day work, night work, laundries, and doctors' offices."[37] In contrast to farm environments, Atlanta's coal- and woodburning stoves and coal-powered trains left the air profoundly polluted. One newcomer said, "I wanted to go back home so bad, where I could be clean."[38] Public venues were segregated in the 1910s; Black Americans could not go to a city park until 1920, unless they were caring for white children. They weren't allowed to eat downtown, and if they purchased food they had to return to the Black districts to eat it. Black washerwomen were further stigmatized, since they were widely considered the most likely carriers of tuberculosis.[39]

On the other hand, Atlanta was a pacesetter in Black popular culture. It was home to the Southern Amusement Company's Auditorium Theatre, the finest Black-owned playhouse in the South and a favorite stop on Black vaudeville and road show circuits. Extending one entire city block on Auburn Avenue, it could seat over seven hundred on the first floor and more than five hundred in the gallery.[40] Ironically, Martin's future partner, Thomas A. Dorsey, would have been playing blues at smaller venues on nearby Decatur Street by 1917. Dorsey recalled that he played a "lowdown type music, they put any kind of words to it they wanted . . . In these places, they'd shine out with anything, say 'Yeah!,' you know, so I think that's why they called it barrelhouse, you'd go down to where they'd opened a keg, and you'd hear anything, did anything, you could get arrested."[41] Blues singer destined for stardom Bessie Smith (1894–1937) also spent time in Decatur Street's Eighty-One Theater as a teenager.

As a lodger in Atlanta, Martin may have remained true to her promise not to frequent clubs, but she found herself pregnant and unwed in late 1914. She gave birth to her only offspring, a son named Joel, on August 25, 1915. Later that year, she met Wallace Martin (1899–1950) a native of Madison, Georgia, twenty-five miles distant from Penfield. He would soon become her husband and the stepfather to her son.[42] She recalled,

> I met a real man and, of course, I really thought, he was so tall and heavy and one thing and another. I thought, you know, he's 22, 23, or 24, because I was 20. So, we got to talking and his mother said, "well, you know, he's just 18." I said "18!" But it just continued on until I married Wally Martin.[43]

If their life in Atlanta was happy, their stay there was short-lived.

On a windy day in May of 1917, a fire broke out on Auburn Avenue and eventually destroyed seventy-three square blocks, leaving ten thousand Black and white people homeless (see figure 1.3). The hastily constructed, densely crowded homes of African Americans in the Fourth Ward burned like tinder as available pumper and hose wagons were sent to the white neighborhoods. Even streetcar wires and poles were consumed by the blaze. Whites and Blacks survived the night together in Piedmont Park.

Eventually, houses were dynamited to stop the spread. As Martin recalled,

> It just seemed that [the fire] had circled the town and it would just leap from house to house. . . . When it got to the East side, of course, the first part of it was mostly Black. . . . They got something to blow the houses down in front of it. That was the only way they got it stopped. So then my husband said, "we're getting our things," but it seemed like the fire was coming [to] where we packed our things . . . and I said, "let's leave here."[44]

The Martins thus abandoned their life in Atlanta and continued their own Great Migration to Cleveland, Ohio, with a group organized by Rev. C. C.

FIGURE 1.3. View of a postcard labeled by Beverly DuBose Sr., "Negro dwellings in which conflagration started," Atlanta Fire of 1917. Kenan Research Center at the Atlanta History Center. Used with permission.

Ailer.[45] They shared a Cleveland apartment with Wallace's brother, Felix Martin; cousin Joseph Johnson; and a lodger, Sudie Johnson. Wallace found work at a plant that manufactured nuts and bolts.[46] "In Cleveland," Martin recalled, "it was always cloudy. Especially through the winter, we didn't see any sunshine. And that just kills me. I don't care how downlike I'm feeling, when the sun comes up, it gives me the desire to go forth."[47]

Seemingly untouched by World War I and the 1918–1920 Spanish flu pandemic, Sallie, Wallace, and Joel Martin nevertheless faced deep challenges during their first midwestern winter.[48] The weather was so cold and gray, Sallie remembered, that it "made me crazy momentarily." In addition, corporate recruitment of immigrants as strikebreakers continued to drastically affect available jobs for Black Americans; in particular, said Martin, "the Polish people made it so hard for us to work."[49] Then came the recession linked to the return of war veterans. Martin recalled, "I think it was 1919 that the panic was on. Everything was slow, nobody couldn't find any job. I was working on the West Side for a school which caused me to have to get up in the morning and get dressed early but, however, I needed it."

Desperate for a second income, Sallie and Wallace came up with a plan based on their close proximity to a church.

> So finally, I said to him, "you're an usher in the church. I'm singing in the choir and we're next door." He said, "You know what I thought about? I thought about I would sell some hamburgers or something like that and why not?" So finally he worked it up until where he put a place out in the yard that was large enough . . . and he started a little business. So that went on until, I guess, around about 1922, I think it was.[50]

Wallace soon embellished his pop-up sandwich stand by offering gambling and sales of bootleg liquor. Sallie was adamantly opposed and did not anticipate changing her convictions. At some point in 1919, she had taken a train to Chicago and wanted to move there immediately, but the economy hadn't then favored relocation. She had found the new city more to her liking, while Wallace had discovered a way to capitalize on the vices so prevalent around him. Sallie Martin left Cleveland for good in 1923.

Wallace Martin soon followed his wife and they reconciled briefly in the Windy City. The only work she could find was at the "Contagious Hospital," which may have been Chicago Communicable Disease Hospital on the North Side. "We were making fifty dollars a week and that was good money then," she recalled. But conflicts continued.

> When he would get off work, he'd have games and playing, men in the house drinking, and would gamble all night. So I didn't say anything. . . . Finally it came to a head. . . . That was not my life and [I was] not changing. So we separated. We stayed separated until he passed away.[51]

Chicago would live up to Sallie's hopes; by 1929, she had discovered and nurtured a promising route not only to solvency, but to national renown.[52]

CHAPTER 2

Chicago, 1923–1933

Fertile Ground for Sallie Martin and Gospel

> When I came [to Chicago in 1919] . . . it was raining, and as soon as the rain was over the sun came out. I said, "This is the place for me." I went back to Cleveland and I told my husband. Well, he wasn't so eager about it. . . . And of course, he began to get just a little bit off the hook and I just said, "Well, now, I'm going to Chicago."
>
> —Sallie Martin

Sallie Martin was twenty-eight years old in 1923 when, unwilling to compromise about her husband's involvement in gambling and Prohibition-era drinking, she left Cleveland for good. She may have been unmarried when her son Joel was born in 1915, but for the rest of her life, she upheld a strict moral code. Her final conversion to Christianity while in Atlanta played a significant role in those values; "I'm very happy I was saved in a Holiness church, cause I got some principles from them and I'd *never* lose, *never* lose, never."[1]

Wallace Martin joined his wife in Chicago soon after her move; during the next census, Sallie, Wallace, and Joel lived together at 5212 Prairie Avenue in what later would be dubbed Bronzeville.[2] Had Martin hoped to resolve their differences over partying and gambling, she would have found the South Side of Chicago a challenging environment. The region pulsed with jazz and blues and their concomitant attachment to the liquor, marijuana, cocaine, and sex trades. The Stroll, an entertainment district on State Street that extended from 31st to 39th Streets, was a brief trolley or streetcar ride from the Martins' rooming house.[3]

Political corruption in 1920s Chicago is now legendary. In 1927, William Hale "Big Bill" Thompson (1869–1944) was elected for a third term as mayor, assisted by "advisor," Al Capone. After his defeat in 1931, the *Chicago Tribune* reported,

> For Chicago, Thompson has meant filth, corruption, obscenity, idiocy and bankruptcy. . . . He has given the city an international reputation for moronic buffoonery, barbaric crime, triumphant hoodlumism, unchecked graft, and a dejected citizenship. He nearly ruined the property and completely destroyed the pride of the city. He made Chicago a byword for the collapse of American civilization.[4]

Times were tough, indeed, and as Martin remembered, "Mr. Cermak was the mayor and he simply wasn't paying anybody, but at least I had my room and board."[5]

Newly arrived migrants continued to experience the internal conflict facing all African Americans after the Civil War. W. E. B. Du Bois called it double consciousness.

> It is a peculiar sensation . . . this sense of always looking at one's self through the eyes of others, of measuring one's soul by the tape of a world that looks on in amused contempt and pity. One ever feels his twoness, an American, a Negro; two souls, two thoughts, two unreconciled strivings; two warring ideals in one dark body, whose dogged strength alone keeps it from being torn asunder.[6]

On the South Side, white and Black Chicagoans alike participated in the marginalization of people who looked like Sallie Martin. The Chicago career of classical music educator, performer, and composer Florence B. Price (1887–1953) exemplifies that caste system.

Price grew up in a middle-class family in Little Rock, Arkansas, then attended the New England Conservatory after high school. She taught music at several Black colleges in and around Little Rock and in Atlanta, then married an attorney, and in 1927, moved with her family to Chicago. Owing as much to her musical gifts as to the fact that she could pass for white, Price was readily accepted into white women's clubs, and her compositions actively promoted by them. Her light complexion and musical expertise landed Price in an interstice of race and class—she was remarkable enough as a pianist to earn accolades in the well-established classical music community, and light-skinned enough to avoid censorship, even if it was known she was Black. The contrast between Price and Martin is nowhere more obvious than in the fact that Price affiliated with Chicago's Grace Presbyterian Church soon after her arrival in Chicago. Brown writes,

"Grace was a church that attracted only fair-skinned blacks who were middleclass and well-educated professionals. . . . The members were staid in their manners, and they prided themselves on their sophisticated and unemotional participation in the worship service."[7] Her skin a deep brown and her soul animated by Sanctified convictions, Sallie Martin would not have moved in Florence Price's circles.

Instead, Martin worshipped in churches that encouraged what she had embraced in Atlanta: dramatic speech-singing, zealous shouts, and stylized bodily movements. She gravitated toward the groups that met in church buildings and storefronts alike. She first met Thomas A. Dorsey, the future Father of Gospel Music, in 1929, then rapidly proved herself capable of marketing his songs and organizing his business. At first, they demonstrated his music wherever they could, but many congregations were not ready for gospel. They encountered strong resistance and outright rejection in mainline, uplift-conscious churches more accustomed to anthems by Handel and Mozart. As they labored, Martin and Dorsey began the process of cultivating a musical middle ground where blues stylings, syncopation, and embodiment were still present, but vocal delivery, harmonization, and bodily movement were tempered. They had set their sights on influential mainline Chicago churches with hundreds of members on the roll and thriving music departments.

After describing the institutional substructure of the new gospel blues, this chapter details the relatively short time span during which gospel's social status evolved from middle-class outsider to insider. Architects of that watershed movement are considered. This discussion ends in 1933, as Martin, along with Magnolia Lewis-Butts, Thomas A. Dorsey, and Theodore Frye first imagined a National Convention of Gospel Choirs and Choruses (NCGCC, today's "Dorsey Convention"). That organization provided the institutional framework that Sallie Martin and her cohort of gospel pioneers steered into national renown. In the decade between 1923 and 1933, Martin discovered her path to becoming "somebody."

Grandparents of Gospel: Baptist Infrastructure and Sanctified Aesthetics

Before the Revolutionary War, many African diasporic people responded to Christianity only outwardly, as a result of coercion, and others syncretized Christianity with their orally transmitted belief practices. One denomination was an early favorite of Black people after the Civil War; by 1790, 13 percent of all Baptist church members in the United States were Black, likely because the Baptist faith was popular in the South (see chapter 1).[8]

FIGURE 2.1. National Baptist Convention circa 1927, Detroit, Blackpast.org.

Before and after the Civil War, Black Baptists founded their own churches and the organizations that connected them: the Foreign Mission Baptist Convention (1880), American National Baptist Convention (1886), and National Baptist Education Convention (1893).[9] By 1906, writes Paul Harvey, "the Baptist faith was firmly entrenched as the dominant institutional expression of African American religious culture."[10] When some of these parent groups incorporated as the National Baptist Convention, USA, in 1916, they formed the third largest religious organization, white or Black, in the country.[11] The NBC's leadership and infrastructure provided pioneers like Sallie Martin with role models and blueprints she adopted as she built her career as a Black businesswoman.

In contrast to Sanctified religions, Baptists did not ordain women as ministers. Working within those limitations, a Baptist Women's Convention was approved by churches prior to 1900. Its progressive founder, Nannie Helen Burroughs (1879–1961), urged Black Baptists to cooperate with the National Association for the Advancement of Colored People

(NAACP), the country's first civil rights organization, in 1909.[12] That year also saw the opening of Burroughs's National Training School for Women and Girls in Washington, DC.[13] Burroughs's promotion of female agency, educational values, and civil rights provided a foretaste of the cultural work Black women would accomplish in the twentieth century. Under her influence, Baptist women also drove the 1920s temperance movement from their leadership positions within NBC–affiliated churches.

The NBC also set precedents in the Black sacred publishing world. The National Baptist Publishing Board opened for business in 1896 in Nashville, the city chosen by the white Southern Baptist Convention (SBC) for its publishing wing (the Sunday School Board). Richard Boyd (1843–1922) became the head of the NBC press in the year of its charter.[14] He adopted best practices of the publishing business from James M. Frost (1848–1916), his white counterpart, who had run the SBC's Sunday School Board since 1891.

> With assistance from James Frost, Boyd sold his publications to churches throughout the country. Starting with virtually nothing in the mid 1890s, by 1906 the publishing board had accumulated a business valued at $160,152. By 1910, the board's presses pumped out over eleven million pieces of literature each year and employed over 150 black workers. By 1915, the board reported a cumulative total of over $2,500,000 worth of business. Boyd plowed back into the enterprise his yearly profits. He set up subsidiary companies to supply churches with pews, benches, hymnbooks, pulpits, choir robes, and children's dolls. His enterprise held together the diffuse and loosely organized National Baptist Convention.[15]

Though financial controversy ultimately tarnished Boyd's reputation and caused a split over ownership in 1915, the press continued to thrive. In 1921, it released *Gospel Pearls*, a watershed, pre-gospel book of 163 hymns, set mostly in four-part arrangements. The collection included Baptist favorites by the likes of William B. Bradbury, Fanny J. Crosby, Isaac Watts, and Charles Wesley; white gospel songs by James D. Vaughan and Crosby; acclamations and responses such as Old 100th (Doxology); and patriotic hymns. Black composers are represented by, among others, Charles Albert Tindley (1851–1933) the foremost transitional composer between Black hymnody and gospel. Tindley's "Leave It There" and "We'll Understand It Better By and By" appear alongside Thomas A. Dorsey's "If I Don't Get There," Lucie E. Campbell's "The Lord Is My Shepherd," and spirituals arranged by the brothers John W. Work Jr. and Frederick Jerome Work. *Gospel Pearls* preserves the moment in time when Black sacred music was poised for the emergence of Chicago gospel.

Martin's childhood worship experiences were Baptist, but during her time in Atlanta, she aligned with sanctified practices that were foundational to her faith, worship, and vocality. The term "sanctified" is applied to any congregation—Holiness, Pentecostal, and Apostolic, for example—which embraces John Wesley's principle of entire sanctification. That goal—achieving spiritual perfection which paves the way for oneness with God—was the driving force behind the Holiness movement of the 1860s and '70s. With a few like-minded ministers in Jackson, Mississippi, Charles Price Jones (1865–1949) founded the Church of Christ (Holiness) in 1897, after leaving his Baptist church. Faith healing and belief in entire sanctification characterized Jones's church.

On the West Coast, preacher William J. Seymour (1870–1922), who had navigated through the Catholic, Baptist, and Methodist Episcopal faiths, led a wildly popular, racially integrated revival movement in Los Angeles from 1906 to around 1915. Highlighting the expression of spiritual ecstasy called "speaking in tongues" (glossolalia), as recorded in the second chapter of the biblical book of Acts, the movement established what is known as Pentecostalism.[16] Seymour's extended series of worship services is now known as the Azusa Street Revival, named after the address of its first permanent headquarters.

In contrast to mainline denominations, sanctified faiths provided Black women the opportunity to organize congregations and preach. Reverend Lucy Turner Smith (1875–1952) grew up in Oglethorpe County, Georgia, adjacent to Sallie Martin's Greene County. Smith moved to Chicago in 1910, spent time in a few congregations, then founded All Nations Pentecostal Church in 1920. That denomination emphasizes a personal relationship with God and baptism by the Holy Spirit, evidenced in the ability to speak in tongues and heal the sick, among other spiritual gifts. Also known for circulating "anointed handkerchiefs" after her services, Smith began to preach on Chicago radio in 1926. Her bombastic style drew ridicule from those who embraced new visions of Black identity based on self-knowledge and best expressed in poetry, art, and education.[17] For them, Lucy Turner Smith perpetuated Locke's idea of the "Old Negro," a fictional character born of racist stereotyping. Louis A. Dulaney's piece in the September 1, 1934, *Chicago Defender* described Smith's sermon as "ignorance personified":

> Here are just a few excerpts from the "sermon," if it may be called that . . . feets for the plural of foot; us going, for we are going; heah, for here; dat for that; Chuesday for Tuesday . . . Further, the solo, "I Don't Know What I'd Do Without My Lord" was a perfect number for some of the

> fan dancers or any cabaret. If that is their best effort for a hymn, Lord help them, I pray.[18]

Mainline Chicago ministers tried to discourage radio evangelism for this reason, but charismatic churches like Smith's and the medium that broadcast such services inevitably infiltrated broader Black religious practice. Radio contributed to the gradual thawing of class distinctions, creating an environment where the seeds of gospel music found fertile ground.

Gospel's Parent Churches in Chicago

Arguably, the Black Chicago Sallie Martin encountered in 1923 was as influenced by religious institutions and musicians as it was by jazz players, bootlegging, gambling, and prostitution. "In 1927, Chicago was home to 55 black Baptist churches with an estimated 65,000 congregants."[19] Smaller storefront or home worship groups, many sanctified, were estimated at 266 in the late 1930s.[20]

Throughout the 1920s, however, the most influential mainstream ministers held fast to their preference for professional-level performances of European choral masterworks and concert arrangements of spirituals, fitting accompaniments to their lofty eruditions. At the end of the decade, the first mainline congregation initiated a process of gospel infiltration. The nonsectarian, nondenominational Metropolitan Community Church (the Met) was founded in a storefront in 1920 by W. D. Cook, a disillusioned American Methodist Episcopal (AME) minister. Soon, Cook hired the most renowned choral musician in Chicago, J. Wesley Jones, to lead his choir. Jones also conducted a community group, the Progressive Choral Club, which was known for its inspiring features on Chicago radio, including a performance of Handel's *Esther* oratorio in 1920. A young soloist and choral musician named Magnolia Lewis (1880–1949) helped prepare Jones's choir for that performance. She became his primary soloist in 1926 and founded a Met youth chorus to sing at funerals in 1929, at Jones's request. Quietly, it seems, Lewis began to program gospel music at the Met, despite Jones's abhorrence of the style. Magnolia Lewis was thus the first person to conduct a gospel choir at a mainstream church[21] (see chapter 4).

Ebenezer Baptist Church opened in 1921 at 4501 South Vincennes Avenue, and by 1928 could boast a 6,000-member congregation. Rev. James Howard Lorenzo Smith hired Theodore R. Frye, a fledgling gospel composer who had moved to Chicago in 1927, as his director of music. Smith then added pianist Thomas A. Dorsey to the musical roster. Dorsey was a 1916 arrival to Chicago who had spent most of the 1920s playing blues and jazz. Frye and Dorsey, a truly dynamic duo, debuted their 100-member gospel youth choir in January of 1932. The congregation was thrilled and appalled in equal measure, but a door to gospel had been opened in a big way at Ebenezer's main service. There would be no going back.

Pilgrim Baptist Church, located for decades at 33rd Street and Indiana, began in 1922. By 1928, it was home to 7,500 members. When the gospel choir from Ebenezer Baptist Church made a guest appearance there in February of 1932, Pilgrim's Rev. Junius C. Austin wasted little time. Understanding that the new music would greatly benefit his ministry, he hired Thomas A. Dorsey away from Ebenezer to conduct a gospel choir. In the face of strong resistance from a board of deacons that at first refused to pay Dorsey, and the resignation of his esteemed classical conductor, Edward Boatner, Austin set about convincing his congregation that the decorous atmosphere he had demanded in the worship space could be enlivened by a gospel choir.[22] Church archives at the Chicago Public Library summarize gospel's tipping point:

> In January 1932, after only a month of rehearsals, the Ebenezer gospel chorus made its debut in a church filled to capacity. The 100-member chorus wowed the congregation with their soulful Southern-influenced spiritual sound. Six weeks after the chorus made its initial public appearance, Dorsey left Ebenezer to direct a new gospel chorus at Pilgrim Baptist Church.[23]

Dorsey would remain the Director of Music at Pilgrim Baptist for fifty years.

Outside the Met, Ebenezer, and Pilgrim churches, the texture of Chicago's gospel infrastructure strengthened as multitalented innovators established, then traded, influential jobs. Publisher and composer Charles Henry Pace (1886–1963) moved to Chicago in 1915. He conducted the choir at Beth Eden Baptist Church in Morgan Park and founded a choir called the Pace Jubilee Singers, for which Thomas A. Dorsey was briefly the pianist. While managing his own Pace House Publishing and the Jubilee Singers, he became house arranger for one of his rivals, publisher Lillian Mae Bowles (married name, Pannell, 1884–1949), who opened for business in 1929. Pace remained there until 1934 (see chapter 4). Kenneth Morris, Sallie Martin's future partner, immediately assumed Pace's vacant position in the Bowles company.

Martin's Pre-1929 Worship Experiences

Little is known about Sallie Martin's activities between 1923 and 1929, though it's fair to assume that she worked to support herself outside of music and sang in churches, some of which met in rented commercial spaces. An eyewitness to storefront meetings described "weird pleading of voices pitched to the tone of jubilee songs. . . . incessant clatter of tambourines. . . . clapping of hands, the jerking and shouting, and dancing of spirit-filled souls."[24] As it had on the radio, this demonstrative worship drew many detractors; in 1926, Black scholar Ira De Augustine Reid grumbled that storefront churches were "a general nuisance," and their founders conducted services "on such days as he feels disposed mentally and indisposed financially. To this gentleman of the cloth . . . the church is a legitimate business."[25] Storefront churches might even attract worshippers by working lucky gambling combinations into religious services.[26] Though Sallie Martin's early Chicago worship experiences also included worship at influential mainline churches such as Pilgrim Baptist, she and other like-minded, spirit-filled migrants could freely express themselves and think of home in sanctified services.

In her 1972 reminiscences with Laurraine Goreau, Sallie Martin thought of these early days in Chicago. To a query about Mahalia Jackson, who arrived in Chicago in 1927, Martin recalled,

> I deem that she and the group—she was with the Johnson Singers—must have undoubtedly worked the west side because we didn't come in contact with her. When I did, I had been on the road somewhere and came back in and I heard that they were gonna be at Ebenezer [Baptist Church] and I went over and that's the first time I saw Mahalia. I didn't get a chance to talk with her that day, but later on . . . I met her again. I had been going to a lot of the churches here and, of course, some of the churches . . . didn't receive her too well.[27]

Jackson was fifteen years younger than Martin, who took the newcomer under her wing. She was particularly concerned by Jackson's dresses, with hems falling at the knee.

> I remember once when we were going to a church down here on Forty-fifth street, I believe it was, and I said, "now, listen, Mahala, you must get a [choir] robe or . . . something, because when you get in the pulpit" [you might show too much] and of course she didn't have much in the way of clothes. You see, I'm the first gospel singer I've ever known to have a robe.[28]

Martin sang with the young singer in the early 1930s when others, believing Jackson's music sounded too secular, would not.[29] In Martin's words,

> Oh, now, we didn't travel all the time, we just [went] here at times then other places. [Mahala would say], "Sallie, come on and go with me here." I said all right because . . . the other singers tried to be a little high-minded [where Jackson was concerned]. . . . The Roberta Martin Singers

> . . . I had them with me several places and they [never connected with Jackson] in any way, but I would go with her to small churches [storefronts]. Most of the big churches wouldn't accept [Jackson] so I would go with her.[30]

Martin would live to see Jackson, a singer she at first described as no bigger "than a minute," eclipse her own fame. Still, they were friends until Jackson's death in 1972 (see chapter 4).

Prior to meeting Dorsey in 1929, Martin's musical repertoire would have included a wide range of songs transmitted both orally, in Baptist and sanctified worship, and in print. She probably sang from *Gospel Pearls*, a collection she later sold from her co-owned business. None of the hymns in that collection could be called gospel, though some bore traces of the style to come. As Martin recalled, prior to Dorsey's gospel, "nobody [was] singing what you would call 'gospel' . . . you were either in a choir and you . . . sang from a hymn book or either a gospel book . . . [you were] just doing church work and singing."[31] About her own sanctified style, she recounted: "people were patting [i.e., only subtly keeping time] because ministers were leery of too much rhythm. But nobody was shaking but me."[32] Shaking probably referred to toned-down bodily movements that she adopted when she performed outside sanctified churches. Such an adjustment was crucial in the popularization of gospel. After the new style was accepted more widely by conservative churches, Sallie Martin was able to add back a repertoire of arm gestures, torso movements, and hip sways that punctuated emotional crescendos in performance. In Heilbut's words, "When [Sallie Martin] sings, practically every note has its physical brother."[33] Rejecting ostentation, Martin maintained that she moved in ecstatic ways only when God caused it. She professed little regard for mere showmanship without divine inspiration.

"The First National Gospel Singer" and Thomas A. Dorsey[34]

Gospel musician Kenny Ulmer later described the early resistance to Black gospel: "You have to remember that Thomas Dorsey and Sallie Martin were kicked out of a lot of churches."[35] Horace Clarence Boyer summarized this dilemma:

> There was the feeling that the more white you acted, the more you would be accepted by white people. There was not that kind of pride about having lived through slavery. . . . The whole emphasis was ridding every Negro of everything that was Negroid . . . including the church service

> ritual. So all of a sudden, now, we get Brahms and Handel. . . . And here we begin to get a whole conflict between the ways people are going to worship. And many preachers said, "Don't sing those slave songs [at all]."[36]

When Sallie Martin first encountered Thomas A. Dorsey in 1929, neither had discovered how a livelihood could be made in the sacred music business. She heard about him through word of mouth:

> I went to [a church] rehearsal [and] came across one of his songs, "How About You." A girl brought it to me at the church. And I said, "where'd you find [that song]?" and she said, "oh, it's an old fellow over on 40th Street. . . . ." I said, "Oh well, I certainly would like to meet him . . . I'm going over."[37]

Dorsey's ideal of a lead singer was shaped by memories of his father's pastoral rhetoric and the delivery style of Rev. W. M. Nix, whom he heard at the 1921 NBC convention in Chicago.[38]

Regarding hymn texts, US revival movements of the late eighteenth and early nineteenth centuries introduced Christians of all races to hymns that exemplified a personal relationship with God. By the 1920s, African Americans who once identified with the fourth verse of Isaac Watts's 1707 hymn "Am I a Soldier of the Cross?", number 48 in *Gospel Pearls*—"Sure, I must fight, if I would reign; Increase my courage, Lord; I'll bear the toil, endure the pain, Supported by thy word"[39]—now daily experienced persistent racism in post–Great War America. They required deeper relevance and vernacular speech in their religious songs. Dorsey's "How About You?" begins this way;

> How well do I remember how Jesus brought me through.
> I prayed and walked the floor a night or two.
> I said, "Lord, take and use me; that's all that I can do."
> And I gave my heart to Jesus, how about you?
>
> Chorus:
> How about you, how about you?
> I hope my Savior is your Savior, too.
> I said, "Lord, take and use me; that's all that I can do."
> And I gave my heart to Jesus, how about you?[40]

Dorsey sets the third verse in the most intimate of spaces and, in language that mainstream churches at first found too vivid and unsophisticated, describes the realities of the dying process.

> When I press my dying pillow and I know my life is through,
> And there's no more that earthly friends can do.

> When my sight begins to fail me and my fingernails turn blue,
> Then He'll take me home to glory, how about you?[41]

Veterans of charismatic revival services recognize the altar call, aimed at winning souls to Christ, in this song. Harris wrote,

> By some standards, this text would be considered little more than religious doggerel. But it was precisely this profound simplification—almost transparency—of doctrinal concepts that allowed Dorsey's songs—like Nix's sermons—to speak to virtually anyone who would listen.[42]

Small wonder, then, that Sallie Martin heard something she liked in Dorsey's "How About You" and made her way immediately to meet the composer of that song. At Dorsey's, she remembered that

> [Someone's] daughter was playing [piano] but she couldn't transpose. That made the song be just a little high for me, so after the rehearsal was over, Mr. Dorsey said, "Well, you have a nice voice. . . . Would you like to work with a group?" and I said, "Oh, I wouldn't mind." . . . So we met together and got started, and for a number of years there, I guess three or four years, [Dorsey's] group sang together and we traveled around a good many parts of Illinois. . . . I worked with him and the group one year before I sang a solo, even though I knew that I was just as good as those that he had.[43]

Her cool objectivity (i.e., "I wouldn't mind") was a typical Martin spin on real events. At the time, she was probably thrilled to be offered such an opportunity (see the introduction to this book for more on her personal relationship with Dorsey).

Beyond lyrics and blues coloring, Dorsey knew that the success of gospel blues would be tied to finding a person whose song-leading was dynamic, expressive, and powerful.[44] Dorsey found his first ideal "caller" in Sallie Martin when, at their first encounter, he heard her deliver a dramatic reading.[45] In the words of Kenneth Woods Jr.,

> [Other singers] were a little bit too polished for Mr. Dorsey at that time. Coming out of blues, he wanted something that had a rough edge to it. . . . So here comes Sallie Martin. Sallie Martin didn't have a beautiful voice but she had a presence. And that's what Mr. Dorsey had coming up playing with Ma Rainey. . . . He liked that rough edge . . . you see. He liked that style.[46]

Sallie Martin filled the bill. She described how, later, she landed her first vocal solo.

> We were down in Danville, IL, for a service that night. We'd always rehearse the group before the service. When we got through, I said to him, "Prof—what about me doing a solo tonight?" . . . If you didn't really have [the gumption] in you to [volunteer], there was no encouragement. [Dorsey responded] "You think you can do something?" "I said well, yes," [to which Dorsey replied] "All right, what will it be?" I said "I Claim Jesus First of All and That's Enough for Me." And from that night on, [for eight years I remained] a soloist and I've never had to ask any more about it.[47]

Martin's career path rapidly opened up to her.

Dorsey's earliest vocal group also included Dettie Gay and Rebecca Talbot.[48] Martin's contralto voice provided the perfect harmonic foundation for Dorsey's musical arrangements, her dramatic style filled his need for a caller, and her business sense would prove critical to his financial success. Yet, he never referred to Martin as his business partner. Roxanne Reed points out that

> Sallie Martin, unlike Dorsey, bore no title affirming her status as a major figure in the building of Gospel, but she traveled with Dorsey demonstrating, organizing and managing the sale of his music, which eventually became the Thomas A. Dorsey Gospel Songs Publishing Company.[49]

What may be her first mention in the newspaper was, "A Line or So from Chicago," published in the *Atlanta Daily World* of November 27, 1932.[50] John G. Hunter reported that Martin had been the featured dramatic reader when Pilgrim Baptist Church of Chicago hosted "the ten best gospel choirs" in Chicago on November 14.

Soon after joining Dorsey's team of singers, Martin noticed that he had no accounting system. Instead, he kept his cash in a drawer from which household and professional expenses were casually paid. The singers rehearsed in the bedroom he rented from his uncle, which, Martin recalls, "had an iron [bed] . . . no rug on the floor, and an old desk."[51] Martin had been responsible for her own upkeep since her teen years and was the mother of a sixteen-year-old son. Seizing an opportunity, she saw fit to take Dorsey's business in hand. After a few rehearsals, she said to him, "You know, you have something here, but you don't know what to do with it."[52] The upshot of that statement was that she began to manage his business—for which she earned four dollars a week. Three quarters of that sum went to renting a room at the Ritz Hotel, on 355 East 56th Street, not quite a block from Dorsey's home. Dorsey also split, fifty-fifty, the profit from music sales she made at choir rehearsals, added incentive she capitalized upon.[53] Martin had engineered a way to live by gospel music.

Martin, Dorsey, and the National Convention of Gospel Choirs and Choruses (NCGCC)

The National Baptist Convention met to celebrate its fiftieth year at Chicago's Olivet Baptist Church from August 14 to 25, 1930.[54] Though Dorsey's music was demonstrated at that Convention, Martin and Dorsey had not yet garnered the reputation necessary to be mentioned in the *Chicago Defender*'s accounts of the meeting. Martin remembered, "Mr. Dorsey [presented] 1 or 2 songs and one of them was, I think, 'If you see my Savior' (1927). That's where we got the idea of a gospel song."[55] The next couple of years after the NBC convention of 1930 were crucial to the gospel music industry, witnessing the initiation of gospel groups at the Metropolitan Community Church (the Met), Ebenezer Baptist Church, and Pilgrim Baptist Church. Those groups participated in a musicale (a monthly music festival) at the Met in August of 1933. Contrary to popular thought, Dorsey could not have been the one to imagine the largescale marketing of his songs after that Met confab because he had written so few by then and had been focused on solo gospel.[56] Instead, Dorsey's part in the momentous events of August 1933 was the recognition that the performance practice of choral gospel had to be taught. He had been leading workshops as a sort of independent contractor to the many choirs that popped up after the spring of 1933. The NCGCC would not be founded solely at his instigation.

The organization's history page reads,

> As Dr. Thomas A. Dorsey traveled, the popularity of Gospel choirs or choruses began to spread throughout the country. Through this, Dr. Dorsey saw a need to organize these choirs collectively into unions. As such, he founded the National Convention of Gospel Choirs and Choruses (NCGCC) in 1932.
>
> Increased awareness of NCGCC gave rise to organizing a convention. Dr. Dorsey contacted many Gospel choir directors out of town to accomplish this. He, Professor Theodore Frye, Magnolia Lewis Butts, Sallie Martin, and Henry J. Carruthers organized the first convention in 1933. Unions from Chicago, IL, St. Louis, MO, and Cincinnati, OH, were the first to join the NCGCC. The organizers published the first bylaws that year and elected Dr. Thomas A. Dorsey president.[57]

This laudatory account likely overstates the extent of Dorsey's travels and may misrepresent the founding purpose of the organization. That musicale was, nonetheless, significant; the key players called the other gospel choirs in Chicago together the next month for a Convention at Pilgrim Baptist Church.[58]

Readers of the *Chicago Defender* understood that they should consider the Convention a watershed event.

> A new epoch in the musical world was realized when the Gospel Choral Union [GCU] of the city of Chicago entertained the National Convention of Gospel Choirs and Choruses in its first annual session at Pilgrim Baptist, 33rd Street and Indiana Ave., Aug 30, 31, and Sept 1. Fifty-two delegates [and] 600 choir members from the Chicago GCU [attended]. . . . Sallie Martin was elected corresponding secretary.[59]

The reporter's opening hyperbole reflected a larger watershed in Chicago history, the $37.5 million "Century of Progress" World's Fair, which had opened on May 27, 1933. Fair attractions included Admiral Richard E. Byrd's Polar Expedition ship, *City of New York*; the arrival of the German airship *Graf-Zeppelin*; the first Major League Baseball All-Star Game; streamlined trains of the Union Pacific and other railroads; and the Balboa Monument, a gift from Benito Mussolini. Timing the foundation of the NCGCC during this affair was a masterstroke. Dorsey's Pilgrim Baptist Church choir performed in the Hall of Religion at the Fair.[60] By the time of its next convening in St. Louis in 1934, the NCGCC was well on its way.

The Century of Progress fair provided Sallie Martin the opportunity to boost her reputation; her photo was featured in a *Chicago Defender* piece of April 8, 1933 with the lines: "The popular contralto and member of the gospel chorus at Pilgrim Baptist . . . is an active contestant in *the Chicago Defender*'s great World's Fair contest, with financial support of the chorus, members of the church, and the Gospel Choral Union." In other articles marking the leadup to the 1933 NCGCC meeting, the *Defender* noted that Martin sang with the Pilgrim Baptist Church Trio.

Martin traveled back to Cleveland in 1933 to organize a Gospel Choral Union there, implementing the NCGCC plan for expansion. She would create similar groups throughout the South and Midwest.[61] Choral unions from Chicago, St. Louis, and Cincinnati were among the first to join the NCGCC in 1933. The organizers published the first bylaws and elected "Dr." Thomas A. Dorsey as president, an office he retained for almost six decades. That year only, Martin was designated secretary of the convention; in 1934 and afterward, her designation was a much more elevated—and descriptive—"National Organizer" of the Gospel Choral Unions. By that time, the organization today known as the Dorsey Convention was on firm footing, but Sallie Martin had made only a regional name for herself. Chapter 3 follows the crafting of her image through the press and growth of her career as a result of untold hours on the road and a change of business partners.

CHAPTER 3

Curating an Identity with Business Partners, 1933–1949

Sallie Martin's livelihood involved performing and selling songs: first, with Thomas A. Dorsey from 1929 through 1939, and then with Kenneth Morris from 1940 to 1973. Both partnerships flourished, due in large part to Martin's activities as touring demonstrator and marketer, director of youth choirs, founder of Gospel Choral Unions (GCUs), and officer in the National Convention of Gospel Choirs and Choruses (NCGCC).[1] Black newspapers in Chicago, Pittsburgh, Cleveland, St. Louis, Atlanta, Indianapolis, New York, Philadelphia, Los Angeles, Seattle, and Washington, DC, among other cities, chronicle her construction of a public identity during this period. Her workplaces also published music strategically promoting her brand, with phrases like "sung by Sallie Martin, Queen of Contraltos."[2] Almost certainly the author of these soubriquets, Martin had begun to practice the art of self-promotion. With the post-1939 groups she headlined—the Sallie Martin Singers, Sallie Martin Gospel Singers, or Sallie Martin and Her Singers of Joy—the gospel singer became a household name. This chapter follows her career trajectory through the first arc of her celebrity, when she managed tour dates, collaborations, accommodations, and transportation in support of gospel music. Capitalizing on the Black press's willingness to support musical entrepreneurs, she curated a public persona that brought her—and many of those who traveled with her—fame, wealth, and respect.[3]

Early Press Coverage for Martin and the NCGCC

After 1933, Sallie Martin was mentioned regularly in the Black press in conjunction with the August meetings of the NCGCC, its board of directors meetings held in February, and the September conventions of the NBC. Even before the first NCGCC meeting, however, Sallie Martin's name and visage had appeared in the *Chicago Defender*. In January of 1933, she was entered in its nationwide contest focused on crowning the twenty-one "most popular race girls [over eighteen years old, married or single] in the country."[4] Contestants were required to submit a nomination form (published in the newspaper and good for five thousand votes), and Chicagoans were encouraged to mail in voting coupons, each worth one hundred votes, for their favorites. Winners from outside Chicago would receive all-expense-paid trips to Chicago's Century of Progress World's Fair in July. Winners who hailed from Chicago would be treated, instead, to a week in Atlantic City.

The April 8, 1933, *Defender* ran an attractive head shot of contestant Sallie Martin, who represented Dorsey's choir at Pilgrim Baptist Church and Chicago's Gospel Choral Union, the latter of which she cofounded.[5] By May 13, Martin had garnered 60,200 votes (cast by 552 people), but she had fallen out of the top twenty-one contestants and was eliminated. Another gospel celebrity, organist Mabel Sanford Lewis from Ebenezer Baptist Church, had received 478,200 (4,732 individual votes) and occupied fourth place. Ultimately, the top prize went to Lillian Jackson, a teacher from Tulsa, Oklahoma, who had amassed 1,008,200 votes (cast by 10,032 people); Lewis finished third with 661,600 votes from 6,566 people. Buzz around the World's Fair intensified alongside that of the contest.

Sallie Martin must not have felt the contest loss too sharply, busy as she was collaborating on the NCGCC's first meeting, to be held while the Fair was in progress. Fifty-two delegates attended that first convention, which kicked off at Pilgrim Baptist with a performance of the 600-member Chicago Gospel Choral Union on August 30. Dorsey, touted as "the Race's greatest gospel song writer," conducted that massed choir.[6] Magnolia Lewis, director of the W. D. Cook Gospel Choir at Metropolitan Community Church, emceed the concert (see chapter 2). The next morning saw the election of thirteen officers, with Dorsey taking the helm as national president. Five vice presidents represented the metropolitan areas that had sent delegates: St. Louis (Gus A. Evans), Chicago (Lewis), Detroit (Artelia Hutchins), East St. Louis (J. B. Harris), and Indianapolis (Miss McGavock). Other officers—including Sallie Martin, elected corresponding secretary—hailed from Chicago. From the outset, women outnumbered men among the vice presidents (three of five), as well as in the total slate (nine of thirteen). From its beginning, the NCGCC was driven in large part by a sisterhood of musical women upholding Dorsey as the figurehead.

In his first annual address, Dorsey laid out his hopes for the organization.

> I recommend that the gospel singers of this national convention have a home or headquarters, with departments to study, rehearse and develop the highest type of gospel singing with the very best interpretation of the spirituals and heart songs. That the headquarters be a place for gospel singers to stop over when traveling through the city and that the place be kept free from any activity or doings unbecoming for a Christian home: a place to reach the young singer and help the older one to reach the highest accomplishment along this line.[7]

These lofty aims resonated with Depression-Era Black Americans. The organization would offer a gospel curriculum that educated participants in all elements of musicianship and, specifically, in the performance practice of gospel. Its leaders also hoped to provide what the society at large did not, a safe haven for travelers.[8] Finally, Dorsey pledged particular attention to youth education in order to guide promising talents toward sacred music, the genre that had recently replaced the blues in his own life.

The second annual meeting of the NCGCC was held at the First Baptist Church of St. Louis, Missouri, from July 25 to 28, 1934.[9] "Five busses and two automobiles" transported two hundred singers from Chicago. Sallie Martin received praise in the *Defender* for her solo singing. At that convening, she traded the office of corresponding secretary for national organizer of the Gospel Choral Unions, a more prestigious role that was perfectly suited to her administrative talents.[10] Importantly for Dorsey's stated goals and the broader history of Black gospel, the NCGCC's Junior Department was established that year and Chicagoan Roberta Martin (not related to Sallie) became its national supervisor.[11] Sallie Martin sometimes acted as the NCGCC's youth fundraising chair in the 1930s and '40s. She also established and conducted youth choruses, including Chicago's South Side Inspirational Choir and the Dorsey Junior Choir in 1936.[12]

The first annual meeting of the NCGCC Board of Directors took place in February of 1935 at Ebenezer Baptist in Chicago.[13] Thirty out-of-town directors and twenty-five from Chicago attended this steering committee. Each director represented at least one choir; a conservative estimate of thirty singers per director brings the total gospel singers represented at the board meeting to 1,650. Important work was conducted at these meetings; for example, in 1936, the Board made further plans to establish a school for educating Black youth about gospel music, an initiative that would come to fruition in 1945.[14] Gospel music was on a steep growth curve, facilitated by these meetings and corresponding reportage.

Snapshots of Touring and Self-Naming in the 1930s

Sallie Martin's profile-raising performances extended beyond the reach of Chicago's influential GCU and the NCGCC, however. Along with the continuation of the Century of Progress Fair, the year 1934 also saw the formation of Dorsey's first female Gospel Quartette, comprising Sallie Martin, Mattie Wilson, Dettie Gay, and Bertha Armstrong.[15] This ensemble provided Martin regular opportunities as front woman, solo singer, ensemble director, and tour manager. The Dorsey Quartette was among the first ensembles in the country to feature women only.

In the role of Dorsey's caller, or declamatory lead singer, Martin remembered being responsible for demonstrating more than a dozen songs in one event, with no one to relieve her in the lead position.[16] Later, Martin acknowledged that she had damaged her voice in those years, when microphones weren't widely available.[17] Vocal damage and exhaustion posed significant challenges to singers who made a living on their vocal chords prior to readily available amplification. Early Black American singer America Robinson described the problem during an 1877 Fisk Jubilee Singers tour of Britain:

> Rest is the thing most desired among us just now. Jennie [Jackson] does not get better. She had three very bad days last week. She was screaming with pain. Maggie Porter is singing but always complaining of her chest. Maggie Carnes has been sick over a week.... This week I told Mr. Cravath [president of Fisk] I would be obliged to have some rest soon.[18]

Management of the Fisk singers and proponents of early gospel felt a similar urgency to capitalize on a revolutionary new marketing potential. Time for rest seemed an indulgence; in gospel, competing groups increasingly vied for the best audiences and venues. Further, Sallie Martin lacked any sort of vocal training that might have led her to sing half-voice to avoid vocal fatigue. She had begun sanctified, shout-style singing while living in Atlanta, then received scant instruction from Dorsey (most likely, diction lessons) after damaging patterns had been established. She treated her voice as she did the automobiles that transported her around the United States. As long as she kept up basic maintenance, her vocal instrument continued to serve its purpose.

At the beginning of 1933, Sallie Martin had been known to Black Chicago, if at all, as Pilgrim Baptist's entry in a popularity contest. Soon afterward, as gospel music neared its tipping point, she had a personal brand to manage. For women in her position, self-naming required meticulous attention to detail; early news releases described Martin as Dorsey's secretary or assistant and it took several years to adjust that impression. When she directed massed choirs at a 1934 meeting of the Protestant churches in Maywood, Illinois, her membership in Dorsey's Gospel Singers was duly noted in the *Chicago Defender* blurb.[19] The reporter also took care to mention that combined choirs under Martin's direction presented "jubilee and Negro spirituals" at the (white) First Methodist Church to a "mixed [race] audience." In a single release, *Defender* readers learned of her versatility as a choral director and Dorsey Quartette member, and prestige as a soloist among Black and white believers.

Traveling US roads by car was a fraught proposition in the 1930s. In later life, Martin especially loved retelling "road stories" from the longer automobile tours that took her vocal ensembles to rural areas in the Deep South. Southern motels open to African Americans in the 1930s were notoriously more unsanitary and unsafe than those serving white clientele. Martin, Mahalia Jackson, and others traveled with disinfectant and cleaning equipment in their cars. One evening, Martin and her group stopped at a particularly uninspiring hotel near Lake Pontchartrain in Louisiana.

> See, at that time . . . the barrier [i.e., discrimination against Blacks] . . . [was in full force] and oh, this hotel I'm telling you, it was nothing. I was scared to death. We got this room and I went up in it and I picked up [and cleaned under] the beds and everything else.[20]

An especially chilling event occurred when she briefly joined forces with the Roberta Martin Singers during the mid-1930s for a trip down South.[21] Reagon reproduced a photo that likely represents the same group, known briefly as the Martin and Martin Singers, which shows Roberta Martin (1907–1969), Sallie Martin, and the teenaged boys of the Martin/Frye quartet: Willie Webb (1919–after 1990), Robert Anderson (1919–1995), and Eugene Smith (1921–2009).[22] Sallie remembered that she "carried them on the road with me and that's the reason, why, we could have swept this country because the people thought [Roberta and I] were sisters."

One unforgettable night, Anderson was driving.

> On our way out of Selma, AL, going to Atlanta, an officer stopped us and we said, "What happened, officer?" He said, "This boy [can't] pass

> anyone on the right side. Why, he'll get somebody killed." I said "The error was, he figured it was a cross road and . . . you were going across, and he just pulled to the right." The officer says, "Where is your license?" So Robert [Anderson] was always so unconcerned, talks slower, and he was so long finding the license . . . so the [officer] got provoked. In the [police] car was an elderly officer [who] came back and he said, "What's the trouble here?" Robert's still not saying anything, so [the first officer] said—he used a curse word—"you get in the car and you all follow us." [I] got under the [steering] wheel, they [started to book] him in a little old place—a little caboose or something—so I jumped out of the car and said, "Officer, you have us under the wrong impression. I'm on my way to Atlanta, Georgia, for a revival in the morning and I just closed out in southern Alabama. We're not somebody just around gallivanting and out for a big time. . . . He said, "What have you got to show that you're doing some evangelist work?" . . . Roberta had published her first book and on the back was Christ on the cross, and I said, "well, here's some literature, so I opened the trunk and that was the first thing he saw. . . . When he came back, he said, "you have to learn this n----- how to talk. If I had my black jack I'd beat him to death." I said, "Well, I'm sure that you don't understand it, he's not a fast talker. It's not a matter that he's trying to ignore [you], it's just simply his makeup." . . . [The officer replied], "Well, I'll tell you, you'd better teach this damn n----- how to talk cause he's way down south."[23]

When Martin told this story to Standifer in 1981, she added that one of the lawmen "gave [Anderson] a wham right in the face" before putting him in their car. Such terrifying experiences would have persuaded the less courageous to stay close to home. Anderson's unhurried response to white authority had exacerbated a racially charged situation, but Sallie Martin's experience and confidence, though perhaps embroidered in her memory, nonetheless defused a potentially deadly scenario. This seems reasonable; her childhood and adolescence in rural Georgia had given her ample experience with racial tension and the capacity to judge when it was time to resist, when to retreat with a "yes, sir," and when to assume the authority to explain (see chapter 1).

Sallie's and Roberta's joint touring was short-lived. Sallie gave her perspective on their incompatibility—competing egos, surely—in another memory. According to Sallie, the Superintendent of a Sunday School Congress in Alabama said that he didn't like Roberta Martin's attitude.[24] Perhaps referring to the same tour, Sallie recalled that Roberta was dissatisfied that the two Martins had received equal billing in Texas. Obviously they were each more comfortable as headliners than as half of a duo. In late-in-life interviews, Sallie didn't hesitate to relay her impressions of that shared tour, but just as often, Sallie reiterated her respect: "[the Roberta Martin Singers] were good singers. They were good singers."[25]

Hiatus, Then a Return to the Spotlight

Black newspapers, otherwise reliable sources for Sallie Martin's activities during the 1930s, published very little about her between the 1934 and 1936 NCGCC summer meetings.[26] This curious gap may be explained by a health issue or, perhaps, events in the life of her son, Joel. On April 24, 1934, the twenty-year-old Joel had married Katherine Johnson (b. 1919–ca. 1971), a native of Seattle, Washington. They would have three children: Earlene (1934–2005), Earl Joel (1936–2008), and Yvonne (b. about 1939). Sallie may have been occupied with her son's family immediately after her first grandchild was born, perhaps even undertaking childcare.[27]

Regular coverage of Sallie Martin returned to the *Chicago Defender*'s pages in the summer of 1936, when she chaired the Chicago GCU's junior scholarship fund.[28] In the same month, she headed to Los Angeles with the Dorsey Quartette for a convocation of the Colored Methodist Episcopal (CME) denomination (see chapter 5). She was accompanied by pianist Beatrice Brown from Indianapolis, an important colleague in the NCGCC, and Rev. A. W. Womack, the influential minister at Brown's church.[29] The Quartette kicked off their tour with an appearance at the Indianapolis church of Brown and Womack, Phillips Temple CME. The July 25, 1936, *Defender* announcement had led with "Sallie Martin, national gospel singer and secretary to Thomas A. Dorsey, noted gospel writer, left July 10 for California." The choice of "secretary" to describe Martin shows the diligence required to maintain her identity as a professional in her own right; such terms appear rarely after this announcement.

About the Los Angeles convocation, the *Indianapolis Recorder* reported that on "men's and women's day," "Dr. Arthur W. Womack . . . was speaker for [the men in attendance] from the subject, 'Man, God's Masterpiece.'"[30] The *Defender* recorded that, "The Hall Johnson male chorus sang [and also,] Madam Sallie Martin, special representative of Prof. Thomas A. Dorsey of Chicago."[31] According to the newspapers, the convocation drew five hundred ministers, delegates, and friends hailing from Ohio, Pennsylvania, Kentucky, Indiana, West Virginia, New Mexico, Texas, Arizona, and California.

While on the West Coast, Martin and the Quartette fulfilled several other engagements, including one at L.A.'s 28th Street YMCA, before heading back to Chicago. They sang in El Paso before stopping in Dallas, Texas, where they planned to perform at the Texas Centennial World's

Fair. Other singing engagements in Oklahoma City, Kansas City, and St. Louis punctuated the trip home. Stopping points on the trip likely represent a combination of trusted performance venues, revenue potential, and overnight accommodations during the long car trip. African American women would have welcomed the safety of home stays as they negotiated the racist motel, gasoline, and automobile repair industries. A notation in Martin's address book, written in her hand and dating to around 1940, mentions one runout to Ohio. The first page is titled "Where Miss Martin Goes," followed by an indication that her group would sing in Columbus on a Sunday, then would arrive at a Steubenville address on Monday (see figure 3.1).

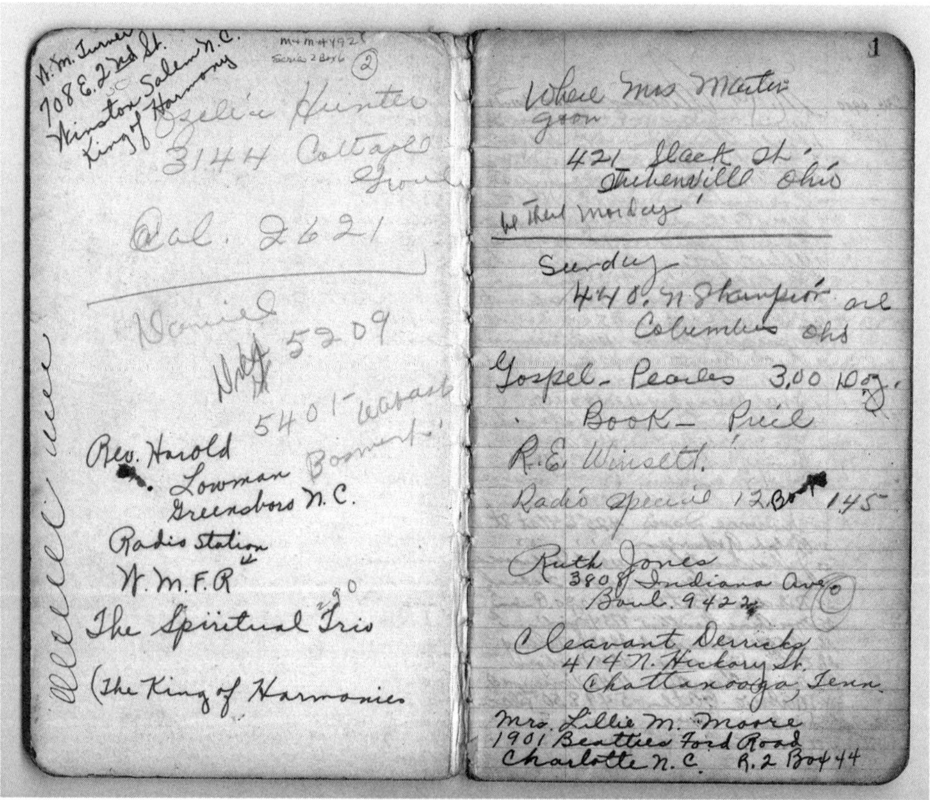

FIGURE 3.1. Martin's undated "Agent Book," with "Where Mrs. Martin goes" in Sallie Martin's hand, followed by a mixture of music orders and contact information. The Chicago address and phone number of Ruth Jones (Dinah Washington), suggests dating of this page to 1940 or '41. Martin and Morris Music Company Records, series 2, 6. Used with permission.

Martin continued her crafting of news reports after her return from Los Angeles. "Mrs." or "Miss" more frequently prefaced her name and she regularly included one of her repertory of taglines. The *Indianapolis Recorder* reported that she, "the great gospel singer," would be at Terre Haute's Free Will Baptist Church to organize a GCU in that city[32] and a 1936 *Pittsburgh Courier* article announced that Martin, "the popular soloist from Chicago" would be presented in a musical program Friday, October 30, at Truelight Baptist Church in St. Louis.[33]

Meanwhile, Martin carried out her duties as National Organizer of GCU's for the NCGCC. During each of her 1936 and 1937 visits to Fort Wayne, Terre Haute, Indianapolis, and Dayton, she founded a new GCU or gave a workshop for an existing one in preparation for the 1937 NCGCC convention in Indianapolis. When the NCGCC board met in in Dayton, the *Pittsburgh Courier* ran photos of Martin and Dorsey to illustrate the title, "Gospel Choral Union Heads."[34] She and Dorsey also traveled outside the Midwest to celebrate the first anniversary of New York's GCU, which took place on May 17, 1937. "Professor Dorsey" was pictured in a photo captioned "America's Foremost Gospel Song Writer" and "Mrs. Sallie Martin" was described as a "National Gospel Singer." The main event took place at Bethel Baptist Church in Brooklyn, but the duo also performed at Mount Zion Church, People's Institutional Methodist Church, and Salem Baptist Church that week.[35] By the late 1930s, Martin was rarely described as secretary or assistant to Dorsey in the newspapers and, occasionally, Dorsey's reputation was even deemphasized, as in the *Pittsburgh Courier* announcement of Martin's participation in a 1938 gospel singing contest in New Orleans. Also appearing on the program of this "most unique affair in the Crescent City" was Thomas A. Dorsey, the "famous tenor."[36]

The NCGCC and an Anti-Lynching Bill

At the 1937 NCGCC convention in Indianapolis, Martin and the other officers registered their views in an important national debate, likely at the urging of minister-activist A. W. Womack.[37] One thousand delegates from ten states attended the gospel convention. President Dorsey read his annual address, the scholarship competition was held, and the "Artists Night" (a concert of popular singers) featured Sallie Martin, among others. Less routine business included a Board resolution, wired to senators from the ten states represented at the Convention, to "use their influence to fight for passage of the Wagner-Costigan antilynching bill," since it was stalled in Congress.

In the 1930s, the persistence of vigilantism could scarcely be ignored by the average American; New Yorkers were regularly reminded by a banner that hung outside the Fifth Avenue offices of the NAACP reading "A Man Was Lynched Yesterday."[38] The Black press was faithful to report such violence, as well. Late in life, Martin was pressed about lynchings that she was aware of during her childhood. At first she responded, "Being young, it didn't stick in my mind."[39] In fact, a horrific mass shooting took place about twenty-five miles from her home.

> A mob went to the Oconee County jail in Watkinsville and pulled out nine of the 10 prisoners accused of various serious crimes. The mob tied the nine men, eight black and one white, to a fence and shot them. One of the nine survived, but the eight who died made the Oconee lynching one of the largest ever recorded.[40]

Prompted repeatedly by Standifer in the 1981 interview, Martin finally shared her memory: "They seemed like they were lining them up on the side of the walls or something, with their backs to them. And that was the reason why this man when they're falling and somebody fell on him. And, of course, he just acted as though he was dead." Her memory was that of a ten-year-old.

The Ku Klux Klan (KKK) had been reinvigorated by D. W. Griffith's film *The Birth of a Nation* (1915); lynchings again increased after Black servicemen, who had experienced more equitable treatment overseas, returned from World War I. The US House of Representatives passed antilynching legislation in 1922, but Senate Democrats filibustered and the majority-Republican Senate had allowed the bill to die. By the mid-1920s, Klan membership had exploded to around four million.[41] The election of Roosevelt in 1932 led many to believe that an antilynching law would finally be passed. In 1934, Eleanor Roosevelt began to collaborate with NAACP Executive Secretary Walter White, with hopes of reviving the antilynching bill that had been drafted that year by Robert F. Wagner of New York and Edward Costigan of Colorado. It proposed federal trials for any law enforcement officers who failed to exercise their responsibilities during a lynching incident. Despite the efforts of the NAACP, the musical NCGCC, his own wife, and other forces, President Roosevelt did not sign the bill because he relied so heavily on the southern Democratic voting bloc for his reelection and New Deal agendas. Ironically, Martin still remembered Roosevelt fondly when asked about the Depression in 1972. "Oh yes, I could never forget my Roosevelt. . . . When [the crash] happened . . . I didn't have but just a few dollars . . . I guess about $50, and lost that in the bank." Asked if she had been afraid to keep her money in banks after that, Martin replied, "I imagine almost everybody was, but after Roosevelt fixed it, . . . I never worried about it anymore."[42] Despite her admiration of FDR, she was a leader in the group that took a definitive stand for justice in 1937 (see chapters 4 and 6).

Endings, Beginnings, and a Singular Benefactor: Rev. Clarence Cobbs

Sallie Martin formally discontinued her business association with Dorsey sometime in late 1939, but the event still rankled many decades later. "Well, you know the thing about it," she said, was that "he was satisfied with the way I was running [the business], but . . . he wanted to [believe] what somebody else said and [Dorsey didn't] have enough grit to just say, 'well, she's doing a mighty fine job with the business.'"[43] That confrontation ended with Martin deciding she would strike out on her own. She had invested a great deal of energy in helping Dorsey build his brand over ten years and established her own reputation in the places they had traveled. The unacknowledged partnership, for such it was, had run its course, though they would cooperate in their shared work for the NCGCC until Martin's death in 1988. Mahalia Jackson, one of Dorsey's featured singers at Pilgrim Baptist Church, would become his primary song demonstrator after Sallie Martin.[44] Martin soon found a situation over which she had more authority.

With only a few dollars and an automobile to her name, Sallie Martin was introduced to an ideal new business partner in Kenneth Morris (1917–1988).[45] By then, Martin had transcended the grim realities of her childhood in the Deep South, where all three of her custodial adults died before she was sixteen. She had completed all or nearly all of the schooling that was available to her and, in rapid succession, she had become a single mother, lost her home in a fire, and joined the Great Migration to Cleveland, then Chicago. Kenneth Morris, twenty-three years old at their first meeting in 1940, grew up as a comparatively advantaged child in New York City. He attended the City College of New York for three years while also receiving musical training at the Manhattan Conservatory.[46] In 1934, Morris ditched his formal training in piano and composition and followed the siren call of jazz, which took him to Chicago.

Sallie Martin ended her association with Thomas A. Dorsey the same year that Kenneth Morris left the employ of another Black Chicago music publisher, Lillian M. Bowles (see chapter 4). Morris's fertile mind and equal facility in church music and jazz equipped him well for the new gospel style. In 1937, he became the arranger/accompanist for Bowles's company. About his job there, Morris recalled, "Somehow or other, I'd have to get the song out of [a person's] head and on to paper."[47] Prophetically, Bowles introduced Morris to the minister who would become so influential in his life.

The Martin-Morris partnership, destined to lead the longest-lived and most successful Black-owned music publishing company in US history to date, was the brainchild of influential minister Clarence Henry Cobbs (1908–1979). A native of Nashville, Cobbs began his Chicago church experience at Pilgrim Baptist around 1926. He then converted to the Spiritual faith, a combination of Black Protestantism and Catholicism that embraced psychic spiritual guidance. Cobbs founded his own Spiritual congregation, the First Church of Deliverance, in 1929. Beginning in 1935, he capitalized on radio to advertise his gospel-infused religious services. To outsiders, the Spiritual denomination seemed to emphasize communication with the dead and endowment of objects such as flowers and handkerchiefs with healing power. One WPA writer remarked that Cobbs's followers obtained these icons like "hungry children at a picnic."[48] In the late 1930s, Cobbs hired Kenneth Morris, a jazz-trained pianist whose gifts extended beyond composition and arranging, as his church music director. When Cobbs purchased a Hammond organ at First Church, Morris fully exploited the musical marvel, forever changing the sound of Black gospel music. Cobbs knew that underwriting a new venture run by the dynamic musician and businesswoman, Sallie Martin, and the musical innovator, Kenneth Morris, was an excellent investment. With funds left over from his successful building campaign, Cobbs provided them the requisite startup money to open a business in 1940.

A charismatic leader, Cobbs was also a magnet for controversy. Tristan Cabello estimates that in the 1940s,

> Bronzeville's most powerful man was probably Reverend Clarence Cobbs. . . . From its beginnings as a small religious organization of just thirteen members, the First Church of Deliverance boasted more than 9,000 members at the beginning of the 1940s, after constructing a huge building at 4315 S. Wabash, [and] becoming one of the country's largest churches.[49]

Martin's life-changing relationship with Cobbs is especially interesting because widespread speculation had come to a head mere months before Cobbs financed the new publishing business. The *Chicago Defender* had published innuendoes that linked Cobbs with homosexuality in late 1939, and same-sex relations were far from acceptable in the eyes of the religious.[50]

Martin could hardly have been unaware of the accusation, given the sensational banner with which the *Defender* superseded its November 25, 1939, masthead: "State's Attorney Probes Scandal on Rev. Cobb" [*sic*], on page one. Immediately below, an unsigned article quoted the minister's statement from a radio broadcast: "I am full man, don't believe any gossip you hear circulating about me."[51] Cobbs swiftly countered the *Defender*'s articles head-on. On December 9, 1939, the *Defender* topped page nine with the banner, "Radio Pastor Sues *Defender* for $250,000," with the subtitle: "Says 'Virtue and Integrity Were Injured.'"[52] Cobbs's official complaint in libel was reprinted in full, along with his request for a jury trial. The absence of follow-up reportage in the *Defender* suggests that the suit was dropped, settled out of court, or otherwise resolved.[53] At any rate, just before Sallie Martin benefitted from Cobbs's largesse, editors at the *Defender* had called attention to what they thought was an inconsistency between his public and private personas, and Cobbs gave back defiance in equal measure. Guided by interviews with First Church of Deliverance insiders as well as outsiders, Cabello believes that

> Very few people . . . did discuss the matter [of Cobbs's sexual identity]: they accepted it without decrying it. Cobbs wished to, and indeed could, control his image, due to a complex web of power relations, combined from his religious activities, control of the media, his own publicity, and his dominant status in the neighborhood . . . which resulted in respect for him.[54]

Informed by oral history, Best argues further that First Church of Deliverance was a well-known safe space for homosexual men in the 1940s.[55] Sallie Martin's alliance with Cobbs may explain why she later gave financial support to young male gospel performers purported to be homosexual (see chapter 7).

Judging the veracity of unsubstantiated reports about a historical figure is always tricky. Cobbs left behind substantial evidence of personal choices that historians have woven into a persuasive picture of homosexuality, but the Reverend never, himself, stated that he was gay. Currently, those to whom it matters least assume he was, while the entire topic is studiously avoided by a large subsection of Chicago church folk (see the introduction to this volume).

In any case, from the outset of their joint enterprise, Sallie Martin and Kenneth Morris were indebted to a dominant but controversial public figure in Chicago's Black religious scene. Though Cobbs's relationship with the *Chicago Defender* was broken at least temporarily, owners of the Martin and Morris Music Studio enjoyed many years of positive press.

Workings of the MMMS in the First Decade

To their musical partnership, the 45-year-old Martin brought a decade's experience as a song demonstrator, financial manager, and impresaria, while Morris, about half her age, contributed uncommon skill in composition, arranging, keyboard performance, and piano teaching.[56] He was willing to headquarter in Chicago, while Martin liked the touring life. The team rented a store at 4315 South Indiana Avenue for fifty dollars per month, bought showcases, and informed competitors Dorsey and Roberta Martin about the new business. They first named the venture the Martin and Morris Music and Studio Teaching School, but soon shortened the name to Martin and Morris Music Studio (MMMS). Sometime between 1946 and 1949, they moved across the street into a larger space—a former post office encompassing 4312 and 4314 South Indiana.[57]

Figure 3.2. Unidentified photographer, Martin and Morris Music Studio (MMMS) storefront, 4312–4314 South Indiana Street, Chicago, mid-1940s. Martin and Morris Music Company Records, series 5, 8. Used with permission.

In its first year, the MMMS published its own single-page octavos such as "I Am Coming, Open Up the Door" (words and music by Curtis Madison, arr. Kenneth Morris), and anthologies like the 24-page *Three Stars Gospel Song Book*, compiled by the owners. It featured twenty-one songs, a hefty percentage composed and/or arranged by Kenneth Morris, some by Theodore Frye (the other "star"), and one composed by Morris's future wife, Necie (Eunice) Gwendolyn Seaberry (1919–2005). Boyer estimated that about seventy of Morris's career total of more than three hundred compositions were copyrighted in 1940 by the MMMS, though only about thirty were composed in that year.[58] Morris's "I'll Be a Servant for the Lord" was his first to attract wide attention, in part because the Wings Over Jordan Choir sang it on their coast-to-coast radio broadcasts originating at Cleveland's CBS affiliate.[59]

Figure 3.3. Unidentified photographer, portrait of Sallie Martin at the MMMS, mid-1940s. Martin and Morris Company Records, series 5, 8. Used with permission.

Figure 3.4. Unidentified photographer, portrait of Kenneth Morris at the MMMS, mid-1940s. Martin and Morris Company Records, series 5, 8. Used with permission.

Kenneth Morris's most familiar arrangement is the perennial "Just a Closer Walk with Thee," based on an anonymous tune he heard sung by William R. Hurse's Kansas City choir in 1940.[60] When asked the origin of the song, Hurse told Morris he had no idea; he had heard it all his life. Morris notated it on the spot and soon published an arrangement. The Sallie Martin Singers performed it at a National Baptist Convention and, according to Morris, "that is what put us on the map." However,

> We weren't too careful about getting copyrights so [my arrangement of "Just a Closer Walk with Thee"] was stolen from me. . . . You have to remember that we didn't have any business sense at all. . . . We knew nothing about copyrighting or any of that end of it. . . . At ten cents a copy, there was no money involved . . . the expense of copyrighting was about two dollars, so it wasn't even worthwhile. . . . We just put the copyright notice on the song, just put it on there. . . . When [the white Southern publisher Winsett] took my song . . . that woke me up. . . . After 1944, we started copyrighting all our music.[61]

A handwritten letter signed by Robert Anderson sufficed as a contract to publish in 1942, while later agreements necessarily sorted out the rights of music written by a customer, published by the MMMS, and recorded by labels such as Savoy and Specialty. Though the US Copyright Act of 1909 had differentiated performance and mechanical rights, and in 1914, ASCAP had simplified the distribution of royalty payments, Martin and Morris were not alone in their loss of ownership and revenue as a result of the complexities of the copyright system.[62] Black entrepreneurs would swiftly educate themselves in order to maintain control of their intellectual property.

Working with the Rayner Dalheim Company, a well-established printer and engraver, the MMMS sold Morris's original and arranged gospel songs, as well as those of other composers. The MMMS also initiated an endeavor that relied on Kenneth Morris's seemingly limitless capacity to generate new gospel melodies, his text-setting expertise, and facility with harmonization. The company's Songwriters Service provided anyone in the country a chance to see their names in print as author or composer on the cover of a gospel octavo, copies of which could then be sold to local choir directors. People from all walks of life and regions in the United States paid a nominal fee to have their gospel poems, melodies, and lead sheets transformed into products ranging from a harmonized melody (returned in Morris's manuscript score) to multiple copies of a published, solo-plus-accompaniment or choral arrangement. Some submissions were rejected, but if he or Martin saw promise in the kernel of a song, Morris could turn out a deft harmonic setting—the mere skeleton of a full-blown gospel performance, but a gospel song, nonetheless—in a day (see figure 3.5). Making his creative work so affordable generated income and expanded the gospel music audience. Morris also sold and demonstrated music in the store and learned on the fly about running a publishing business. He remembered, "I gave lessons. We were not looking forward to the sale of music to make a living"; i.e., they weren't naïve enough to believe they could make a living selling music without teaching lessons.[63] They would soon realize that they had underestimated the potential of selling music.

Prior to 1952, the MMMS communicated its fee structure in individual letters and invoices (see table 3.1). That year, if a customer submitted a poem only, the MMMS provided two copies of a typeset melody with accompaniment for $25. Additional copies of anything that had been typeset were $5 for 500. A customer received 1,000 typeset copies of a Kenneth Morris melody and accompaniment for a poem for $35. Each copy of that new gospel song thus cost 3.5 cents. With luck, the customer might sell all thousand for ten cents each, resulting in a gross profit of $100 and a net gain of $65.74.

At some point before May of 1952, Martin and Morris printed the first Songwriters Service flyer and began to send it out with shipped orders and distribute it on tours. A new fee structure retained the $25 charge for two copies of a new Morris melody (now returned to the customer in manuscript) and $10 for two manuscript copies of a four-part vocal arrangement by Morris. One thousand typeset copies of a Morris arrangement now cost $55, so the conversion of a submitted poem to 1,000 copies of a melodized, harmonized, typeset, and printed octavo therefore cost $90: $25 for the melody, $10 for the arrangement, and $55 for the copies.[64]

In 1960, the complete cost for returning that thousand copies to a customer who had supplied a poem only was $115. If the customer sent in a tape recording of his song, MMMS would publish a four-part, voice-plus-piano arrangement and 1,000 octavo-sized, black-and-white copies for $120. On this final extant version of the Songwriters Service flyer, the owners spelled out their policies governing deposits, return of materials, and refunds. Advertising on a publication's back cover cost extra and responsibility for copyrighting songs rested with the customer.

As the company's reputation grew, Martin and Morris followed the leads of Frye, Dorsey, Pace, and Bowles by publishing song anthologies in booklet form. That practice extended well into the 1960s and produced booklets such as *Special Song Book #2* (1946) and #15 (1949); books containing numbers popularized by prominent groups (Pilgrim Travelers, 1951, as *All Star Gospel Song Book* #30 [1962]); and *The Best of James Cleveland* as *All Star*

FIGURE 3.5. Kenneth Morris's 1940s manuscript arrangement of Pearl Bryant's text, "The Victory of Love." Martin and Morris Company Records, series 1, 1. Used with permission.

TABLE 3.1. Prices and Services of the MMMS Songwriter Service: 1942, 1952, and 1960. Martin and Morris Company Records, series 1, 1–2.

4 May 1942					
If Customer Submits:	MMMS Provides	Cost	Copies	Layout (Inches)	Down Payment
Poem only	Typeset melody/ accompaniment	$25	2	8.5 x 11	$2–$5
Poem and melody	4-part arrangement, typeset	$12	500	1 octavo page	
	Additional copies of above	$5	500		
August 1952*#					
If Customer Submits:	MMMS Provides	Cost	Copies	Layout (Inches)	Down Payment+
Poem only	Suitable melody, MS	$25	2	8.5 x 11	$15 w/ contract
Poem and melody	Vocal/piano arrangement, MS	$10	2	8.5 x 11	
Poem, melody, 4-part arr.	Typeset submitted arrangement	$55	1,000	4 octavo pages	$30 w/ contract
	Photo on cover and/or back cover	"extra"			
November 1960*					
If Customer Submits:	MMMS Provides	Cost	Copies	Layout (Inches)	Down Payment+
Poem only	Suitable melody	$35	2	8.5 x 11	$20 w/ contract
Poem and melody	Vocal/piano arrangement, pen MS	$15	2	8.5 x 11	
Poem, melody, 4-part arr.	Submitted arrangement, typeset	$65	1,000	4 octavo pages	$50 w/ contract
	Photo on cover and/or back cover	"extra"			

*"We are not responsible for the return of your material unless accompanied by postal stamps sufficient for return."

"We will help you get your song on the market through our nation-wide contacts and mailing list."

+ The flyer included a contractual agreement—"I agree to pay . . . the balance COD when the work is finished"—and a signature line.

Song Book #5 (1965). These would have been sold at the NCGCC and NBC conventions alongside similar volumes and octavos of their competitors, and advertised in any mailings leaving the MMMS store (see figures 3.6 and 3.7).

Morris also capitalized on his position as gospel thought leader by publishing prose booklets, comprising aphorisms intended as sermon illustrations, practical instructions for church ushers, inspirational poems by various authors, and practical guides for choir directors. His small monograph, *Improving the Music in the Church* (1949), contains chapters on the value of church music, music history, rudiments of music, ways to test and choose suitable repertoire, duties of church officers, and how to plan a program.[65] Guest author Thomas A. Dorsey contributed a chapter entitled "Ministry of Music in the Church." Morris valued congregational singing, but saw the choral director and choir as guardians of musical quality; he urged discipline in rehearsals and regular introduction of new songs to retain interest. To combat the vocal wear and tear Sallie Martin had experienced, he advocated half-voice rehearsals. He paid careful attention to choral processions and recessions, and conservative dress: "It is not the loudness or gaudiness of costumes which makes a choir beautiful, but the cleanliness, neatness, and complete uniformity of all the members."[66]

The Chicago Public Library acquired 1,500 separate MMMS publications, one each of the remaining inventory, in two batches dated 1986 and 1988. Kenneth Morris had composed 134 of those. Other prominent gospel figures are represented in the total; ninety were composed by James Cleveland, fifty-six by Alex Bradford, thirty-nine by Roberta Martin, twenty-five by Thomas A. Dorsey, twenty-one by Dorothy Love Coates, fourteen by Clara Ward, ten by Cora Martin, and eight were the works of Sallie Martin.[67] Approximately 150 additional authors were represented by only one MMMS publication, only one of which, Adolphe Adam's "O Holy Night," was an arranged classic. In 1972, a "robust," 55-year-old Kenneth Morris proudly told interviewer Anthony Griggs that he had composed or arranged at least 80 percent of all printed gospel music in circulation at that time, a claim that could plausibly withstand challenge. By Morris's reckoning in 1972, the MMMS still shipped music to every state in the United States and to England, France, the West Indies, and Liberia. He explained that international sales were bolstered by Black GIs who ordered music during World War II and the Korean conflict.[68]

Kenneth Morris and Sallie Martin contributed great intellect and energy into building the MMMS from a startup to a thriving concern in record time. It moved successfully into the second half of the century following a simple formula: Morris created the product and Martin marketed it.

1944 - JUST OFF THE PRESS - 1944

Yes God is Real 10c
Have You Forsaken Your Old Mother 10c
Oh Lord Hear My Plea 10c
Just Smile Awhile 10c
Well You've Never Seen The Like Before 10c
Oh The Joy That's Never Been Told 10c
Is It Well With Your Soul 10c
I've Borne A Heavy Load 10c
I Know I Have Another Building 10c
I Love Jesus 10c
You Gotta Be Real And Pure In Heart 10c
Nothing Can Keep Me From Serving The Lord 10c
Just Hold On 10c
I'm Trying To Make Heaven My Home 10c
I've Had A Hard Time Seeking For My Lord 10c
He Will Explain It All To You 10c
Get Away Jordan 10c
I Know He Has Prepared A Place For Me 10c
Just To Know 10c
Holding Jesus In Thine Arms 10c

1944 — BRAND NEW! - 1944

Hold Out Your Light 15c
I Want To Be Dear Lord Just What You Want Me To Be 15c
I Have An Interest Over There 15c
If This World Only Knew 10c
God Leads His Dear Children Along 15c

BEST SELLERS

If I Can Just Make It In 15c
Does Jesus Care 15c
Jesus I Love You 10c
You Must Be Born Again 15c
Till We Meet Again (New Dismissal Song) 15c

PLACE YOUR ORDER NOW

" MARTIN & MORRIS" Gospel Gems No. 1, 2, 4 and 5

Price 35c Each **$3.50 Per Dozen**

ORDER NOW! AVOID DELAY!

"THREE STARS" GOSPEL SONG BOOK

Price 35c Each **$3.50 Per Dozen**

! BRAND NEW !

Gospel Song Books by "Martin & Morris"

NATIONAL GOSPEL SINGER

Price 35c Each **$3.50 Per Dozen**

GOLDEN STARS No. 1

Order Today From

MARTIN & MORRIS MUSIC STUDIO

4315 INDIANA AVENUE **CHICAGO 15, ILLINOIS**

FIGURE 3.6. Back Cover Ad, 1944. Martin and Morris Company Records, series 4, 1. Used with permission.

FIGURE 3.7. Poetry Book Cover. Martin and Morris Company Records, series 4, 1. Used with permission.

Returns on their investment of time and energy were unprecedented: Morris recalled that annual sales fluctuated between $70,000 and $100,000 (1940s values) in the company's "first years" and a steadier $100,000 per year from 1944 to 1954. The company's zenith spanned the years 1955 through 1964, during which time gross sales ranged between $160,000 and $200,000 per year.[69] More about Martin's touring and recording life are forthcoming in chapters 5 and 6; chapter 4 suspends the chronological progression of this book to consider Sallie Martin in the company of several female peers.

CHAPTER 4

Interconnected Spheres of Influence

Sallie Martin and Early Peers

Early 1930s gospel music gave religious women entrée into a livelihood that had formerly been closed to them. Sallie Martin and her fellow pioneers need no longer hesitate to travel and sing, lest they be classified as blues singers like Ma Rainey (Dorsey's former employer) or Bessie Smith. In reconciling their culture's expectations of Black female propriety with gospel's syncopated rhythms and blues inflections, these women performers, managers, and publishers were trailblazers.

This chapter outlines a spectrum of female success in the first full decade of gospel blues by considering several women whose professional lives intersected with or paralleled Sallie Martin's. They were roughly of the same generation and began their careers in the 1920s or '30s.[1] Whether personal or professional; warm, amicable, or antagonistic; their relationships and independent routes clarify the crucial work carried out by the first generation of gospel women. Some of them worked closely with Martin over several decades, demonstrating a quality previously unexamined in writings about Martin—cooperation within long-term relationships. A synthesis of the work accomplished by the eight women briefly visited here closes the chapter.

My case studies include Lucie Eddie Campbell of Memphis (1885–1963), the most outspoken advocate of women's rights in the group, who by 1930 was the musical tastemaker in the all-important National Baptist Convention. Lillian Mae Bowles Pannell (1885–1967) opened the first female-owned and -run gospel music publishing business in Chicago in 1929. Magnolia Lewis-Butts (1895–1949) was a classically trained vocalist and pianist who led from the position of director of the junior choir at Chicago's Metropolitan Community Church. Gertrude Ward of Philadelphia (1901–1981) is best known as the impresaria of the Clara Ward Singers (founded 1943), but her own gospel journey began in 1932. Before establishing another family-based group, Willie Mae Ford Smith of St. Louis (1904–1994) at first mirrored the patterns of Sallie Martin's musical tours and likewise commanded respect in the NCGCC. Though Roberta Martin (1907–1969) falls between Sallie's generation and the next, she is considered here because she opened her Chicago publishing business a few months prior to the founding of the Martin and Morris Music Studio in 1940. Documentation about Chicago composer, conductor, and publisher Emma L. Jackson (1910–1946[?]) is sparse, but she belongs among the women publishers and performers in this discussion. She and Mahalia Jackson (1911–1972), the latter of whose relationship with Martin is better documented, represent a point of articulation between the older and younger generations. Mahalia's popularity within and outside of religious institutions eclipsed that of the other women in this group, though she began by singing in 1930s storefront churches with Sallie Martin in Chicago.

Lucie Eddie Campbell

In gospel circles and the history of Black women, the name of Lucie E. Campbell is spoken with reverence and respect. Her place of origin was the rural Deep South, but her migration ended in Memphis, where Ida B. Wells (1862–1931) had already shattered the expectation that disadvantage would forever follow poor southern Black girls. A formidable organizer, teacher, and choir director, Campbell's influence was felt throughout the nation. She made her mark in three areas. First, she led the way for Black women composers; her "Something Within" was included in the landmark NBC hymnal of 1921, *Gospel Pearls*.[2] After 1940, Campbell turned her attention more fully from teaching to composing. Having established herself professionally before the widespread acceptance of gospel, Campbell favored hymnlike songs in moderate tempos, but embraced tinges of gospel in "Something Within" (1919) and her crossover-to-gospel song, "Jesus Gave Me Water" (1946).[3]

Campbell's second major contribution to history was her civil rights advocacy for women and Black Americans. In her youth, composers like Theodore Frye could preach a message and punctuate it with his own singing, a position of influence denied Campbell because of her membership in the Baptist church and its ban on women preachers. Rather than accepting subordination, she infiltrated the male-dominated administrative structure of her Memphis churches. She pushed her agendas hard and was even expunged from the church rolls on more than one occasion—once for refusing to apologize to a male deacon.[4] Campbell's male cohorts found her brash, stern, and prickly, but as often, they (like Sallie Martin's detractors) benefited from her self-knowledge, clear thinking, and organizational skills. She even resisted the status quo in delaying her marriage to her long-term partner, C. R. Williams, because she would have been expected to give up her teaching position as a married woman. Campbell and Williams married in 1960 and formed a publishing company.

Third, Campbell had a singular influence over the early acceptance of gospel, which, in turn, had a tremendous impact on Sallie Martin's career. Prior to Campbell's influential work within the National Baptist Convention, she welcomed Beale Street blues musicians into her Music Club. Such a group was featured at the 1903 NBC Convention in Birmingham. A dozen persistent years later, Campbell was elected the NBC's Music Director and became its musical tastemaker and gatekeeper: significantly, one who had no problem with the blues. By the time Willie Mae Ford Smith performed Dorsey's "If You See My Savior" at the 1930 National Baptist Convention in Chicago and the composer was summoned to sell copies, Campbell had solidified her position as arbiter of musical taste for that organization. In her decision to allow Dorsey to sell his music at the convention, she accomplished several things: she gave early gospel her imprimatur, she advanced the music department of the organization and thus positioned it at the headwaters of the gospel movement, and she opened doors for a handful of composers and fledgling businesses in exponentially significant ways. She also founded and directed Convention choirs and facilitated the early career of W. Herbert Brewster of Memphis, whose "Move On Up a Little Higher" (1946) became a Mahalia Jackson standard. Another Brewster tune, "Surely God Is Able" (1950), was a calling card of the Clara Ward Singers. Sallie Martin recalled to Luvenia A. George in 1983, "[Campbell] was beautiful; she had 'grace' enough to bring Black music out of the hymn writing tradition."[5]

Boyer and George provide valuable coverage of Campbell's gospel work in the NBC, her musical legacy, and her advocacy for racial justice in *We'll Understand It Better By and By*.[6] In the same volume, Rev. Charles Walker relates firsthand experiences with the musical icon. Famously strict, Campbell taught English and American History at Booker T. Washington High School in Memphis. She was also administratively responsible for an entire floor of students in the building. Bearing the "uncanny ability" to tell if a student were pregnant, Campbell demanded on one occasion that a girl sit out of rehearsal for a graduation ceremony: "You'll never disgrace this school with two of you in line! Both of you can't march in this line, baby.

Sit down. I'll mail you your diploma!"[7] In enforcing her high expectations of those in her charge, Campbell mirrors Sallie Martin's no-nonsense tour policies (see chapter 5).

Roxanne Reed pointed out that values of uplift (whose essential element is spirituality) and universality (where one succeeds, all succeed) characterize Campbell's relentless efforts.[8] Her personality was grounded in a clear vision of personal power, but geographical place was also crucial, as it was for Martin. As the home of social gospel advocate Mary McLeod Bethune, Memphis provided Campbell with antecedents of resistance and power that she personalized, then wielded both within and outside the institutional structures that witnessed her greatest successes. Like Sallie Martin, Campbell was saved, then nurtured in the affirming ground of the Sanctified church, where female exhorters who blended preaching with testimony were welcomed. Baptist misogyny might succeed in limiting a woman like Campbell, but it could not erase her potential to lead.

Lillian Mae Bowles Pannell

Lillian Bowles, songwriter and arranger, was among the first music publishers in Chicago.[9] Whereas her predecessor in the business, Charles Henry Pace (1886–1963), published his own arrangements of spirituals from his home in Chicago beginning in 1915, Bowles Music House (1929) set a precedent for Sallie Martin in selling music by multiple composers. In addition, while Pace handled all his own business dealings in addition to creating fully realized performance editions, Bowles was more comfortable dividing responsibilities. She managed the business side from 4662 South State Street in Chicago and hired an arranger to aid in producing her songs. Pace himself was her arranger for a while, as were Cay Hoyle and Theodore Frye. By 1937, Sallie Martin's future partner, Kenneth Morris, had filled the role of Bowles's arranger. She and Morris arranged the Soul Stirrers' "Walk Around" in 1938.

Being female wasn't the only thing setting Bowles apart in gospel publishing. Pace, Dorsey, and Morris were veterans of the 1920s blues and jazz circuits and had developed their skill in generating new material as they improvised for gigs. Women destined to own their own businesses did not come to gospel with that background. Beholden to far more limiting cultural expectations than were the men of early gospel publishing, Bowles acquired her skills in arranging from formal musical education. Not until Roberta Martin turned her hand to publishing in 1939 would a woman be solely responsible as chief business officer and primary arranger in Chicago, however.

In the 1930s, teams of Black publishers and arrangers formed an open network that shared advice for doing business with the majority white printing industry. Sallie Martin offered her own knowledge when Bowles wanted to expand her inventory. Before she and Morris opened their business in 1940, "Mrs. [Bowles] . . . had asked me, 'Well, how do we set up the book store, and how do you get this, and how do you get that?' I explained it to her."[10] Following the leads of Pace and Dorsey, Bowles established the Bowles Singers to advertise her catalog. Her store also became an access point for made-to-order choir robes, an offering that may have been unique to her.[11]

Bowles married Thomas J. Pannell in 1942, after which time she used the double surname, Bowles Pannell. Thomas, too, was well acquainted with the pioneers of gospel music; at their wedding, his best man was Theodore Frye (1899–1963), the electrifying preacher, choir director, and cofounder with Dorsey of one of the first gospel choirs in Chicago. After her marriage, Bowles Pannell continued to run her publishing business, superintended the Junior Music Department at the influential Olivet Baptist Church, and actively served youth-oriented branches of the NBC. Throughout the twenty-seven years she was at the helm of Bowles Music House, her connection with Sallie Martin remained strong (see chapter 6). Bowles Pannell passed away on a train after attending the NBC's Sunday School and Baptist Training Union conference in June of 1967.

The working relationship maintained by Martin and Bowles Pannell adds texture to persistent accounts of Martin's combative personality. With many Chicago competitors from whom to choose, Bowles Pannell sold her business to Martin around 1959, after which Martin modified operations according to the winning strategy of the Martin and Morris Music Company. She boosted advertising in the *Chicago Defender* and *Los Angeles Sentinel* and continued to sell textbooks, Bibles, hymnals, and literature for Sunday School and Baptist Training Union (BTU).[12] Martin sold formal marriage certificates and missionary licenses from another storefront at 17 East Garfield Boulevard and later renamed the company Martin's House of Music. "Formerly Bowles" continued to appear under the new name in most advertisements, but consumers could purchase tickets for Sallie Martin's musical events through Bowles Music House as late as 1973, the year that Martin sold her interests in Martin and Morris and the Bowles Pannell catalog to Kenneth Morris.

Magnolia Lewis-Butts

Vocalist and composer Magnolia Lewis-Butts is the third of a quartet of professional women considered here who made their professional homes in Chicago. She was born in Tipton, Missouri, where she attended private school and studied the classics, including Western European music and the Delsarte system, a dancelike form of physical education intended to enhance graceful and dramatic performance.[13] A gifted pianist as well, Lewis swiftly put her dramatic and musical training to good use after moving to Chicago in 1918.[14] She married Jesse J. Butts on November 7, 1933, and was thereafter known by a hyphenated surname.

Lewis joined J. Wesley Jones's community group, the Progressive Choral Society, in 1919, the year of its founding.[15] Her earlier training was especially useful when she helped Jones prepare the group for a performance of Handel's oratorio, *Esther* (1718, 1732).[16] This apprenticeship was a coup for Lewis, since Jones would soon be the influential choir director at Metropolitan Community Church (the Met, founded 1920). Jones was a leader and sometime president of the National Association of Negro Musicians and author of a column called "West Side News" for the *Chicago Defender*.[17] Repertoire for the Met and the Progressive Choral Society featured Western classical repertory and spirituals—but no gospel. Jones reportedly wanted nothing to do with gospel's physicality, which he considered regressive, if not sacrilegious.[18]

Magnolia Lewis became an official member of the Metropolitan Community Church around 1925 and Jones's primary vocal soloist in 1926, then was charged with establishing a youth choir to sing at funerals in 1929.[19] Significantly, and despite Jones's disregard for the genre, Lewis had added gospel music to her group's repertoire by August of the next year, when a *Defender* writer commended her choir for its "religious fervor and well-balanced tone."[20] Her choir thus predated the one organized at Ebenezer Baptist Church by Dorsey and Frye.[21] Sometime after the NBC met in Chicago in 1930, Lewis captured Dorsey's attention and further reinforced Sallie Martin's idea that there was a market for his songs.[22] Dorsey remembered the occasion.

> I stumbled into a political meeting one night at the Eighth Regiment Armory in Chicago and there was a slight, short, brown-skinned woman with a big voice singing my song, "How about You." I wanted to know who she was. I found out she was Magnolia Lewis who was soloist in the great Metropolitan Community Church Choir.[23]

Lewis's voice was well known in Chicago; she soloed before a reported audience of 150,000 in 1930 at the inaugural Chicagoland Music Festival.[24]

Lewis was the undisputed catalyst for what became the National Convention of Gospel Choirs and Choruses (NCGCC). After a successful performance at the 1932 NBC in Cleveland, Dorsey remembered Lewis asking, "How come we can't have a convention?"—a thought that struck Dorsey as too "visionary and impractical." She persisted, "But we'll go around and get others and make a national convention out of it." Still, Dorsey was reluctant: "It's all right with me, [but] I don't want all that work." The interchange ended when Lewis and Frye agreed that Thomas A. Dorsey should be the Convention's new president.[25] Others present at this brainstorming event included Sallie Martin. At its inaugural meeting in September of 1933, Magnolia Lewis was elected second vice president and Martin, recording secretary; the next year, Lewis assumed the role of first vice president and Martin became the national organizer of Gospel Choral Unions.[26] The NCGCC convened again at Chicago's Metropolitan Community Church in 1935, on which occasion the pastor celebrated Lewis-Butts's "ken for evoking music from the souls of her singers" and leadership in the church.[27]

Although she held a subordinate position in comparison to Jones's at the Met, Lewis-Butts's leadership of youth choirs had important implications.[28] A 1936 photo of J. Wesley Jones's "award-winning" Met choir captures approximately 190 white-robed adult choir members, evidence of a thriving congregation and choir program.[29] High-quality music education for children and youth in such a music program is implied in that photo; Lewis-Butts clearly worked behind the scenes to recruit for and train young people in a feeder choir for Jones's more publicly celebrated ensemble. In her case, typically female-gendered church work also paid off in a surprising way. Marovich found that her salary was higher than Jones's in 1935 because she also held the more lucrative church stenographer position, which paid $720 annually ($16,690 in 2024 dollars), in addition to her choir director role, which paid an additional $140 ($3,245). All told, she surpassed Jones's salary by $260.[30]

Energetic, gifted, and well prepared for leadership, Lewis-Butts served the National Council of Community Churches and continued her governance roles in the NCGCC, where she was elected to establish the Scholarship Department (for youth) in 1935 and Artists' Night in 1936.[31] She continued this trajectory of leadership and musical education throughout the 1940s to great acclaim: "The W. D. Cook Gospel choir under the dynamic direction of Magnolia Lewis-Butts astounded the audience with a contrapuntal arrangement of 'Ride the Chariot,'" wrote a 1940 *Defender* reviewer.[32]

Shortly before her death on December 10, 1949, the NCGCC realized a long-term goal by purchasing a property worth $50,000 at 4048 Lake Park Avenue, Chicago, where it would establish a headquarters for youth education and training. In addition to catalyzing the foundation of the NCGCC, Lewis-Butts's accomplishments also included nearly twenty-five years as the Met's assistant choral director and offices in her era's Biennial Conference of Community Churches and Gospel Singers of America. She had foreseen, far better than her mentor, J. Wesley Jones, the central place gospel would assume in Chicago's megachurches of midcentury and had trained generations of young singers to perform it with great artistry.

Gertrude Murphy Ward

South Carolina–born Gertrude Murphy Ward (1901–1981) was a conductor, soloist, and pianist, but more than anything, an impresaria, even more laser-focused on fame than was Sallie Martin.[33] After their marriage, Gertrude and husband George Ward moved from Anderson, South Carolina, to Philadelphia, where she gave birth to Willa (1920–2012) and Clara (1924–1973), the latter of whom would provide the keys to Gertrude's fortune. Recognizing the younger daughter's exceptional musical gifts, Gertrude provided both girls with a thorough education in music and experience in gospel from her position as choir leader at Philadelphia's Ebenezer Baptist Church.[34] In 1934, when Willa was fourteen and Clara was ninc, thc sisters first performed in church. By that year, Gertrude was also working as a professional agent around Philadelphia; among the gospel performers she booked in 1934 were Sallie Martin and Thomas A. Dorsey.[35] Martin and the Wards continued to move in the same social circles, as commemorated in an undated photo of a dinner party in Washington, DC, attended by Sallie and Gertrude.[36]

The Ward Gospel Singers' career jumpstart came for them in 1943 as it had for Dorsey before them: in a performance at the NBC in Chicago. Though Sallie Martin, Roberta Martin, Willie Mae Ford Smith, and, to a lesser extent, Bowles and Campbell trained and toured with vocal ensembles, Gertrude Ward was clearly a different sort of stage manager, driven to utilize a wide range of strategies to promote her group both within and outside the gospel field. Her singers were consummate musical artists, but Ward regularly gilded her lilies with onstage hijinks performed for effect. Their Ronettes-style beehive wigs and matching sequined gowns set fashion standards for many all-women gospel and Motown groups who succeeded them. Like Sallie Martin, Gertrude Ward moved liberally while singing, though Martin opposed the choreography for which the

Wards were known: "If the Lord don't move you," Martin opined, "you just stand there."[37]

Not all of Gertrude Ward's bids to stardom were mere attention-getters, however. Early on, the Singers showcased groundbreaking compositions of Rev. W. Herbert Brewster of Memphis, sermons set to music and first promoted by Lucie Campbell.[38] His "Surely God Is Able" catapulted the Wards to greater renown in 1947, the year Marion Williams and Henrietta Waddy joined the Ward roster. Like other savvy gospel personalities such as Kenneth Morris, Gertrude Ward brokered an agreement with Brewster in 1949, which in her case extended for fifteen years. During that period, the outstanding vocal prowess of Clara, Williams, Willa Ward, and occasionally Gertrude herself were expertly showcased in lead-switching arrangements created specifically for them by the Memphis composer.

Gertrude Ward's single-minded ambition brought setbacks not only to Clara, the group's goldmine, but also to other member-singers, according to Willa Ward-Royster.[39] Grossly insignificant salaries and a requirement to pay rent to Gertrude led to the 1958 exodus of Marion Williams and Willa Ward—everyone except Clara. The latter had been controlled and manipulated by her mother since childhood, but was also the only one besides her mother who had been fairly compensated.

Though the Ward Singers remained committed to sacred music, they sang in New York, Hollywood, and Las Vegas nightclubs and even began a seven-year stint at Disneyland in 1962. Darlings of the recording industry, they released important tracks on the Savoy, Capitol, Dot, Verve, MGM, United Artists, and London labels. The Clara Ward Singers toured Vietnam in 1968 at the request of the US State Department and the USO. Clara was a featured singer in Hollywood movies and in Langston Hughes's Broadway play, *Tambourines to Glory*, in 1963. A group under Gertrude's management continued to tour the United States, Europe, Australia, Japan, and Southeast Asia until 1970, despite Clara's failing health.[40] Gertrude Ward thus achieved her goal, leading variously named iterations of her group to unprecedented stardom.[41] Willa Ward-Royster details the downward trajectory of her mother's professional life after Clara's death in 1973 in *How I Got Over*.[42]

Misunderstanding midcentury copyright laws was a costly mistake lamented by Martin's partner, Kenneth Morris, as well as by Dorsey himself. Most Black entrepreneurs were "once bitten, twice shy" of such misunderstandings, and Ward-Royster wrote that Gertrude, too, was bilked out of royalty payments by the white executive of Savoy records, Herman Lubinsky, with whom the MMMS also did business. The resolute Gertrude Ward regularly fashioned new opportunities for herself, sponsoring headliner group tours under the name the Ward Gospel Cavalcade and opening a publishing house of her own. In Los Angeles, she also hosted a popular radio show and founded her own institution, the Miracle Temple of Faith (for All People) Church as a nonprofit, which remained active until at least 1976.[43] Remembered as an evangelist in obituaries, Gertrude Ward was memorialized in a service in April 1983 with performances by James Cleveland, Bessie Griffin, and Raymond Rasberry.

In contrast to the other case studies in this chapter, Gertrude Ward's legacy is tarnished by Willa's tell-all book. Sallie's daughter, Cora, repeatedly expressed respect and appreciation for her mother long after she stepped away from the Sallie Martin Singers, while Norsalus McKissick revered Roberta Martin as a mother figure. Ward, on the other hand, knowingly endangered the health of a young and pregnant Clara, insisting on an exhausting tour itinerary, which contributed to Clara's miscarriage and failed marriage. Gertrude affirmed that a late-in-life trip to the Holy Land and personal experience of the Jordan River made a difference in her life, after which she vowed to "sing better, teach better."[44] Her greatest contributions to gospel are encapsulated in the groups she founded and managed.

Willie Mae Ford Smith

Willie Mae Ford Smith (1904–1994) grew up poor and Baptist in Rolling Fork, Mississippi. Her father, a railroad employee, brought the family to St. Louis by way of Memphis in 1917. With Willie Mae and three of her sisters, Mary, Emma, and Geneva, he organized the Ford Sisters Quartet, which toured the Midwest before their discovery at the NBC in 1922 (Louisville).[45] She married James Peter Smith in 1924. In the NCGCC's second year, 1934, Willie Mae Ford Smith was elected chair of the Soloists Bureau and therefore met regularly with other officers, including Dorsey, Sallie Martin, Magnolia Lewis-Butts, and Roberta Martin. Indeed, it was Smith's performance of Dorsey's "If You See My Savior" that had so impressed NBC music director Lucie E. Campbell in 1930 that the composer's music almost immediately advanced to the status of musical currency at the NBC. Smith was a powerful and agile soprano who toured as a soloist with her adopted daughter, Bertha, as accompanist. She regularly did business with the MMMS (see figure 4.2). Like Lucie Campbell and Gertrude Ward, Smith felt the call to preach and, rather than suppress that vocation, specialized in the sermonette, a blend of singing and declamation that could appease those who felt that women should not be allowed to deliver a homily. Mother Smith, as she came to be called, was an ordained minis-

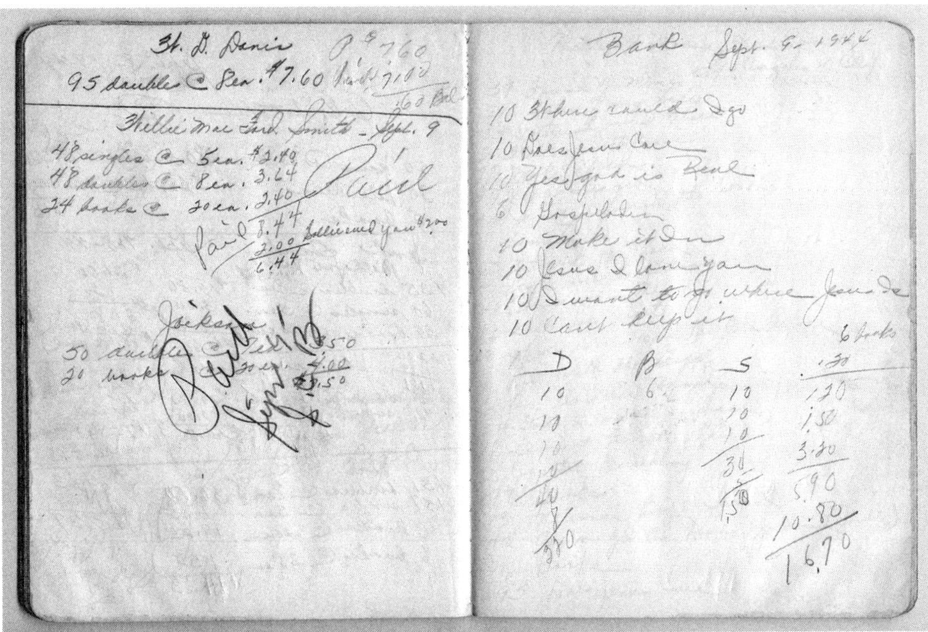

FIGURE 4.1. (Left) Sallie Martin's Ledger 1942–1944. Willie Mae Ford Smith order noted in Sallie Martin's hand, marked paid after a $2.00 credit was deducted. (Right) Martin's calculations for a music order, with titles and prices for doubles (D, i.e., octavos over 4 pages long), books (B), and singles (S, i.e., octavos 4 pages and under). Martin and Morris Music Company Records, series 2, 6. Used with permission.

ter for thirty years in the Lively Stone Apostolic Church in St. Louis. Her professional activities slowed after 1945 and even more after the death of her husband in 1950.

Like several of her confederates in this discussion, Smith enjoyed her celebrity, donning a silken cape, keeping congregations waiting for her late arrivals, and instructing pullman porters to bow when she stepped off a train.[46] Her conversion to Pentecostalism (Church of God Apostolic) in 1939 placed her in a milieu where women were encouraged to preach and pastor. Despite the growing capitalization of gospel, Smith refused to accept payment for her musical performances, instead requesting free-will offerings which apparently were never equal to her financial needs. Despite a few recordings, radio performances, and outstanding appearances later in life, including the 1972 Newport Jazz Festival, she might have retired into anonymity were it not for the 1981 documentary *Say Amen, Somebody!*[47] The film captured rare footage of NCGCC convention performances honoring Smith by the likes of the Barrett Sisters and the

O'Neal Twins. In one scene, Smith made a revelation familiar to all professional women: marriage and children had seriously complicated her chance to live out the same dreams pursued by her male contemporaries. Her husband complained bitterly about the fact that she was home only one week per month for about ten years. These and other scenes from the documentary—one filmed in the Smith kitchen and another with her offspring at the rail platform where Smith so frequently left them behind—highlighted Smith's legacy before her death. In many ways, *Say Amen, Somebody!* is an homage to Smith and Dorsey.

Sallie Martin was also spotlighted in the film. Seated in a quiet room during the Convention, she and Dorsey half-sang along with an early recording of his "If You See My Savior," musical ground they had covered together countless times in the past. Willie Mae Ford Smith joins them after the song and the conversation turns to the founding of the NCGCC, which Smith insists occurred in St. Louis. Martin would have none of that opinion, firmly insisting on the Chicago origins of the very Convention that was meeting while the scene was filmed. Tension builds between them for a bit, then Dorsey intervenes with a smile and soothing scriptural quotation. The moment highlights a debate that persists to the time of this writing and, further, suggests a simmering animosity between the two gospel mavens. Yet, Martin presented Smith in Los Angeles on several occasions, and Smith sang several times to honor Martin. Dorsey, perhaps averse to confrontation, left behind the general observation that "There was more rivalry then among church singers than show [Hollywood] folk," but it's also worth considering that Dorsey may have been highly sensitive to the forthrightness of women like Smith and Martin.[48] His own discomfort may have exaggerated the import of normal and natural clashes between large personalities.

Like Sallie Martin, Gertrude Ward, and Mahalia Jackson, Smith is remembered for gesturing and moving about freely while she sang. Women aspiring to expand beyond Sanctified congregations were criticized for that physicality in the 1930s, as pioneers labored to have gospel accepted by influential Baptist and Methodist churches. Yet for them, faith was wedded to movement. Sallie Martin is called the Mother of Gospel Music and Brother Joe May bestowed the moniker "Mother Willie Mae Ford Smith" on the St. Louis icon, but both women projected a maternal aura not solely instigated by those nicknames. Barnes wrote that Smith possessed a "wonderful, charismatic blend of pride and humility" and Anthony Heilbut wrote that she exuded an "Ethel Waters–like maternal piety."[49] Smith was named a National Endowment for the Arts National Heritage Fellow in 1988.

Roberta Martin

Roberta Martin (Roberta Evelyn Winston, 1907–1969) grew up in Helena, Arkansas. She began piano study at the age of six and moved to Chicago in 1917, where she continued her music education. Her younger brother, Fontaine Winston, remembered that there was always a baby grand in the family's Chicago home.[50] What an advantage, in the context of the other women discussed here! Like that of Magnolia Lewis-Butts, Roberta Martin's career was shaped by formal training, but she readily immersed herself in gospel, as well.[51] Roberta Martin auditioned for Dorsey and Theodore Frye's Young People's Choir at Ebenezer Baptist Church in 1932, became its accompanist, and, later, music director. Under Frye's imprimatur, she organized the Martin-Frye quartet in 1933, for which her youth choir supplied the personnel: Robert Anderson and Willie Webb (age fourteen), James Lawrence (thirteen), Eugene Smith (twelve), and Norsalus McKissick (ten).[52] Roberta Martin's early tenure at Ebenezer Baptist Church bore fruit for many young singers there and at Shiloh Baptist, where she produced musicales every fourth Sunday.

Like Sallie Martin, Roberta turned early to publishing and distributing gospel music as a stable source of income. She opened the Roberta Martin Gospel Music Studio on East 43rd Street in 1939, a decade after Lillian Bowles established her company, but a few months in advance of the Martin and Morris Music Studio's opening.[53] Buttressed by her formal musical training, she composed, arranged, secured publication for, and distributed her group's repertoire, thus collapsing the more typical two-person business model of the Bowles, Dorsey, and Martin-Morris ventures. She married James Austin in December of 1947 and they adopted a son, Leonard, the next year,[54] which led Roberta to discontinue touring and pass the role of tour manager to member Eugene Smith. Martin and her husband then opened their own printing business, which allowed Roberta to avoid working with white executives of the industry. Roberta Martin stayed close to Chicago for the final two decades of her life.

In contrast to Sallie Martin's four decades on the road, Roberta toured with her Singers for a decade only. Further distinguishing her group from others was Roberta's classical training and flair for training young voices. Veterans of her group stress values reminiscent of a secondary school choral curriculum. Bessie Folk, the first female to join Martin's Quartet in 1939, said that Martin taught her how to avoid stage fright and how to deliver a message.[55] Baritone Romance Watson said that Roberta Martin emphasized phrasing, continuing that "she taught us how to breathe [and] how to enunciate so that people will know what you're singing about."[56] An original member of the Martin-Frye Quartet, Norsalus McKissick mentioned that Martin "happened to pick us out at random" for the first quartet from the Ebenezer Junior Choir when he was seven years old, though she likely chose him for his musical gifts. Because McKissick's mother had died early in his life, Martin negotiated with his father about bringing the teenager on board. Norsalus concluded that she was "more or less my mother."[57]

Sallie Martin often mentored other groups by joining them on a tour and introducing them in her own trustworthy stops. Sometime in the late 1930s, she agreed on an automobile tour—a double bill—with the Roberta Martin Singers, through the Deep South. Trouble soon brewed. Sallie remembered that "[Roberta] had a young man [Eugene Smith] with her that was so jealous that . . . if you said Sallie and didn't say Roberta, he thought you had committed a crime."[58] Advertisements touting performances of the "Sallie Martin and the Roberta Martin Singers" apparently exacerbated the issue until it came to a head somewhere in Louisiana, where they also had a frightening encounter with law enforcement (see chapter 3). Roberta and Sallie agreed to part ways once they got to Atlanta. Though Sallie believed that the Roberta Martin Singers suffered from a superiority complex, she bore no professional grudge against Roberta or other members of the group. Sallie narrated a tribute to Roberta Martin in August of 1966.[59]

Though she had been on the Chicago scene since 1917, Roberta Martin is not named among the group that first envisioned the NCGCC. Nevertheless, known and respected, the younger Martin participated in the first convention in 1933. When its junior department was established at the 1934 convention, she was named its national supervisor. Thereafter, one day at each Convention would be dedicated to raising scholarship funds to support convention attendance by musically gifted youth, funding that would support luminaries such as Della Reese, Dinah Washington, and Aretha Franklin.[60] As part of her NCGCC service and work at Shiloh Baptist Church in Chicago, Roberta Martin influenced dozens, if not hundreds of young singers.

The many extant recordings of the Roberta Martin Singers feature rich, well-balanced harmonies from the vocalists. Martin decorated the piano part with fluid runs and arpeggios and an innovative use of dissonance—elements few of her generation had mastered. Boyer described her pianism as embodying "the nuances of a Horowitz, inventions of an Ellington, and the power of an Erroll Garner," though she performed sacred music exclusively.[61] Her vocal arrangements, often expanded to seven parts, left space in the lower register in order to emphasize her own deep, rich contralto. Voicing featured timbral homogeneity and dynamic nuances that ebbed and flowed with facility. Like Duke Ellington, Martin recruited soloists who were also gifted stylists; she arranged and chose keys in order to capitalize on the strengths of each featured singer.

At the apex of their renown, in 1963, the Roberta Martin Singers appeared at Gian-Carlo Menotti's Spoleto Festival in Italy. In all, they recorded over a hundred compositions in forty years, first with Apollo in the 1940s and in the next two decades with Savoy. The recording industry's strict time limitations usually curtailed the lengthy improvisations so central to the Roberta Martin Singers' style, but they did record a full-length, live album in 1963 for Savoy. All their recordings provided models for generations of gospel singers. Roberta Martin composed seventy songs and published 280—she arranged all except one of that total. "Didn't It Rain," "God Is Still on the Throne," and "Only a Look" are widely known arrangements and compositions of hers.

Roberta Martin was a persuasive speaker, gifted conductor, and a wholesome role model, as illustrated by the care she took in establishing "no public smoking or drinking" rules on tour. As a result of all her high standards for musical performance and behavior, she left behind a dynasty of gospel singers and a sizable corpus of canonic music.

Emma L. Jackson

Jackson (1910–1946[?]) was born in Ruston, Louisiana, and ran a gospel distribution business in Shreveport in the early 1930s.[62] Alongside fellow performers Sallie Martin, Magnolia Lewis, and Roberta Martin, Jackson was commended for her singing at the second NCGCC meeting in 1934. Boyer credits her with introducing Dorsey's "Precious Lord, Take My Hand" at the National Baptist Convention in the mid-1930s.[63] Like Magnolia Lewis, Emma Jackson was known in the NCGCC as a conductor; she led the six hundred singers of the Chicago Gospel Choral Union at its third anniversary celebration in June of 1935 at the Met. Jackson therefore moved in the same institutional circles, the NBC and the NCGCC, as Sallie Martin and several other gospel pioneers discussed here.

Jackson's notable compositions include "I'm Going to Die with My Staff in My Hand" (1941), which she first performed at the National Baptist Convention in the mid-1940s. At some point, she opened the Emma L. Jackson Music Studio at 3704 South Parkway in Chicago, and from there, published her own works, including "Don't Forget the Family Prayer" (1945).

Sparse documentation makes certainty impossible, but Jackson may have died in October of 1946. If that is the case, someone continued selling music from her company after her death. A 1951 *Defender* ad promised same-day shipping and special discounts from Jackson's company, and in 1964, a 64-page songbook was offered for sale. Like Roberta Martin, Jackson taught lessons in her studio and toured with her own singing group, the Emma Jackson Singers. One such outing saw Jackson and her group headed to "Dixie" via Muskogee, Oklahoma, where her uncle was pastor at Central Baptist Church.[64]

Goreau identified Emma as a member of the gospel circle who met at Mahalia Jackson's salon (see below). Apparently, Emma kept track of available pianists for those in need of accompanists. Being in the know about personnel for choirs and small groups would have been a valuable function in the thriving business that gospel had become. Because Emma L. Jackson was a foundational influence on Gwendolyn Cooper Lightner, an important second-generation gospel pianist and educator who toured at least once with Sallie Martin, it's worth contemplating that Martin may have learned of Lightner through Emma Jackson (see chapter 5).

Mahalia Jackson

Mahalia Jackson (1911–1972), the internationally acclaimed soloist, singing evangelist, and Civil Rights activist, hardly belongs in a discussion of women who labored mainly within institutional structures—churches, conventions, and businesses—to capitalize on gospel music. Yet Jackson's career began in ways similar to Sallie Martin's and she was no less an entrepreneur. Before long, however, Mahalia Jackson had deeply affected the collective consciousness of music consumers in the United States and fans on several other continents—she was a star of Hollywood proportions. Her relocation to Chicago from New Orleans occurred in 1931, by which time Sallie Martin had established herself in the Dorsey enterprise. Martin was the 36-year-old mother of a teenager; her son Joel was born in 1914, just three years after Jackson's birth.[65] Martin recalls seeing Jackson perform for the first time with the Johnson Singers of Greater Salem Baptist Church at Ebenezer Baptist Church, when Theodore Frye was director of music. At first, Martin offered maternal advice to the homesick newcomer, insisting that she wear a choir robe for reasons of modesty when performing at a venue that required her to sit on a raised platform.[66]

During her first decade in Chicago, the highly social Jackson faced the universal challenge for migrants, how to make a living. She earned small amounts singing for funerals and other church meetings, then began to perform at political meetings—first, Republican, then after Roosevelt's reelection in 1936, Democratic, reflecting the Black South Side's changing politics. Jackson also sold beauty products out of her apartment, then obtained her beautician's license around 1940. She soon opened Mahalia's Beauty Salon on South Indiana Avenue, just down the street from the Martin and Morris Music Studio. Like so many manifestations of racial uplift, Black women's hair and complexion were culturally and politically coded. Stereotypes ranging from sheet music covers to Margaret Mitchell's *Gone with the Wind* (1935) equated natural, untreated Black hair and deep ebony complexion with ignorance and slovenliness. Professional Black women with the means to do so favored straightened and re-curled locks or wigs and chemically or cosmetically lightened complexions. Jackson's business thus provided essential support for a central concern, Black beauty. It was also a meeting place for the gospel community, including locals like Emma L. Jackson and Robert Anderson, as well as those touring through Chicago such as Sister Rosetta Tharpe, Ernestine Washington, and the Ward Singers.[67]

In the early 1930s, Sallie Martin and Jackson sang together at storefront churches or runouts to nearby towns. Martin did this at least in part because "other singers tried to be a little high minded" about Jackson, the green newcomer who moved around freely as she sang and clung tightly to her rustic sincerity.[68] Martin and Jackson never toured together in a formal way; in fact, Jackson was Martin's replacement as Dorsey's song demonstrator after Martin's departure in 1939. The two singers moved in distinctly different directions beginning in 1940. Between them, Jackson had the far more agile voice and, consequently, the capacity for finely grained interpretations of hits ranging from spirituals to religious ballads to up-tempo jubilee songs. Jackson's reputation was firmly established after she performed Dorsey's songs in the Midwest, East Coast, and Atlanta, especially from 1941 to 1944.[69]

Jackson's combination of musical and performative gifts, her training with Dorsey, and fortuitous timing, which facilitated her success with the nascent race record industry, differentiates Jackson from the other women discussed here. Whereas Sallie Martin's shout-style of gospel performance—reliant on audience participation—did not transfer well to radio or recordings, Mahalia Jackson was recording gold. Her 1946 Apollo release of Brewster's "Move On Up a Little Higher" was a watershed both for her and for the gospel industry.[70] Resonant with Sallie Martin's damaging commitment to sing as many songs as required of her in the 1930s, Jackson incurred vocal damage by remaining faithful to a demanding contract with Apollo. She returned from her first European tour in 1952 vocally tired and physically shattered.[71] She nevertheless remained a prized commodity in the minds of record executives and managers.

The 1950s saw Jackson's rise to individual stardom, while Sallie Martin continued to pour energy into nationwide touring with her Singers, founding Gospel Choral Unions, and working the convention circuits. Two television series entitled *Mahalia Jackson Sings* featured a series of five-minute musical spots; the show was nationally syndicated. In 1956, Jackson sang at the Democratic National Convention and marched in the Montgomery Bus Boycott. Whereas Sallie Martin had been the favorite singer of Martin Luther King Sr., Jackson was the friend and confidante of that Atlanta pastor's iconic and tragically short-lived son.

About her relationship with Jackson, Sallie Martin remembered, "Mahalia really gave respect to me, more than any of them that I know . . . she knew that I'd just been the same [in my early career] . . . she always said that I never, even when she was trying to make it, I never looked over her even though I was going everywhere I wanted to go."[72] In 1959, Jackson made a gesture to repay the figure who had treated her with kindness in the 1930s. In his coverage of a large-scale salute to Rev. Clarence H. Cobbs at the International Amphitheater, a *Defender* critic made it clear how Sallie Martin came to sing with Jackson.

> Mahalia Jackson was somewhat disappointing in her appearance especially when she insisted on another singer, Sallie Martin, joining her in her spot. It was just like going to market to get this and coming away with that. . . . While Miss Martin is an equally noted gospel singer and was scheduled to appear later in the program, the duet just didn't reach home for me.[73]

To be fair, the critic complained about more performances than he applauded at that event. More importantly, he documented one outcome of the relationship the two divas had enjoyed for many years.

Jackson rode her meteoric career through the 1960s, but her health began to fail. Goreau interviewed Martin soon after Jackson's death in 1972. When asked to describe the woman with whom she had experienced so much, Martin stressed Jackson's kindness, but also a self-destructive stubbornness and resentment over the fact that she was not getting her just due because of her race. While Martin thought it expedient to negotiate with whites, Jackson was less likely to accommodate white hegemony without resistance. In these philosophies are seen most clearly the sixteen years that separated them in age. Martin clearly cared for Jackson and, though she was included on the roster to speak (but not sing) at Jackson's funeral service, she made a last-minute choice to give her spot to the Barrett Sisters. The benedictory song at that service was delivered by Aretha Franklin, and the audience included Sammy Davis Jr., Harry Belafonte, Pearl Bailey, Ray Charles, and Ella Fitzgerald (see chapter 6).

Career Ways of Sallie Martin's Generation

Gospel musicians considered in this chapter built their careers on a set of commonalities. Most, if not all of them could name a parent or grandparent who had been enslaved—hardly remarkable, given their ages. Second, crucially, they were inspired at some point to respect and pursue the educational opportunities open to them, certainly not universal in rural areas where mere survival often took precedence. Also, like 40 percent of Black Americans between 1910 and 1970, these women or their parents migrated from the rural Deep South to a city further north. The South's publishing industry, though decimated during the Civil War, had recovered somewhat, but the women discussed in this chapter relocated themselves to the advantaged side of the disparity in mass media between the postbellum South and northern cities. Infrastructures conducive to building a gospel musical career were readily available in places like Memphis, Chicago, Philadelphia, and St. Louis. This final point was central to the nascent gospel movement; for gospel to spread as it did, pioneering musicians had not only to leave the South, but also to market their music on paper.

Not everyone who valued music and education and who joined the Great Migration were able to build successful careers in gospel, however. The heritage of slavery and its succeeding cultural offspring—persistent violence and Jim Crow laws governing housing, voting, and self-expression—were permanently crippling for many a Black Southerner. The women featured in this chapter are exemplars in their pursuit of opportunity and their unwavering self-determination. Their varied access to specialized musical training shaped the specifics of their careers. The parents of Magnolia Lewis-Butts and Roberta Martin nurtured an attraction to music and also had the means to provide their young daughters with formal piano and singing lessons. The impoverished parents and grandparents of Lucie E. Campbell, Sallie Martin, Mahalia Jackson, and Willie Mae Ford Smith likewise endowed their daughters with a love of music and performing. Campbell studied piano vicariously through the lessons of her oldest sister, the only child the family could afford to train. Proving that talent and drive will make the most of opportunity, these gospel women enjoyed noteworthy success.

Their native gifts blossomed along infrastructures that included work within the NBC and/or NCGCC, business ownership, tour management, teaching and mentoring of new singers, activism, and church affiliation, the latter of which gave to some the opportunity to preach as well as sing. Each one discovered her unique recipe for success in the 1930s; many in a city where the National Baptist Convention had a strong presence. Incorporated in 1895, the year of Sallie Martin's birth, the NBC was far more than a configuration of churches. It became a mechanism for improving the schooling Black children received in public schools; further, it founded newspapers and journals, and organized US foreign missionary activity in Africa. The NBC was the most powerful Black organization in the United States in the first quarter of the twentieth century. Its infrastructure would be co-opted and its success emulated by secular organizations like the NAACP (founded 1909) and the National Association of Negro Musicians (1919); the reach of the NBC thus extended well beyond the Baptist denomination (see chapter 2).

The National Baptist Convention was the spiritual and leadership home of Lucie Campbell and Emma L. Jackson. Though most of the women discussed here benefitted from career-defining performances at the NBC, it was the NCGCC where Bowles, Lewis-Butts, Sallie Martin, Willie Mae Ford Smith, and Roberta Martin built their careers by working as founding members, long-term officers or board members, and featured performers. Thomas A. Dorsey acknowledged Magnolia Lewis-Butts as the instigator of the entire concept. Sallie Martin's immersion in activities of the NCGCC as performer and National Organizer of Gospel Choral Unions provided structure for her touring life, but also is responsible in part for the rapid growth of the organization. Willie Mae Ford Smith was Sallie Martin's counterpart in the Dorsey Convention's Soloist Bureau and Roberta Martin manifested her heart for education in its Youth Department. As Burford writes, the name of Mahalia Jackson "is never mentioned in the voluminous newspaper coverage of the NCGCC,"[74] but early on, she was acknowledged and promoted by its leaders and thus built her renown only one step removed from the Convention's administration via her associates such as Dorsey and Sallie Martin. Likewise, Gertrude Ward's Singers appeared frequently on Convention programs, but Gertrude appears not to have been an active member who carried out duties for the organization. The further these women operated from the center of NCGCC activities, the more likely they were to take their religious music to secular venues.

On the business trajectory, all the women considered here except Magnolia Lewis-Butts either partly or solely owned a gospel music business. Lewis-Butts, instead, was a longtime junior choir director, voice teacher, and church secretary at another institution, Metropolitan Community Church, which provided her a good living and a place to apply her musical and performative gifts. Campbell's labor in her business was secondary to her leadership roles in the NBC and Smith's was incidental to managing her singing group, while Mahalia Jackson began with the Dorsey publishing company, but soon became the individual singer most sought after by publishers and record companies. Business ownership was central to the two Martins and Bowles Pannell, and half of what little is known about Emma L. Jackson is tied to her company.

Those deeply involved in publishing music were obligated to market it outside their home cities, a venture demanding that they create set lists from an increasing flow of new compositions, test them out in local venues, and embark on financially risky tours to distant locations. Traveling cost money, which was hard to come by in the 1930s. Sallie Martin mentions that early on, sales of music paid for the trip as they went. If they didn't sell enough music one night, they had no choice but to circle back home the next day. To counter such a precarious business plan for her own business after 1940, Martin kept a directory of addresses and phone numbers which was used as much for arranging tours as for shipping music (see Sallie Martin's undated "Agent Book," figure 3.1). She probably relied first on friends' and family members' churches, then added new stopovers to her itineraries each year. The Martin and Morris Music Company Records do not specify if host churches kept part of the profits collected by Martin's Singers, but such an arrangement would have made sense.

All the pioneers discussed here were self-employed during the Great Depression, managing much of their workforce and bearing personal responsibility for success or failure. Business acumen among these first-generation gospel pioneers, especially those who specialized in booking tours or facilitating the running of a company, also had its roots in family values. Someone in the early lives of these women planted a belief in education, one of the mechanisms of uplift that had been so prevalent in the first decades of the twentieth century. The Martin and Morris Music Company Papers show that Sallie Martin was a meticulous recordkeeper and correspondent. Like Martin, Lucie Campbell, Magnolia Lewis-Butts, and Roberta Martin held their singers to high standards of performance and behavior. For them, the goal of perfection was a way to elevate themselves and their people.

Fronting or performing in a touring group in the 1930s, probably required different skills than those required in the next decade, when money flowed more freely and overnight accommodations for Black people were marginally more available, despite Jim Crow laws and the rebirth of the KKK. Sallie Martin, Roberta Martin, Gertrude Ward, and others traveled by automobile, which the US government positioned as an antidote to Depression-era strictures. In a car, Black Americans could avoid the humiliation of public transportation's separate cars and seating zones, and drop in on family members who had migrated to various northern cities. Victor Hugo Green's *Negro Motorist Green Book*, first appearing in 1936, documents a network that first coalesced by shared experience. Increasingly, in subsequent generations, the *Green Book* insured that there were safe routes for Black Americans, even in the Deep South.

Several of these women chose a particular denomination of Christianity within which to worship and work, one that facilitated female ordination, preaching, or both. Sanctified churches were obvious destinations if gospel women desired to evangelize through word, as well as song. In the late 1970s or early '80s, Sallie Martin was ordained as a minister by Rev. Clarence Cobbs at First Church of Deliverance. Willie Mae Ford Smith remained active as a singer and preacher into the last decade of her life, and Gertrude Ward preached in Philadelphia, then founded her own church in Los Angeles.

Activism is a prism that sharply differentiates the legacies of these women. In advocating for herself in a conservative Baptist congregation, Campbell paved new pathways for women in religious and sacred musical circles. Twenty-six years her junior, Mahalia Jackson became deeply involved in the Civil Rights Movement and appeared frequently on stage with Martin Luther King Jr. Apparently favoring cooperation with whites to more visible civil engagement, Sallie Martin nonetheless considered her very work as Black female entrepreneur as a resistance to and a restructuring of the status quo.

Pioneers in this group facilitated the grooming of new musical talent to supply their own performance needs, in service to the educational tenets of the NCGCC, and later in life, simply because they had the means to do so. Men and women who were introduced, mentored, and supported financially by the subjects of this chapter are too numerous to name, but such a roster would feature relationships between Lucie Eddie Campbell, Marian Anderson, and J. Robert Bradley; Gertrude and Clara Ward, Marion Williams, and Aretha Franklin; Willie Mae Ford Smith and the O'Neal Twins and Brother Joe May; Roberta Martin and Robert Anderson, Norsalus McKissick, Willie Webb, Eugene Smith, and Bessie Folk; Emma L. Jackson and Gwendolyn Cooper Lightner and Vernon Oliver Price; Mahalia Jackson and Robert Anderson and Brother John Sellers; and Sallie Martin and Julia Smith Whitfield, Lightner, Dorothy Simmons, Doris Akers, and Cora Martin-Moore. Chapter 5 looks selectively at men and women closely associated with Sallie Martin in the context of her expansion work in Los Angeles.

CHAPTER 5

Los Angeles, the Sallie Martin Singers, and Recordings, 1940–1956

Sallie Martin's first trip to Los Angeles in July of 1936 had been as lead singer of the Dorsey Quartette. While the composer himself remained in Chicago, the singers and pianist traveled by car to the annual convention of the Colored Methodist Episcopal (CME) churches (see chapter 3). Fully inhabiting the role of tour manager, Martin booked performances along the route in both directions, singing and selling music to pay travel expenses. While in Los Angeles, she also worshipped at Aimee Semple McPherson's Angelus Temple (Church of the Foursquare Gospel). Martin recalled, "She used to say, 'Now who's here tonight for the first time? Now come up cross the pulpit, I'm gonna give you a rose.'" McPherson's services were integrated and Martin remembered, "They always did get happy there."[1]

A new goal was planted in Sallie Martin's fertile mind on that Los Angeles trip. Soon after the 1940 founding of the MMMS, she initiated expansion into a new metropolis, one offering mild winter weather and abundant marketing potential. Though distant, the city was linked to Chicago via Route 66, or, for those like Martin who could afford it, the "Chief" line of the Atchison, Topeka, and Santa Fe Railroad could make the trip in about thirty-nine hours. To advertise her new plans and prosperity, she placed a notice in the *Chicago Defender* with a photo of herself, "wearing her white squirrel coat" as she boarded the Santa Fe Chief. Her stated purpose in this December 1940 notice was to participate in the "celebration of the second anniversary of her West Coast operation" which, at that point, was anchored in the music stores of a couple of her agents. She made the trip with Julia Smith, Cora Martin, and Charlie Lomax, and before the year was out, the Martin and Morris Singers had made their first recordings.

This chapter shows how Sallie Martin's entrepreneurial efforts in Los Angeles advanced gospel music, her own reputation, and the financial health of the MMMS beginning in 1940. Like the previous chapter, it documents early gospel's interconnected web of music, institutions, and performers, but additionally, this chapter positions Sallie Martin's orbit as a launching pad for an impressive number of second-generation gospel pioneers. A brief visit to gospel's genesis in Los Angeles offers background for Martin's westward career expansion.

The chapter also sheds light on the earliest documented group of singers Martin fronted after cofounding the Martin and Morris Music Studio in 1940, as well as distinguished musicians who performed in later versions of the Sallie Martin Singers (SMS), either as mainstays or short-term substitutes. Between 1940 and 1956, longer tours with the SMS, radio and television performances featuring Martin as soloist or ensemble member, and recordings were added to an already busy work calendar for Sallie Martin.[2] In 1947, she gave the name Gospel Music Mart to MMMS's West Coast branch, which she had been operating informally. The *Los Angeles Sentinel* joined the ranks of the *Chicago Defender*, *Atlanta Daily World*, *Cleveland Call and Post*, *Indianapolis Recorder*, and other Black newspapers in promoting Martin's brand. The chapter closes with a curious event that reflects Martin's celebrity status—her unlikely marriage in July of 1956 to handsome Chicago nightclub owner and socialite Joe Langham. Though that union made little difference in the way Sallie Martin did business, becoming part of a highly visible couple fit well with her Los Angeles persona and brought further attention to her as a gospel star.

L.A.'s Fertile Fields for Gospel

The Southern Pacific and Transcontinental Railroads facilitated the Great Migration westward. By 1910, a decade before the Second Great Migration, Los Angeles was home to about 7,600 Black Americans, drawn by jobs in farming and, later, the need for skilled aeronautical laborers and shipbuilders in the defense industry. A branch of the NAACP opened in 1914. The next year saw 55,000 street cars in the city and the opening of direct steamship service to Japan, which, along with a sizable Chinese immigrant population, would differentiate the L.A. job market from that of Chicago. Los Angeles's first radio stations—KFI, KHJ, and KNX—took to the air in 1922. The first western convention of the NAACP was held on Central Avenue in 1928. Local newspapers such as *The California Eagle* (founded as the *California Owl*, 1879–1964) and the still-active *Sentinel* (founded 1933) eased the transition for several waves of Black newcomers. By 1940, the Black population in Los Angeles had risen to 63,700.

Class consciousness and uplift still dictated musical tastes in some mainline Baptist, AME, and CME denominations, where musical repertory included songs like Lewis Edgar Jones's "Power in the Blood" (1889) and "Brighten the Corner" (1915), the latter popularized by white musical evangelist Homer Rodeheaver, and C. Austin Miles's "Dwelling in Beulah Land" (1911).[3] Black and white mainline congregations often sang very similar repertoires. To gain traction in these congregations, gospel music required a starter, a catalyst, like the essential ingredient for sourdough bread. In Chicago, the spark had been a confluence of composers/arrangers, Lucie Campbell's endorsement of a Dorsey song at an NBC convention, and mainline ministers persuaded by Frye's and Dorsey's gospel blues in the early 1930s. For Los Angeles, the starter was the nineteenth-century Holiness movement and the subsequent founding of several Sanctified congregations. Sallie Martin was right at home in Holiness-influenced Los Angeles, having found her faith in such an Atlanta church in the mid-1910s.

People affiliated with Holiness or Sanctified religions sought an embodied expression of Christian zeal—improvised handclapping, swaying, and shouting—in more rhythmically complex, antiphonal, and heterophonic styles than could be seen in mainline performance practice.[4] Timbres and pronunciations celebrated the vernacular; rhythms and textures deemed acceptable for worship were far less controlled in Sanctified churches than in most self-conscious, mainstream denominations.

By the 1930s, Los Angeles was home to a wide array of Black churches and practices, both mainstream and sanctified. The African Methodist Episcopal (AME) denomination had arrived in California in 1872. Black Baptists and AME Zion faiths set up congregations later in the nineteenth century. Religious revivals, beginning at Joseph Smale's First Baptist Church of L.A. in 1905, infused a vital energy into the aesthetics of Christian worship. On the heels of Smale's watershed came William J. Seymour's Azusa Street revivals (see chapter 2). Those meetings attracted ministers of the Holiness faith (founded in Jackson, Mississippi, 1895) and Church of God in Christ (COGIC), founded in 1897 in Lexington, Mississippi. Turn-of-the-century California revivalism engendered a growing acceptance of Sanctified worship practices by Blacks and whites, though more mainstream denominations remained skeptical.

Jacqueline Cogdell DjeDje recognizes four periods in L.A. gospel's evolution; the first, *Pre-gospel*, extended from 1900 to 1930.[5] Next came DjeDje's *Beginnings* era, from 1930 to 1943, during which time Sallie Martin first visited L.A. and Rev. J. C. Austin, the man who had hired Dorsey at Pilgrim Baptist Church in Chicago, preached musically illustrated guest sermons that reinforced the demand for Dorsey's music.[6] *Expansion* occurred between 1943 and 1955, aided by Sallie Martin and second-generation pioneers: notably, James Cleveland, Gwendolyn Cooper Lightner, and Doris Akers. Finally, gospel *Prominence* occurred in L.A. between 1955 and 1969, when Andraé and Sandra Crouch, and the Edwin Hawkins Singers and their riveting soloist, Dorothy Combs Morrison, pointed gospel toward a contemporary era. The Crouches and Hawkinses were the first gospel leaders born in California; prior to their successes, leaders of West Coast gospel had migrated from elsewhere and their music was strongly derivative of Dorsey's style.

The earliest resident performers of Chicago-style gospel in L.A. were the Three Sons of Thunder. The all-male trio was founded and managed by Arthur Atlas Peters (1908–1975), a native of Slidell, Louisiana, who arrived in Los Angeles around 1936, the same year that Martin attended the CME convention. Performing gospel music hardly supported a musician in the 1930s, so Peters also owned a Christian gift shop located at 1057 E. Jefferson Blvd. Peters was an agent for the major publishers in Chicago—Dorsey, Bowles, Martin and Morris, and Roberta Martin—and received a discount on published music, as well as a commission on copies sold.[7] Simultaneously, he directed the music at Phillips Temple CME church until he received the call to preach and founded Victory Baptist Church in 1943.[8] By 1950, that congregation's Voices of Victory, a 75-voice choir, permeated the airwaves via the primetime airing of its Sunday night services on Channel 11, KTTV.[9] Victory Baptist was later a headquarters for Civil Rights–era activism and voter registration campaigns. Martin Luther King Jr. spoke at its twenty-fourth anniversary celebration in 1967.[10]

One of Peters's cohorts in the Three Sons of Thunder was vocalist/composer/evangelist Earl Amos Pleasant (born New Orleans, 1919–1974), who arrived in Los Angeles in 1939.[11] Olga W. Pleasant (née Williams, 1920–2006), Earl's wife, assisted the group on piano. Earl also entered the ministry and founded Mount Moriah Baptist Church in 1945, then hired the dynamic vocalist and arranger Thurston Gilbert Frazier (1930–1973) as his music director.[12] Pleasant's services then became popular on the radio. Of the Three Sons of Thunder, he had the widest reach as a soloist, touring with Mahalia Jackson and soloing before thousands at the first-ever crusade, in Los Angeles, of white evangelist Billy Graham in 1949. Gospel composer Margaret Douroux (b. 1941), the Pleasants' daughter, remembered that Jackson, Sallie Martin, Joe May, and Doris Akers visited their home frequently in her youth.

Eugene Douglass Smallwood (b. Guthrie, OK, 1920, d. 2005) rounded out the Three Sons of Thunder. Late in his teens, he earned a soloist's spot on the program of the 1939 NBC and Baptist Training Union Congress in Tulsa, Oklahoma. With a chuckle, he remembered that at his rehearsal, he asked the accompanist if she knew "He'll Understand and Say Well Done," and if she could play it in the key of B-flat. He was unaware that the pianist, the formidable Lucie E. Campbell, was the composer of that song, and could have played it any key. Even placed directly after a Mahalia Jackson solo, he knew that his song was well received.

Nearing the end of her partnership with Dorsey, Sallie Martin may not have attended that Congress, but she would soon know the name of Eugene Smallwood. He moved to L.A. in 1939, with a collection of Dorsey publications in tow that he kept for the remainder of his life. Upon arriving in the City of Angels, he connected with Peters and Pleasant.[13] Like Peters, Smallwood ran a music company, in his case from 4507 Ascot St., and was an agent for the Martin and Morris Music Studio until 1945.[14] Smallwood founded Opportunity Baptist Church in 1946 and, notably, purchased a Hammond organ for the church, complete with a Leslie attachment, despite the seller's misgivings. Within three weeks, Smallwood remembered, every church in L.A. wanted one.[15]

Both bringing classical music training to their crafts, Smallwood and Pleasant contributed compositions to the gospel repertory and established community choirs: the Venerable-Smallwood Gospel Singers (with C. B. Venerable, late 1940s), and Pleasant's Victory Baptist Choir. The regular members of the Three Sons added the layer of pulpit ministry to Dorsey's proven trajectory for gospel success: opening music publishing businesses, conducting choirs at established churches, and sponsoring Los Angeles appearances of gospel stars like the Sallie Martin Singers, the Roberta Martin Singers, and Bessie Griffin. In their own churches, each of the Three Sons hired outstanding staff musicians and commanded influential radio preaching spots.

The role of the gospel-singing evangelist had been established in Chicago. Even viewed alongside the Three Sons of Thunder, Chicagoan John L. Branham (d. 1984) was foremost among Reverend-musicians responsible for transplanting Chicago gospel to Los Angeles.[16] After his ordination at Chicago's gospel music–infused Olivet Baptist Church, he pastored in San Diego for a while, then returned to Chicago in 1940, but eventually assumed the leadership position at Saint Paul Baptist in Los Angeles in 1943. He hired James Earle Hines (1916–1960) of Cincinnati, Ohio, as choral director, and Chicago-born accompanist/arranger Gwendolyn Cooper. The team at Saint Paul "set a standard of excellence" for L.A. Gospel.[17] Branham, Hines, and

Cooper founded the Echoes of Eden choir in 1946 and it debuted in 1947 on KFWB radio. The listening public responded enthusiastically to live radio broadcasts recorded during the 7:30 p.m. Sunday worship service. This live spectacle, for such it was, eventually drew Hollywood and recording stars such as Hattie McDaniel and Nat King Cole.[18] Cooper transformed hymn standards such as "I'm So Glad Jesus Lifted Me," (a mainstay at Chicago's First Church of Deliverance) into an enthusiastic, up-tempo number for the Echoes that became their broadcast theme music.[19] In demand nationally, Hines took the National Baptist Convention's New Goodwill Singers on tour in 1948, during which time "famed gospel composer Sallie Martin became the director of The Saint Paul Choir of Los Angeles."[20] By this time, Sallie and her adopted daughter, Cora Martin, were fully integrated into the music scene at Saint Paul.

These men—Branham, Peters, Pleasant, and Smallwood—led the churches most significant to the early development of gospel in L.A. Each headquartered their ministries within the Baptist faith, which by the mid-1940s was largely on board with the gospel movement. Being Baptist meant that men remained at the captaincy of the most influential gospel churches in Los Angeles, but women commanded influential musical positions within church musical hierarchies.

The First Sallie Martin Singers and Early Recordings

When Sallie Martin walked away from her business agreement with Dorsey in 1939, she faced an immediate dilemma (see chapter 2). She had the voice, reputation, and business experience to be successful, but unlike Dorsey, Roberta Martin, and others of her generation, she could not play the piano for her own group. A late 1939 notice in the *Chicago Defender* advised that Edna Mae Quarles would be Martin's accompanist for an upcoming Boston appearance, either Martin's last as a Dorsey agent or her first independent engagement.[21] For the longer term and to her great fortune, Martin teamed up with the gifted twenty-year-old whom she and Dorsey had recently recruited from Springfield, Ohio: Julia Mae Smith (1918–1998), who would stay with Martin for a decade.[22]

Martin's vocal style was best showcased with backup singers; she and Morris wasted little time after opening their Chicago business in forming an all-female gospel ensemble, with Martin and Julia Mae Smith at the core. When Smith was unavailable, Martin drafted short-term talent; an undated newspaper photo, labeled "Original Sallie Martin Singers, Virginia Revival, 1940," and showing Sallie, pianist Ruth Jones (a.k.a., Dinah

Washington), Necie (Eunice) Morris (wife of Martin's business partner), and Sarah Daniel, is a very early iteration of the Martin and Morris group.[23]

Martin's first long-term ensemble comprised Julia Mae Smith as pianist and vocalist, Dorothy Simmons (1910–1966), Charlie Mae Lomax (early 1920s–1980), and Cora Brewer (1927–2005). When Martin and the other members of the ensemble moved their households to Los Angeles in 1947, Smith elected to remain in Chicago, where she captured one of the plum gospel piano jobs in the South Side: accompanist for the W. D. Cook Gospel Choir at Metropolitan Community Church—the group founded by Magnolia Lewis-Butts. An arranger and singer (later dubbed "Chicago's Song Bird") as well as gifted pianist, Smith then became the accompanist for Dorsey's gospel chorus at Pilgrim Baptist Church in 1949—more proof of her versatility and finesse—and occasionally sang with Dorsey's Celestial Trio.[24] Also active in the NCGCC, Smith periodically served as its financial secretary and sang in the Chicago Gospel Choral Union. Her own group, the Julia Smith Choralaires, debuted in the late 1940s. They appeared alongside the Sallie Martin Singers several times afterward, most often in Atlanta. Martin thus supported Smith's career and Smith, in turn, widened Martin's circle of influence.[25] Julia Mae Smith Whitfield assisted Dorsey at Pilgrim Baptist until 1992, mere months before Dorsey's death.

Sallie Martin's first long-term ensemble was further solidified with the addition of the precocious teenager Cora Juanita Brewer, born in Chicago to Lucius and Annie Brewer in 1927. Before joining Sallie Martin's entourage, Cora sang for Mount Pleasant Baptist Church. Sallie was drawn to Cora's preternaturally mature voice, and after her only child, Joel, was killed in action in Tunisia in 1942, she adopted Cora in an informal agreement with Brewer's parents.[26] Cora Brewer was thereafter known as Cora Martin until her marriage to Henry Moore (1907–2004), when she became Cora Martin-Moore.[27] Cora may have dropped out of high school to tour with Sallie Martin's groups, but she would later attend the University of California–Dominguez Hills, in addition to running the Los Angeles Gospel Music Mart, hosting a radio show, composing and arranging dozens of gospel songs, and serving Saint Paul Baptist Church as choir director from 1958 until her death in 2005, with only a few years' hiatus.

A less permanent member who recorded early on with the Martin and Morris Singers was Charlie Mae Lomax (née Crawford, early 1920s–1980), whom Sallie Martin met in Los Angeles, probably at a National Baptist Convention meeting. Charlie Mae Crawford was born in Groesbeck, Texas, in the early 1920s and moved with her family to California when Charlie Mae was eleven years old.[28] She attended USC as a music major and earned a BA degree in social work at San Francisco State University. She married

Reverend Thurston Lomax in 1939 and was considered the "first lady" of his congregation, Second Baptist Church of Long Beach, until his death in 1941. She then married Reverend Frederick Douglas Haynes in 1945 and moved to San Francisco. Lomax recorded with Sallie Martin's group in 1940 and, possibly, again in 1945.

Rounding out the first iteration of the Martin and Morris Singers to make a recording was Dorothy Vernell Simmons (1910–1996), who was born in Powhatan, Louisiana, then moved to Chicago in about 1917. At one time, she clerked in the MMMS store. After moving to Los Angeles, Simmons left Martin's group and cofounded the Simmons-Akers Singers, which featured Simmons's "sweetly soaring soprano," Hattie Hawkins, and Doris Akers, a mezzosoprano-alto.[29] The Simmons-Akers ensemble was most active in the 1950s and disbanded in 1957.[30]

Early Recordings and Tours of the Sallie Martin Singers

Under the moniker "The Martin and Morris Singers," Sallie Martin, Cora Martin, Lomax, and Simmons, with Smith on piano, recorded four sides for the Bronze label in 1940: "I Know I Have Another Building," "I'm Walking with My Jesus," "On the Jericho Road," and one that was not released, "It Must Be Jesus' Love Divine" (see Selected Discography). Metrically rock-solid, but reflecting the highly controlled inflections of early gospel, Julia Smith's pianistic complement imbues the first three songs with lightness and grace.[31] Block-chord vocal arrangements celebrate the singers' capacity to blend with each other—quite an accomplishment for timbral opposites like contralto Cora Martin and soprano Dorothy Simmons. Cora's sound is naturally brassy and widely vibrating, while Simmons delicately lilts along the top lines. Call-and-response delivery characterizes Donald S. McCrossan's "On the Jericho Road" (1933), which by 1940 was beloved in both white and Black gospel circles.[32] In these three recordings, balance, restraint, well-tuned harmonies, and clearly articulated texts were the priorities. These cuts sound tame in comparison to their later recordings for the Specialty label, where white owner Art Rupe encouraged Black singers not to whitewash their sound. The restraint evident on the Bronze sides hearkens back to the class consciousness of mainline denominations; the stereotypically "whiter" a group sounded, the better they would be received by influential churches and the larger their consumer base would be. That pastel aesthetic would not last long, for Black gospel or the Sallie Martin Singers.

Three other recordings of the early 1940s deserve mention here. Neither studio nor personnel is documented for "There Must Be a Heaven Somewhere," but the two Martins' voices are recognizable. The rest of the ensemble seems much the same as the singers for the 1940 Bronze sides, except for the pianist. The upbeat introduction, weaving together of thematic snippets, facile chromaticism, and syncopated alternation of hands, sets up a far more exuberant atmosphere than that heard on the Bronze recordings. This recording feels less "conducted" and more spontaneous, and though the vocalists take similar care with lyrics, the once self-conscious enunciation and phrasing has become more natural. The impression of spontaneity—akin to what happens in a live setting—and newly established knowledge that the Black audience could sustain a gospel recording industry, had profound effects on style. If this is Julia Smith on piano, she had severely curtailed her rhythmic drive and melodic fertility in the earlier Bronze sessions.

Kenneth Morris may also have been the collaborative pianist on these recordings, since the latter two sides were released on the short-lived Martin and Morris label in 1945. Martin's final pianist, Kenneth Woods Jr., made a statement that helps to differentiate the pianistic styles heard in the 1940s recordings: "When I think about it now, Mr. Dorsey was blues and ragtime style. Kenneth Morris [played with] more of a swing style, which was popular in the '30s."[33] "There Must Be a Heaven Somewhere," along with "I'm Going to Bury Myself in Jesus' Arms" and "Joy in My Soul," surely were accompanied by the same pianist. "Joy in My Soul" is more light-handed, but the pianist uses some of the same decorative, introductory motives in "There Must Be a Heaven" and "I'm Going to Bury Myself."[34] In synch with the pianist, the singers seem more interested in spirit as opposed to technique and, thus, more stylistically predictive of the Golden Age of gospel. Their cut of "There Must Be a Heaven Somewhere" is among the first times the group recorded as The Sallie Martin Singers of Joy, and for the other two numbers they were credited as the Sallie Martin Gospel Singers on the Martin and Morris label.

Early recordings show that Sallie Martin's first group—whether called the Martin and Morris Singers, the Sallie Martin Singers, or Sallie Martin's Singers of Joy—grew more cohesive as they made a living singing and selling music. Nothing refines ensemble blend and fertilizes improvisation more efficiently than regular performances of the same repertoire. Early on, the Sallie Martin Singers essentially replicated the style that Martin had been demonstrating with Dorsey on the nascent NCGCC circuit. However, as the 1940s progressed, competing vocal ensembles sprang up all over the nation and the NCGCC, a thriving enterprise, gave them regular opportunities to show off, compete for consumers, and absorb the most attractive riffs they heard from others.

Sallie Martin readily utilized the convention circuits. "You see," she remembered, "what I [did was] to make every National Baptist Convention and I [carried] the music." If a song happened to be hot, Martin could sell between 500 and 1,000 piano/vocal octavos to conventioneers. "That's the way I built my business: taking copies, selling them on the road, [and] paying expenses [with the proceeds.].[35] Sons of Thunder vocalist and minister Eugene Smallwood offered further details about what happened at the conventions.

> [Organizers of the NBC and the NCGCC conventions] would let singers practice to "sort of warm up the meetings" and help gather people together for the main events. If [the convention delegates] were out for lunch at 12:00 and the afternoon session started at 2:00, the gospel singers would get in about 1:00 . . . and start singing their new numbers. The people would come in to hear the new numbers, because they'd have different people go through the audience and sell [the music]. . . . When the pastors would go back to their various churches, then they would bring the music back with them.[36]

The combination of worship, musical performance, merchandising, and administering the organizations made for a vibrant scene, one that persists in these organizations and those founded after them.

Martin's utilization of newspaper advertising and her labors as National Organizer of Gospel Choral Unions also kept her singing group in the national spotlight after 1947.

> I was really blessed to be booked from one year through another. . . . We spent about 2 to 3 weeks a year right in Chicago, we'd go to California for the winter, work out there through the winter, leave there in January and go to Miami, Florida, and then [tour] around up until the [NCGCC] convention and . . . then we'd start out again, time to get back to California.[37]

If they traveled by train, Martin maintained control of the tickets throughout the tour, the better to enforce her rules.

> It has always been my way that whoever would sing with me, I'd try to tell them before they'd start: . . . "Well now, you have all day wherever you're going. I'm not going . . . to try to keep up with you where you're going to go. Only thing I want, you . . . keep the way clear that you don't have any trouble, but remember when services are over at night we go

> home. We have a meal and if it's . . . games or something that you want to play or the piano or something we do that, but we do not go to taverns and . . . carry on when the service is over, we don't do that at all. I tell you before you go with me so that you'll know because I keep your railroad fare with me and I will send you home." . . . I had grown people too, I didn't have children, but . . . that was my way, and everywhere I've been, I can go [back]. I don't have to take chances.
>
> My main purpose out there [was] trying to give a message to help others . . . that's the reason I couldn't be out there now because you can't find folks now that . . . want to do the right thing. They get through . . . and they want to go to drinking . . . well I just can't have that.[38]

Traveling by train or automobile, but mainly propelled by native temperament and necessity, she enforced high expectations for her singers. Still, the train didn't go to every location on Martin's itineraries, and she spent most of her time traveling by automobile. "One reason for driving," she said, was that "you could pull aside and sleep in the car."[39]

The irrepressible Martin loved a good story and got a lot of mileage from recounting her brief affiliation with Ruth Jones (a.k.a., Dinah Washington [1924–1963]).[40] Another prodigy like Cora Brewer, Jones dropped out of high school to tour with the Sallie Martin Singers in 1940. Martin told Goreau in 1972,

> [Ruth] had been traveling with me and she was just a little over 16 and she was so wild, . . . Mercy, she was a beautiful singer, but [when] she'd play for me . . . she would . . . spot somebody, some man in that crowd [in church] and before you could say "praise God from whom all blessings flow and say amen," . . . she was back at the door [meeting him].[41]

Martin later explained, "I know that her Mother trusted her with me, so I just had to tell Mrs. Jones, 'I just have to leave [Ruth in Chicago] because I can't be responsible for her.'"[42] Martin's uncompromising position contributed to her stern reputation, but her reasoning was sound. As she told Goreau, "Well quite naturally, whatever happens through them, it's on you."[43]As Dinah Washington, the flirtatious Jones soon accrued fame as a blues and jazz singer in Lionel Hampton's band. The Sallie Martin Singers embraced a new member and continued on its way.

Martin was a firm believer in newspaper advertisement and considered Dorsey's unwillingness to advertise in the 1930s a great failing. Notices in the Black press outline the perimeters of her travels with the Singers. With Chicago as hub until 1947, runouts to local or nearby churches weren't usually advertised, but trips to larger or more distant cities were noted in Chicago, Atlanta, Pittsburgh, Cleveland, Indianapolis, Shreveport

(LA), and Saint Joseph (MI) newspapers. A fledgling Singers group gave a "midsummer recital" in Indianapolis in July of 1940, accompanied by that city's Cosmopolitan Music Study Chorus, a Gospel Choral Union (GCU) chapter of the NCGCC, and at the NCGCC in Chicago that August. Performances drawing press coverage the next year included multiple stops in Terre Haute, Cleveland, and Pittsburgh. A 1941 Cleveland performance documents Ruth Jones's time with the group; she and Martin were featured on the selection "My Father Watches Over Me."[44] The same year, Martin's solo concert in New Jersey was advertised in the Passaic *Herald-News*. The NCGCC's 1942 board meeting took the Singers to Atlanta for a performance with the Atlanta GCU. After the fall 1942 NCGCC meeting in St. Louis, they again headed "off to California," according to the December 11, 1942, *Defender*. This was the month when Sallie's only child by birth, Joel Martin, lost his life in the North African Campaign of World War II.[45]

Even as war raged in Europe and the Pacific, the NCGCC's spring board meeting of 1943 took place in Huntington, West Virginia. The late-summer convention followed in Cleveland, where the Sallie Martin Singers performed before an audience of 700 singers and 500 visitors. Martin and the group sang at Atlanta's Ebenezer Baptist Church, pastored by Martin Luther King Sr., on June 12, 1944; again before a crowd of 1,500 in late August of that year at the NCGCC in Huntingdon, West Virginia; and for an estimated 20,000 visitors and delegates at the Dallas NBC in the second week of September. Performing Kenneth Morris's arrangement of "Just a Closer Walk with Thee" at that convention would be a watershed; as Morris stated, "that is what put us on the map."[46] Roads to these destinations would have been dotted with performance stops, largely unnoticed by the press.

Martin's handwritten records of agents' addresses and sheet music orders show just how meticulously she managed the complicated business of touring, though increasingly, facilitators in each concert location did a variety of local jobs that supported the Singers and the MMMS: distributing music, managing performance venues, and arranging for overnight stays.[47] During the NBC where she introduced "Just a Closer Walk with Thee," Martin drafted a letter to Lillian Doty, by then her Los Angeles booking agent.[48]

> Aug. 8–1944
> My dear Miss Doty.
> I'm sure it's time we were thinking it over about our engagement for November and the first three weeks in Dec. I'm coming home for Chris[tmas]. First I want to say I don't want to come unless you are certain of a stopping place before I leave. I have decide[d] that I would like

> to open with the big program on Nov. 5. This could be at the Embassy [Auditorium, Ambassador Hotel, Los Angeles], and as I said see Rev Collins. Rev Russell and I have just talked with Rev Henderson of First Baptist. He would like for us to open with him after our big program. I told him you were taking care of this and I'm sure would talk with him at once.[49]

No records suggest that these L.A. appearances occurred or if, as she suggested, Martin abandoned the idea when stopping places for performances en route could not be found.

During the remainder of the 1940s, the ambitus of the Sallie Martin Singers extended to Buffalo, New York; Louisville, Kentucky; and Washington, DC. Martin's advertising flair is seen in a May 1948 *Indianapolis Recorder* announcement; the "Famous Sallie Martin and her Singers of Chicago and Los Angeles" would favor an Indianapolis audience with "He Is All I Need" and "Move On Up a Little Higher."[50]

Even as she maintained an active national touring schedule, Martin tended the professional garden she had planted in Los Angeles with the first Bronze recording session and the Gospel Choral Union she founded there in 1942. An ad for the Sallie Martin Singers' "farewell appearance" before heading back to Chicago in January of 1946, designed to fuel a fear of missing out among readers, was their first notice in the *Los Angeles Sentinel.* Blaine Venerable, soon to partner with Eugene Smallwood in founding a choir, was named as sponsor.[51] That event and an identically advertised one a year later took place at Neighborhood Community (COGIC) Church at San Pedro and 47th Place. The SMS then performed at the Second Baptist Church in March of 1947. For that event, the ensemble comprised Martin, Julia Smith (piano), Dorothy Simmons, Cora Brewer, and Hattie Hawkins. Tickets were available at Martin's Gospel Music Mart and the Dunbar Hotel (4225 S. Central Ave.), which long had been a recommended stop in the *Negro Travelers' Green Book.*[52]

As always, Martin accepted new opportunities to promote her music and her brand. "In 1950, Sallie Martin became one of the first female announcers in L.A. when she went on the air in March and was dubbed 'California's First Religious Disc Jockette' by the *California Eagle.*"[53] Later, Cora Martin Moore spent two years as a gospel announcer in L.A.

The Gospel Music Mart

Significant as it was in spreading Chicago gospel to the West Coast, the Gospel Music Mart (GMM) apparently did not operate from a rented store in its early years. Especially before she moved her household to L.A. in

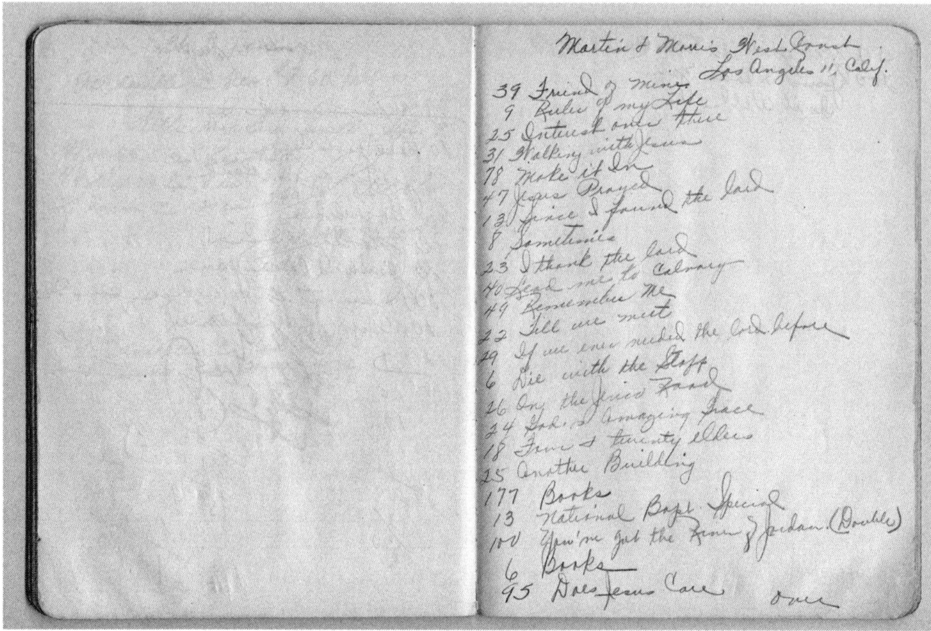

Martin & Morris West Coast
Los Angeles 11, Calif.
39 Friend of mine
9 Ruler of my Life
25 Intercede over there
31 Walking with Jesus
78 Make it In
47 Jesus Prayed
13 Since I found the Lord
8 Sometimes
23 I thank the Lord
40 Lead me to Calvary
49 Remember Me
22 Till we meet
29 If we ever needed the Lord before
6 Die with the Staff
26 On the Jesus Road
24 God's Amazing Grace
18 Four & twenty elders
25 Another Building
177 Books
13 National Bapt. Special
100 You've got the Room of Jordan (Double)
6 Books
95 Does Jesus Care
once

FIGURE 5.1. Page of Sallie Martin's Waste Book, Martin's hand, West Coast inventory, headed "Martin & Morris West Coast, Los Angeles 11, Calif." Martin and Morris Music Company Records, series 2, 6. Used with permission.

1947, Martin simply brought sheet music along as she and the Singers commuted annually from Chicago to Los Angeles for the winter. Her base of operations would have been wherever she resided and sales were part of each performance. A combination address and order book dated 1942–1943 records transactions with Arthur Atlas Peters and Eugene Smallwood, and a "waste book" lists the music she brought along in late 1942 or early 1943.[54] Sales in Los Angeles seem to have been folded into the accounting of the Chicago store both before and after Martin rented a space at 4707 Avalon Boulevard for the Gospel Music Mart in 1947 (see figure 5.1). A 1956 phone directory showed the address of the GMM as 4365½ South Central Avenue. Acting on Martin's behalf, Lillian Doty hired Gwendolyn Cooper Lightner to manage the store in 1948.[55] The Gospel Music Mart was more than a place to buy sheet music and records, however. Just as her mentor, Kenneth Morris, did in the Chicago MMMS store, Lightner taught voice, harmony, musicianship, and piano as she managed sales and inventory. In addition to locals, she taught students who commuted weekly from San Diego, Long Beach, Riverside, San Francisco, and Bakersfield because, as she said, "We were the only studio in the city." A committed pedagogue, Lightner traveled to one of those fairly distant locations monthly to teach a music theory class. Her own career-building therefore served to extend Sallie Martin's California influence. Cora Martin managed the Gospel Music Mart from 1953 to 1962.

In 1947, Sallie Martin made Los Angeles her primary home and retained a residence there until at least the late 1950s.[56] The 1950 census shows that she and Cora lived at 4387½ East 42nd Place. At that time, Sallie described herself as a business owner, occupied in the singing chorus industry, with a reported income of $5,000 a year, about $67,000 in 2024 dollars.

Further Established on the West Coast: The GCU and Recordings

As National Organizer of the NCGCC, Martin founded, rehearsed, and advised Gospel Choral Unions (GCUs), the Convention's de facto regional chapters. She established the Los Angeles GCU in 1942, after which the real work of recruiting church choirs for its membership began. Rehearsals and performances of the West Coast group were first advertised in the *Sentinel* in 1946, the year that the NCGCC Board met there in preparation for the 1949 national convention. In the year of its founding, the studio and record store Dolphin's of Hollywood used Sallie Martin's name to add weight to its offerings, including a recording of Martin's own composition, "Jesus," with "Thank You Jesus" on the reverse.[57] An August 1948 Dolphin's ad gave Martin top billing, followed by Roberta Martin and the Ward Singers of Philadelphia.

In the summer of 1949, L.A.'s Gospel Choral Union busily promoted the upcoming NCGCC convention; in July it sponsored the Sallie Martin Singers and the Willie Mae Ford Smith Singers; in early August, a youth choir; and in August, the GCU sang with its sponsored youth finalist, "Miss Foster," in a national singing competition run by the NCGCC.[58] The next month, the National Baptists Convention, also in Los Angeles, was celebrated by a *Pittsburgh Courier* photo featuring three musicians on top of the world: Sallie Martin wearing a bright smile, her arms linked with Kenneth Morris to her right and Thomas A. Dorsey on her left.[59]

Martin's visibility was also boosted by her promotion of Christian foreign missions in the late 1940s (see chapter 6). She was given a coveted spot on the program of the NBC in Houston to speak on behalf of fundraising for missions work in the "West Indies, Africa, and the Southwest Pacific." Naturally, the Sallie Martin Singers sang on that program.[60]

Sallie Martin had "made it" in L.A., without losing ground in the rest of the country. On February 27, 1948, she, Cora, and the rest of the Singers headlined on a live Capitol recording with the foremost choir on the West Coast, Saint Paul Baptist's Echoes of Eden. In "Just a Closer Walk with Thee," the SMS contribute a plodding background to Ruth Black-Castille's performance of the first verse—pitched stratospherically in E-flat major. Then, Sallie Martin delights the congregation with her equally improbable notes in the contralto range as she solos in the second and third verses. In a notable rendition of the jubilant "Didn't It Rain," Cora Martin takes center stage, backed by Hines's remarkable choir and confidently supported by associate director and pianist Gwendolyn Cooper Lightner. "They say I'm the first to bring the curlicues to Los Angeles," Cora said; the twenty-year-old spins athletic melismas over a suspenseful chant from the choir—"Listen to the Rain"—then leaps effortlessly back into the lead to signal the final chorus.[61] The final song recorded on that session was Kenneth Morris's "Dig a Little Deeper in God's Love," one of Sallie Martin's calling cards. Driven by Cooper's "bounce" piano style, the SMS and the Echoes sing the first verse and chorus, followed by Black-Castille, then a Cora Martin solo. Quite capable of upstaging all comers, Sallie Martin then takes the lead, delighting the audience with her movements (she was liable to use the mic stand as a mock shovel) and her vocal delivery. She seems to be having the time of her life on this recording, knowingly signifying the Sallie Martin persona.

Capitol highlighted the mother-daughter duo, backed by the SMS in 1949, though the new label made little difference in their vocal arrangements. In their performance of "King Jesus Will Roll All Burdens Away," an older-style gospel song by Kenneth Morris, Julia Smith sings soprano and either she or Dave Weston (b. 1923) plays piano. Also on that session was Mahalia Jackson's 1947 hit, "Move On Up a Little Higher," featuring Sallie on lead vocals against the Singers' delivery of W. Herbert Brewster's antiphonal responses. Lastly, Sallie is featured in Morris's rousing "Thank You, Jesus," memorable in part for her initial entrance half a bar early, and the ensemble's seamless accommodation of that hiccup. Rousing and replete with vocal slides and her shout-style timbres, this session kept Martin's reputation going strong.

In September of 1949, Capitol tried a new approach to market Sallie Martin. She and Julia Smith recorded four songs with a trio of swing veterans from the company's rhythm and blues department: "In My Heart" and "He's All I Need," then "The Little Wooden Church on the Hill" and "Jesus Is the Only One." The same group's March 10, 1950, session, this time including Cora, further emphasizes how a change in accompaniment can transform a group. Instrumentalists included "Nappy" Lamare (1905–1988, guitar), Leonard Bibb ("Bibbs," bass), and Zutty Singleton

(1898–1975, drums).[62] Lamare ran several dance bands in Los Angeles after a career playing in New Orleans and New York. A swing bassist and Chicago native, Bibb recorded with various artists including Singleton on Decca, Brunswick, Columbia, and Stash, and also played sessions for Savoy in the 1950s. New Orleans native Singleton recorded with Louis Armstrong on the Hot Five recordings, as well as other notable sessions, then ran L.A. bands that played for movies after 1943. Though they reported for light duty that March day, the rhythm section propelled the singers and Julia Smith fit right in.

"I'm Going to Follow Jesus" opens with Cora's able solo against Sallie's hummed obbligato. While the rhythm section comps steady eighths, Sallie leads on the chorus as Cora responds, then they reverse roles. The bridge features Lamare's banjo-style picking. "Love Like a River in My Soul" (a.k.a. "I've Got Peace Like a River"), too, is enlivened by the rhythm section's forward momentum and occasional decoration. In "Satisfied," Cora's tendency to sing sharp is hard to overlook, but the old standard has all other pieces in place. "Do You Know Him" allows fleeting glimpses of Smith's melodic fertility and Cora's beautiful head tones, which are impeccably pitched. Despite the ravages of time and abuse on Sallie's 54-year-old vocal cords, unisons between Cora and Sallie are mostly true. The elder singer's subtleties with text and enunciation are delightful.

Touring made for an exhausting life. A close listen to these four recordings calls to mind that Cora would lose interest in touring around 1952.[63] To my ears, the 22-year-old sounds vocally tired, but she gave the session all she had, and the public continued to appreciate her singing. A stronger Cora Martin had sung for a fifteen-minute KTLA–TV (Los Angeles) Christmas program featuring the Sallie Martin Singers and an ensemble from the Echoes of Eden choir, under Sallie's direction. The *Sentinel* reviewer described that 1949 holiday broadcast as "one of the biggest Christmas Day thrills for music lovers and TV fans."[64]

Back with Specialty and still in search of a chartbuster like Mahalia Jackson's "Move On Up a Little Higher," which never materialized, Sallie and Cora Martin recorded with various singers and accompanists in 1950 alone. In April, they recorded several times with Brother Joe May (1912–1972), whom Art Rupe described as the "best gospel soloist we have as far as sales go."[65] A native of Macon, Mississippi, May emigrated to East St. Louis in 1941 and was mentored by Willie Mae Ford Smith. Upon moving to Los Angeles in 1949, the gifted tenor was signed by Specialty/Venice.[66] The Martins and May were joined by Theresa Childs on vocals and piano and Dave Weston on vocals and organ. May, Cora, and Sallie each take their solo verses in the barnburner "Oh Yes, He Set Me Free."

That song features May's favorite backing, a fully harmonized and highly rhythmic accompaniment on organ. As the *Billboard* reviewer observed, "Brother Joe doesn't get much to do on this bright, revival-like chant, but the group shouts up a storm."[67] After recording with Weston and Albert Goodson on piano on August 16, the same group, again with May, recorded eight standards on December 15, 1950.[68] Sallie is featured on a ballad based on the story of Shadrach, Meshach, and Abednego (biblical book of Daniel, chapter 3) entitled "God Is a Battle Axe (in the Time of War)." May and Weston lend resonance to Cora's somewhat mediated tones. Theresa Childs decorates her piano accompaniment with runs on the black keys. This genre of gospel song clearly evolved from singing preachers; thus, it suited Sallie down to the ground. May, Cora, and Sallie each have a verse on "Oh Yes, He Set Me Free," where Cora is in especially lustrous voice.

In June of 1951, the Martins were back in the studio with Berda Young Patrick, Lonnie Polk, Dave Weston (vocals and organ), and Albert Goodson (piano). Sallie and Cora then recorded in L.A.'s Elks Auditorium with Theresa Childs, Fred Miller, Charles Brown instead of Weston on organ, and Brother Joe May in March of 1952 ("Until We Meet Again," featuring Cora; and "He's Able to Carry You Through," which May leads). Those tunes were recorded again, before an audience, only a few days after the March 1952 recording session.[69] In the live recording, the Sallie Martin Singers remain very much in the background, though Sallie Martin's words of encouragement ("Sing, Joe," "Tell the Story,") give a good sense of her onstage persona. Before they sing "Hold On to God's Unchanging Hand," Martin banters with the audience. "We're very happy to be here; we don't have a full group . . . we don't have our main lead, but Brother May said he could lead it and if he can lead, I can follow." Then she explains in an aside after her statement, "I was just intending to give Brother May . . . a chance to catch his breath." Backup harmonies by the SMS are homogeneous and well-rehearsed. May's vocal and dramatic control is very much on display as he begins in a soft, prayerful dynamic, then leads a mighty crescendo in "Jesus Is Real to Me." His leadership on Brewster's "Move On Up a Little Higher," has all that, plus an accelerando.

Billboard announced in December of 1952 that the Sallie Martin Singers were represented by a "major booking operation," the Lil Cumber Attraction Agency. Lillian Cumber (1920–2002) set up the business in 1948, after working as Art Rupe's Specialty Records publicity director.[70] Primarily focusing on Specialty's groups, Cumber also represented the Pilgrim Travelers, Brother Joe May, the Soul Stirrers, J. Earle Hines, Sister Wynona Carr, the Original Gospel Harmonettes, the Swan Silvertone Singers, and the Detroiters. She also managed bookings for the Blind Boys of Mississippi and the Spirits of Memphis Quartet (both contracted with

Peacock records). Cumber typically booked several groups as a package, "in ball parks during the warm weather dates and . . . indoors for the winter swings." She also managed Black actors; she is seen, far right, in a 1940s photo with her artists, including Louise Beavers (*Imitation of Life, Holiday Inn*), Lillian Randolph (of radio's *The Great Gildersleeve*), and Academy Award winner (for her role in *Gone with the Wind*) Hattie McDaniel.[71] Sallie Martin's Specialty contract thus put her in league with Hollywood's brightest lights.

As it had for Gwendolyn Cooper Lightner, Sallie's Gospel Music Mart provided a home base and launchpad for Cora Martin beginning in 1953. In April of 1954, she began a radio show on KWKW, entitled "Sister Cora Martin's Spirituals," where she interspersed recordings with her own live performances.[72] She is listed as the director of the L.A. Gospel Choral Union (Sallie Martin, supervisor) in a June 1953 issue of the *Sentinel*. After her tenure with the SMS, Cora appeared regularly as soloist and in combination with her mother's and other groups: a solo at Hays Chapel CME church ("Cora Martin in Recital Plans," *Los Angeles Sentinel*, Oct. 1, 1953, A10) and at Second Baptist church (*Sentinel*, Nov. 19, 1953, A7); and with Sallie at a Masonic Hall benefit at 42nd and Avalon (*Sentinel*, Feb. 4, 1954, A7). By 1955, Cora had established her own thriving career in Los Angeles, publishing an anthology of her compositions with the MMMS in February 1955.

Meanwhile, Sallie Martin continued as before. She was feted for her twenty-five years in gospel (since 1929) at the Independent Community Church (*Los Angeles Sentinel*, Dec. 9, 1954), appearing almost monthly while in L.A. with various singers, including the SMS, the Simmons-Akers Singers, and Robert Anderson. She sang for a February 1957 appearance with Dave Weston (*Sentinel*, Feb. 7, 1957) in Los Angeles, and then was back with her old friend, Rev. Clarence H. Cobbs, who facilitated an appearance for her at Chicago's Orchestra Hall (see below) with his music director at First Church of Deliverance (Ralph Goodpasture). For the remainder of the 1950s, Sallie Martin sang periodically in Los Angeles, Chicago, Cleveland, Indianapolis, Kansas City, Atlanta, and Montgomery, Alabama, likely anchoring her performances around activities of the Gospel Choral Unions she had founded. An ad she placed in *Billboard* states that Sallie Martin sang at London's Royal Albert Hall in 1955.

Marriage to Joe Langham and Conclusions

In interviews with Laurraine Goreau (1972) and James Standifer (1981), Martin detailed the foibles of her first husband, Wallace Martin, but she kept the specifics about her second marriage strictly private. On July 20,

1956, she married Joseph (Joe) Langham (1912–1975), a Chicago gambler and nightclub owner. Reports suggest that he was favored by Chicago's smart set: "The Lloyd (Congo Lounge) Wests gave a 'much too much' party for Joe Langham, former sportsman along the Stroll, who is now making his home in Phoenix, Ariz., and in town on a vacation," read a 1945 *Defender* gossip column. The same event was described as an "epicurean's delight" and "one of the most colorful affairs on the social calendar [of] the past week."[73] Beginning in 1952, Langham owned a place called Joe's Los Angeles Show Bar on 6323 Cottage Grove Avenue, close to the Pershing Hotel in Chicago ("Joe Langham . . . seems to know just what the public wants in the line of entertainment").[74] A couple of weeks after his marriage to Martin, he played host alongside other club owners at Chicago's House of Rock n Roll, where the roster was led by Muddy Waters.[75] For a decade or so after their marriage, Martin sporadically appears as Sallie Martin Langham or Mrs. Joseph (or Joe) Langham in the *Defender*.

Joe Langham was born in Bessemer, Alabama, on March 12, 1909, to Emma (b. 1893) and William H. Langham (b. 1883), the latter a farmer.[76] Emma labored on their farm at home, located in a southern suburb of Birmingham. At some point, Joe married Bessie Taylor and that marriage ended in divorce around 1940.[77] On October 13, 1947, a woman named Christine Burton celebrated the birth of a daughter, JoMarie (Marie), in Chicago. The baby's father was Joe Langham.

A liaison between the strait-laced Sallie Martin of the 1930s and this handsome club-owner is hard to imagine, but by the time of her marriage to Langham, Sallie Martin had amassed a power and influence that befitted her formidable presence. An owner of multiple businesses and properties, she was deeply respected in performance, publishing, recording, and radio. She traveled nationally and internationally, wore the best in women's couture, and was known for her regal deportment. With his livelihood firmly rooted in the secular, Langham appears to have been as ambitious, though not as well known, as Martin herself. After their marriage, the power couple appeared to have retained substantial independence, extending to multiple residences in Los Angeles and Chicago. While they were married, Kenneth Woods Jr. remembers walking the block from his own brownstone, at 8220 Eberhart Avenue in Chicago, to share a dinner that Martin had prepared. Langham, he remembers, was often away from home.[78]

Joe's daughter, Marie Langham, married Leonard Cooper Jr. in January of 1968.[79] A reported five hundred guests attended the reception at the Tiki Room in Chicago. A festive photo shows the newlyweds, the bride's paternal grandmother (Emma Langham), and the bride's parents, Mr. and

Mrs. Joe Langham ("the famed gospel singer, Sallie Martin"). Otherwise, Martin and Langham appear to have moved in largely separate circles during the sixteen years they were married; the couple divorced on October 10, 1972, in Chicago (see chapter 7).[80]

Los Angeles of the 1940s was a perfect location for Sallie Martin's personal and professional evolution; she particularly enjoyed performing for L.A. audiences: "I'll tell you, most of my people that I sang to in Los Angeles were white." When questioned whether or not they responded as Black audiences did, Martin replied "Well, you know, they never get completely like [Black folks]. They let you know anyway. . . . because it's about . . . Christ, they'll let you know that they're enjoying it."[81] Los Angeles was hospitable to Sallie Martin in other ways, as well. In the 1940s alone, she made her first recordings, made MMMS's merchandise accessible from her newly established Gospel Music Mart, founded a Gospel Choral Union, collaborated with the musical leaders at Saint Paul Baptist Church, and gained experience as a radio broadcaster. She gave Gwendolyn Cooper Lightner and Cora Martin opportunities to develop managerial experience in the Gospel Music Mart. Lightner developed the teaching side of the business and expanded the reach of the MMMS brand to other Southern California cities before handing over the reins to Cora Martin, who established herself as a radio announcer and solo performer from the same storefront. In like fashion, Sallie Martin gave many second-generation gospel musicians the chance to appear alongside or to sing within the Sallie Martin Singers.

As DjeDje points out about 1940s Los Angeles gospel, "Only a few of the first generation were prolific as composers; rather, much of their energy was spent in organizing the performance groups and institutions that provided the necessary support for the growth and development of gospel music."[82] The success of this foundation was predicated upon having a flair for recruiting exceptional soloists, choir members, directors, managers, agents, hosts, and sponsors to join the gospel movement. Eminently suited and prepared for this work, Sallie Martin left an indelible imprint on the gospel history of that city. Chapter 6 focuses on a Sallie Martin who no longer needed to establish herself—she had achieved the renown she imagined as a girl in Georgia and fully enjoyed her positions of influence and leadership.

CHAPTER 6

Gospel Stardom, Missions, and Civil Rights, 1960–1973

By the 1960s, Sallie Martin had been a woman of action in the gospel world for more than thirty years. In that decade and the early 1970s, she continued to sing publicly, but also fulfilled roles of speaker, mistress of ceremonies, announcer, and missions fundraising chair. She was honored at anniversaries of her birthday, her 1929 origins in the gospel industry, and her establishment of Gospel Choral Unions in several cities: Chicago, Los Angeles, Cleveland, Atlanta, Pittsburgh, and Baltimore. She also continued to expand her business interests, purchasing Lillian Bowles's company around 1959 and acquiring distribution rights to Martin and Morris publications for which she had composed text, music, or both. Independent, savvy, and still crotchety ("She didn't age well," said Kenneth Woods Jr.), she retained the name Sallie Martin in the Black press with only a few exceptions, despite the continuation of her marriage to Joe Langham until 1972.[1]

This chapter demonstrates the fact that by 1960, Martin had made it as a gospel celebrity who wielded great influence and power. However, as her beloved music continued to transform in answer to popular trends, she increasingly lost currency in the field. In some circles, she was revered but considered old-school; in more hostile quarters, she was nothing more than a has-been. Never daunted, Sallie Martin moved with the times to the extent that she could. She still performed Dorsey-style gospel as a soloist or supplied lead or harmony lines within the Sallie Martin Singers or her Singers of Joy, but revised her group's signature sound by hiring Kenneth Woods Jr. as her arranger and accompanist in the mid-1950s. Inventive and university educated, Woods contributed fresher, more complex melodies and arrangements to her repertoire. In this period extending to her retirement, she performed with or was sponsored by members of first- and second-generation gospel royalty such as Robert Anderson (1919–1995), Raymond Rasberry (1930–1995), Thurston Frazier (1930–1974), and James Cleveland (1931–1991), as well as former mentees such as Julia Smith Whitfield (1918–1998). She sang often at Chicago's Pilgrim Baptist Church and First Church of Deliverance, as well as other Baptist, AME, CME (CMEC), COGIC, Methodist, Presbyterian, and nondenominational churches.[2] She performed "The Little Wooden Church on the Hill" in a July 1960 episode of WTTW's *Time for Religion* TV series in Chicago and sang "Wonderful Jesus" with a youth choir from Washington, DC, on that city's *Gospel Time* TV variety program in 1962. With the 1960s iteration of her Singers—trained and accompanied by Woods—she performed on Chicago's *Jubilee Showcase* TV show in March and April of 1964. In 1966, she headlined a six-week European tour comprising twenty concerts in seventeen cities. Rev. Clarence Cobbs arranged the trip and traveled alongside the First Church of Deliverance choir, directed by Ralph Goodpasteur.

All the while, she remained active as the National Organizer of the NCGCC Gospel Choral Unions and, especially, Chicago's GCU, renamed the Evangelical Choral Chapter in the mid-1960s. Each of two major recording projects with Vee Jay, in 1961 and 1963, featured new Sallie Martin Singers ensembles. In 1969, Martin made a Savoy album with the Evangelical Choral Chapter. In all of these Martin delivered sermonettes as song preludes and, just as fluently, negotiated Woods's updated arrangements.

Tapped frequently as the face and muscle of diverse capital campaigns, she supported her own favorite projects more visibly in the 1960s. Christian missions in Africa held a special significance for her, but she also supported longtime friends and advocates in local efforts. In 1969, she was one of many fundraising captains for Rev. Clarence Cobbs's ambitious efforts to raise $100,000 in sixty days for the establishment of a nursing home near the church.[3] Additionally, Martin was chief fundraiser and building coordinator for the long-delayed completion of the NCGCC's national headquarters at 4048 South Lake Park Avenue.[4] Named Gospel Singers Plaza, the building opened in March of 1971. The eleven-story structure comprised sixty-one apartments and was intended for education, as well as a place for elder gospel singers to retire.[5]

Martin's 1960s and '70s—characterized by stardom, wealth, and Christian missions activities—also placed her in the company of those active in the Civil Rights Movement. In contrast to her friend, Mahalia Jackson, Sallie Martin's presence was never recorded at a rally or political meeting. Still, she was among the officers at the May 1960 NCGCC Board meeting in Huntington, West Virginia, who raised a few dollars to support students who had been arrested in civil rights protests. She also participated in a

1964 event in Chicago that was sponsored in part by the United American Progress Association, a group devoted to economic retribution.[6] If she contributed money to these efforts, that fact was not advertised.

From 1960 until she sold her interests in the MMMS and Martin's House of Music (formerly the Bowles imprint) to Kenneth Morris and discontinued her touring in 1973, Martin's career work of intertwining religion and capitalism remained constant, her performance circles widened, and her worldview expanded through travel to Europe, Africa, and the West Indies. This chapter follows Martin's late-career activities, which bore fruit in worldwide visibility for Chicago gospel performers and their churches.

The MMMS in the 1960s

In the 1960s, Kenneth Morris continued to compose his own songs and to manage all musical arranging, correspondence with composers, lyricists, publishers, and distributors; and communications with the US Copyright Office, organizations like BMI, and recording companies such as Vee Jay, Savoy, Excellorec, and Planet. Martin continued the work of in-person marketing with her Singers. New technologies meant change, however. Morris could forward cassette tape submissions to Martin for approval, wherever she was. He wrote customer Ira Harris of Oakland, California,

> Enclosed you will find our check in the amount of $40.00 covering 2 songs selected by Mrs. Martin and myself for Bowles and Martin & Morris. Mrs. Martin is keeping the tape until she gets a chance to hear all the numbers, and perhaps will select another tune. If not, she will return your tape at an early date.[7]

The MMMS continued business as usual with its longtime printer, the Rayner Dalheim Company of Chicago, with one significant change, likely resulting from the development of photocopying. In January of 1961, Kenneth Morris authorized the destruction of any and all printing plates copyrighted by Martin and Morris Music, Inc. probably in answer to the printer's request. He requested that any plates copyrighted by other persons or firms held in the MMMS files should be retained.[8] Going forward from January of 1964, Morris asked that Rayner Dalheim keep plates for newly copyrighted and printed songs for ninety days only. Martin and Morris continued to patronize the white-run company that had flourished in Chicago since 1908.

Primarily for the Vee Jay recordings of the early 1960s (see below), Sallie Martin oversaw the copyrighting and publication of around twenty songs under the imprint of Lillian M. Bowles's long-established business. She rereleased several publications of Bowles's more popular music, e.g., *Bowles Book of Poems and Helper* number 2, first published in 1945. Martin also published a couple of her own tunes and new songs and arrangements by Kenneth Woods Jr. Table 6.1 is a representative list of songs she copyrighted from 1958 to 1969, under the imprint of Bowles Music House and Book Store, Bowles Music Studio and Store, or Bowles Music House.[9]

As before, the MMMS published Morris's works and newly submitted songs from clients, but also distributed music of well-established colleagues Raymond Rasberry, Beatrice Seay, Lucie E. Campbell, Thomas A. Dorsey, and Thurston G. Frazier/James Cleveland; that of large companies (Boosey & Hawkes, Theodore Presser); and songs copyrighted by record labels (Planemar, Excellorec, and Venice).[10] Unconcerned with market saturation and willing to pay fifty dollars each for rights to print seven songs in perpetuity, the MMMS released its own compilation, *The Best of James Cleveland* in 1965, even as the Frazier and Cleveland company was publishing Cleveland's works between 1962 and 1967.

Sounds and Values of 1960s Gospel

Like all music, gospel adapts as a result of many factors, among them public taste, corporate actors (i.e., publishers, record labels, radio), the national zeitgeist, competing styles, the economy, government regulations, and emerging talent. Flowing with the tides of these influences, gospel readily absorbs its musical surroundings and attracts new consumers. The 1963 release of James Cleveland's "Peace Be Still" is widely considered to have been a shot heard round the nation. For his famous Savoy recording, Cleveland supplied, trained, and conducted the musical talent; Edward Smith played a Sallie Martin role by contributing substantial business acumen; and Lawrence Roberts, gospel producer for Savoy Records, provided the Angelic Choir of Nutley, New Jersey, to record in Newark.[11] Together, says Boyer, collaborators on "Peace Be Still" transformed old-style gospel blues from "music of the church to a music of the nation."[12] Sallie Martin and Cleveland held mutual affection and respect for each other; the latter's drive for innovation would affect Martin's currency in the gospel world in substantial ways.

As an adult singer, James Cleveland mixed "hard and rough and sweet and smooth" tones, all the while retaining the call and response practice of earlier gospel.[13] Further, he emphasized the half preached, half sung styles of his singing evangelist precursors: J. C. Austin of Pilgrim Baptist and a host of others. To the piano and organ, he added drums, electric

TABLE 6.1. Representative list of songs copyrighted by Sallie Martin for Bowles Music House and Book Store (BMHBS) or similar imprint. KWJ—Kenneth Woods Jr. SM—Sallie Martin.

Year, ©, Imprint	Title	Words	Music	Arrangement
1958 © SM BMHBS	"I'm Still on the Glory Road"	SM	SM	KWJ
1960 © Bowles Music House	"One Step at a Time"	James Cleveland Verse 2, SM	James Cleveland	
1961 © SM BMHBS	"Great Day, When Jesus Christ Was Born"	SM	SM	KWJ
1962 © SM BMHBS	"I Need Him"	KWJ	KWJ	KWJ
1963 © SM BMHBS	"God Is Here"	James Herndon	James Herndon	KWJ
1963 © SM BMHBS	"Just as Long as I Live I Will Serve Him"	André McClellan	André McClellan	KWJ
1963 © SM BMHBS	"Keep in Touch with Jesus"	Clyde Bradley	Clyde Bradley	KWJ
1963 © SM BMHBS	"Keep Me, Jesus"	James Herndon	James Herndon	KWJ
1963 © SM Bowles Music House	"When He Comes"	James Herndon	KWJ	KWJ
1965 © SM BMHBS	"He Is a Friend of Mine"	Cora Martin	Cora Martin	KWJ
1966 © SM BMHBS	"A Child of God"	James Herndon	KWJ	KWJ
1969 © SM BMHBS	"They Found No Fault in Him" with "Praying Time Will Be Over Afterwhile"	SM	SM	KWJ

bass, and stringed instruments. In "Peace Be Still," he adorns his solos with long melismas, adds secondary dominants to decorate choral harmonies, and turns up the drama with choral techniques like long crescendos and sudden dynamic shifts. Community choirs and mass choirs like those of Cleveland featured three-part harmony instead of four and a light bass; a prioritization of the upper voices of soprano, tenor, and falsetto; extended vamps with shifting textural variations; and dramatic modulations.[14]

Few of Cleveland's signature gestures are without precedent in gospel or rhythm and blues; however, his stylistic innovations—some unique and some imported—accrued greater power as the socially conscious soul genre individuated from R&B in the 1960s.[15] A decade earlier, singers like Ray Charles and James Brown had already blended secular and sacred sounds in their hits, and Sam Cooke had transplanted the smooth and sophisticated sounds of the omnipresent Soul Stirrers quartet into R&B.[16]

Whether or not James Cleveland ever listened to Brown's "Please, Please, Please" (1956) or Charles's "What'd I Say" (1959), he understood the musical styles that attracted Black and white kids in the 1950s. A consummate musician, Cleveland played, sang, arranged, and composed. He was also an empire builder on the scale of first-generation musicians such as Dorsey, Frye, and Sallie Martin, seemingly always on the lookout for what could become the next big thing.[17] Marovich reports the rumor that Cleveland's 1957 Apollo recording of "That's Why I Love Him So" with the Gospel All-Stars was inspired by Ray Charles's "Hallelujah, I Love Her So" (1955). Ultimately, writes the same author, the unprecedented sales of "Peace Be Still" owes to several elements: the song's haunting, allegorical message delivered (albeit in New Jersey) against the backdrop of the 1963 march on Birmingham; the power of corporate singing in live service recordings; and the fact that record executives were becoming more tolerant of, and even interested in, songs that advocated civil engagement through direct or metaphorical language.[18]

Sallie Martin first knew James Cleveland as a boy, a "little Pilgrim," singing under Dorsey's direction at Pilgrim Baptist Church in Chicago. His was not the only path to gospel innovation in the early 1960s, however. Gwendolyn Cooper Lightner and Kenneth Woods Jr. were inspired to revise their gospel music by collegiate experience, rather than in response to Cleveland's "Peace Be Still." But that song both signaled and catalyzed the acceptance of new ways in gospel and in Black worship. In 1981, almost two decades after its release, Martin complained about new directions in choral gospel in the television age. Groups she heard at conventions were "trying to have a show or something. . . . they're too far out. I'm used to the folks not being [involved in] just a showmanship, but I'm used to them singing . . . let's have a little Holy Ghost singing."[19] She could not fully appreciate Cleveland's infusion of a new aesthetic in "Peace, Be Still," preferring his capacity to sing in the old-timey way.

The Sallie Martin Singers in the Woods Era

Martin's final regular accompanist, Kenneth Woods Jr. (b. 1929), enters the Martin biography in around 1955.[20] A native of Indianapolis, Woods was mentored and trained beginning in 1943 by Martin's close Convention colleague, Beatrice Brown, who at that time served as National Supervisor for NCGCC's Youth Department. As a teenager in 1944, Woods met Sallie Martin while walking along State Street in Chicago with gospel pioneer Emma Jackson (see chapter 4). In 1948, Martin sponsored Beatrice Brown's Singers, of which Woods was a member, in several Los Angeles performances.[21]

Woods spent a couple of years in the US military in Korea, and at some point was a music theory major at Indiana University–Bloomington, Butler University (Indianapolis), and Roosevelt University in Chicago. This training prepared him to respond to, as well as lead, evolving gospel tastes. In 1954, Brother Joe May selected Woods as his accompanist, and they traveled together for a year (see chapter 5). Back in Indianapolis due to his grandmother's illness in March of 1955, Woods received a call from Sallie Martin. She needed a group to accompany her to a revival engagement in Charleston, South Carolina.[22] By then well established in gospel and finished with his yearlong stint with Joe May, Woods filled Martin's requirements, then stayed on in Charleston for about a year. When invited by Martin a few years later, Woods was happy to rehearse and write music for a new version of the Sallie Martin Singers.

In the 1930s and '40s, a plethora of hopefuls had done almost anything necessary to get their feet in the door of gospel and, once there, to stay inside. By the mid-1950s, the industry had shifted enough to offer space for greater individuality, often as a result of formal education, which allowed gospel musicians to acquire teaching positions and other stable sources of income. Woods, for example, did not always tour with the SMS during their two-decade association. Rather than pursue gospel anywhere it took them, as their predecessors had done, Woods's generation had earned the power of choice.

> I didn't like the process of recording. Now, if it's something going to be live, right then and there, I like that. . . . [But] when you go into the studio, you do tracks. I don't like that. They record you and maybe their

> drummer, then record somebody else, then the singer doing something else over there, somebody doing something, [in the end, it] sounds like it's all happening at the same time. And I tell you the reason why [I don't like it]: I play from the top of my head. In other words, I don't always play the same thing twice.[23]

He did enjoy composing and arranging, and Martin and her new group, including soprano Edith Gary, soprano Shirley Bell, and mezzo-soprano Sara Jordan Powell recorded for Vee Jay in December of 1961. Woods was ready with a portfolio of new songs.[24] His tune "That's What He's Done for Me" gave Martin a chance to show that her musical flexibility was alive and well. It features Woods on piano and Jessy Dixon (1938–2011) on organ. Martin imbues the lengthy recitativo section at the beginning and the triple meter central section of "No One Ever Cared for Me Like Jesus" with sincerity and expressiveness. Woods's arrangement fully exploits Shirley Bell's high notes and highlights an otherworldly solo instrumental line played either on musical saw or theremin by J. E. Gaines.[25]

Woods's arrangements featured frequent secondary dominants, extended chords, delayed cadences, and recitativo passages—signs of the times. The 1961 Vee Jay album is a chronicle of his inventiveness within the new gospel sounds of the 1950s and '60s, the Singers' new timbral and harmonic balance, Edith Gary's power and finesse, and Martin's continuing ability to pick up the lead at any time. Everyone shines in "Let Me Cross Over" and "Own Me as a Child," led by Gary. Old meets new in Gary's 1940s stylings against Woods's fresh, lightly adventurous arrangements.

In February of 1963, another Sallie Martin Singers group comprising Martin, soprano Bessie Folk (1924–2001), Shirley Bell, tenor Eugene Burke (Akron, OH), and Kenneth Woods Jr. cut a second album in the Vee Jay studio. Woods's four-part mixed arrangements (with Martin covering low notes), sung across long sections of ad-libbed meter, and Folk's throaty brilliance ("Closer to Jesus" "When He Comes Back"), brought the Sallie Martin Singers firmly into the present. "God Is Here" and "Seeking for Me" juxtapose Shirley Bell's high range with judicious xylophone punctuations—perhaps from the Hammond B3 organ—and Woods's deft piano. Martin is featured in "Let Jesus Come Into Your Heart," while Woods gives the listener ample evidence of his creativity on piano. Added reverb intensifies "Seeking for Me." Vocal backups are bluesy and sharply articulated, allowing Bell's and Woods's improvs to fill the foreground. Eugene Burke ably dispatches "Nothing but the Grace of God" with his seemingly unlimited, full-throated range. Folk inserts a verse of "Amazing Grace," decorated with high whistle tones, then Burke completes the track. Kenneth Morris's challenging composition "Jesus I Love You" stands out with a vocally resplendent Eugene Burke on that 1963 session. These arrangements are full of varied accompaniment colors, chromaticism, and beautifully arranged and rehearsed vocal blend.

Sallie Martin then had a chance to tour in Europe. The choir of First Church of Deliverance and Martin as featured soloist departed in May of 1966 to great fanfare in Chicago. Never satisfied with the commonplace, Rev. Cobbs booked the entire group of thirty-seven singers and himself on the HMS Queen Elizabeth for their departure on May 24.[26] The six-week tour made twenty performance stops in London, Paris, Zurich, Frankfort, Hamburg, Copenhagen, several cities in Sweden, and Oslo. Under the direction of Ralph Goodpasteur, they planned to perform at a Pentecostal Conference in Alingsås, Sweden, before an expected thirty thousand religious leaders. Several other soloists joined the "widely hailed gospel singer and musical symbol, Sallie Martin."[27] This would not be Martin's last European singing engagement, but it did fulfill a dream she had long held, to sing in Paris and London.

She headlined one final album, *The Living Legend: Miss Sallie Martin and the Evangelical Choral Chapter* (Savoy, 1970). The record seems to be as much a vehicle for her sermonettes as for her singing. It was a low-budget production by Fred Mendelsohn and Rev. Lawrence Roberts—ironically evident when actual feedback among microphones is audible in the recording of Dorsey's "It Doesn't Cost Very Much." Nevertheless, pianist Kenneth Woods Jr., organist Jessy Dixon, and J. E. Gaines, with his novel instrumental sounds, bring professionalism and verve, especially in Woods's slightly more jazzily arranged choir responses in "God Put a Rainbow in the Clouds."

Martin's solos are marked by ill-advised growls that extend above her range. A well-worn sermonette prefaces "That Wooden Church on the Hill." Choir members offer easy, worship-service-style commentary, Motown-style "oohs," and lots of body percussion in this 12/8 tune. Martin's words that introduce "I Heard the Voice" highlight her rhetorical gifts:

> It doesn't cost very much to be nice to somebody as you pass along this way. Or to help somebody along the way. I'm glad I can say, not boastfully, but one thing I know, if they gave out any crowns, or if they gonna give any stars, I know I'll have one for helpin' somebody. Cause whatever you do, it'll come back to you.[28]

Kenneth Morris's challenging composition "Yes, God Is Real" does not achieve the momentum this downtempo song requires, but the livelier "Let Us Give Our Best in Service (While We Can)" is propelled throughout by sparkling keyboard playing and hand claps. Martin's ordination as a minister by Rev. Clarence Cobbs at First Church of Deliverance probably occurred at about this time. Nearing seventy-five years of age, it seems that she wanted to leave a record of her preaching ministry.

Black American Missions in Africa and Sallie Martin's Nigeria

Although surviving records of the MMMS occasionally indicate monthly salaries and annual dividends for each owner, the ways Martin spent her money beyond travel, wardrobe, and real estate are hard to guess. One thing is certain: by 1962, she had begun to invest substantial time and money in domestic and foreign Christian missions. Details included here of her philanthropic work rely mainly on accounts in the *Defender*, since independent records from the two churches with which she worked the hardest were either destroyed in a catastrophic fire (Pilgrim Baptist, January 6, 2006), or have been unavailable (First Church of Deliverance). Nevertheless, press reports are good indicators of what Martin considered important. Her special interest in African missions did not simply arise out of nowhere; there was a genuine movement afoot in mid-1900s Chicago. A quick review of the ways the Baptist denomination and African missions are intertwined is helpful here.

Christian conversion through foreign missions is inspired by Jesus Christ's "Great Commission": "Go ye therefore, and teach all nations, baptizing them in the name of the Father, and the Son, and the Holy Spirit: teaching them to observe all things whatsoever I have commanded you" (Matthew 28:19), but missions and colonialism have operated in tandem. Black Baptist interpretation of the Great Commission, though focused on Christianizing the nonbeliever, has also been shaped by African ancestry and messages of liberation.[29] Nineteenth-century Black Baptist missionaries "shared the religious and cultural assumptions of white Baptists and white Christians in general . . . but also a deep sense of racial solidarity with Africans."[30] If Black missionaries were sent to Africa in the first few decades after the Civil War, they were sent by white organizations. Black believers enthusiastically supported missionary work in African countries by the 1960s.[31]

Black Baptists first established the Baptist Foreign Mission Convention, an umbrella organization, in 1880. In the 1890s, that organization was named for Lott Carey (1780–1828), a formerly enslaved man who purchased his freedom and was one of two men sent to Liberia in 1821.[32] In 1895, the Black Baptist Foreign Mission Convention merged with two other organizations in the United States to form the National Baptist Convention (NBC), the entity so fundamental to the dissemination of gospel music in general, and the careers of countless performers, including Sallie Martin, in particular. During the period from 1920 to 1960, few Black missionaries were sent by white missionary boards to Africa. Whites reasoned that that those dispatched might stir up "trouble"; Black missionaries who applied for foreign posts were sent to Asia and Latin America during those decades.

Back in Chicago, gospel music, egalitarianism, and support of African missions began to coalesce at Pilgrim Baptist Church in the 1930s, by then the second largest church of its denomination in the country. Pastored from 1926 to 1968 by Junius C. Austin Sr. (1887–1968), a Garveyite, the congregation had enacted racial uplift through music in the late 1920s (made evident in part by a preference for European classical music in worship). Austin reversed his preference for classical music when he hired Thomas A. Dorsey to direct a choir in 1932 (see chapter 2). He also led efforts in Chicago to support Ethiopian Emperor Haile Selassie's 1935 resistance to Italy's Fascist invasion of his country.[33]

To celebrate Dorsey's third anniversary at Pilgrim Baptist Church, Austin oversaw a service in which six hundred members of the Chicago Gospel Choral Union, together with one thousand in the congregation, performed a song entitled "Sing, Sing, Ethiopia Sing" as a mass choir.[34] Four months later,

> In the program closing out Pilgrim's two-week revival, as the invasion smashed through Ethiopia's forces in November 1935, Sallie Martin and Dorsey were guest artists and former Pilgrim minister V. David Bond reformulated a stalwart of the black sermon repertory, "The Eagle Stirreth Her Nest," to suggest that the war was God's way of exhorting Haile Selassie to develop his country.[35]

In this early instance, Sallie Martin's performance during a public act of resistance is a matter of public record, but her convictions remain elusive.[36] By 1942, Black foreign missionaries from the United States worked in Monrovia, Liberia; Nyasaland (near modern Zimbabwe); Johannesburg, South Africa; British Guiana (Guyana); and Dutch Guiana (Suriname). At that time, Pilgrim Baptist was the only church sending missionaries to Nigeria.

As they did in the Dorsey Convention (NCGCC), women worked tirelessly to advance the NBC's missionary cause. C. C. Adams, newly appointed as secretary of the Foreign Mission Board of the NBC, pointed out:

> While women may not have served as much in pioneership on the foreign field as men, they have had more heart and more leisure for

> consideration of the study of missions and have gone farther along in missionary thinking, giving, and sacrificing than the rest of the church. Our Foreign Mission Board believes that women more largely support and sustain these causes than the other church groups.[37]

By the end of Adams's sixteen-year term (1942–1958), Pilgrim Baptist Church's Nigerian missions project had raised funds, built, and dedicated a 3,000-seat church in Issele-Uku.[38]

The impoverished Nigerian town of Issele-Uku had been brought to the attention of Austin and Pilgrim Baptist by Samuel Wadiei Martin (S. W. Martin, born Olisemeke Nwadiei Nwaonya in 1878, died 1975). Martin-Nwaonya had been converted to Christianity by the US missionary A. K. Martin in Sudan, in the late 1910s. Assuming the surname name of his mentor after his conversion, S. W. Martin traveled with A. K. Martin to Topeka, Kansas, and then moved to Chicago to study at the Moody Bible Institute. S. W. Martin was ordained as a minister in 1918 at Pilgrim Baptist and became an associate pastor there in 1919. He returned to Nigeria in about 1921, then traveled back to Chicago, where the NBC commissioned him to return to Issele-Uku in 1925 as a missionary to Nigeria, with Pilgrim Baptist as his sponsor. A strong advocate for the needs of his people, S. W. Martin returned frequently to Chicago to raise funds.[39]

The National Baptist Convention earmarked Nigerian missions as its focus at the 1948 annual meeting in Houston.[40] In advance of the conference, ads promised performances by Mahalia Jackson, the Ward Singers, the Sallie Martin Singers, the Roberta Martin Singers, and a 500-voice choir conducted by Theodore Frye. National Baptist Convention member ministers were instructed to bring their congregation's donations for Nigeria. The goal for that meeting was set at $15,000, 7.5 percent of the NBC's annual budget of $200,000. That advertised figure was designated for missions to the West Indies, Africa, and the Southwest Pacific.[41]

In 1950, J. C. Austin traveled to several countries in West Africa and wrote, "I saw black clerks and managers working in stores and black officials high in government everywhere I went. I went to Africa only to be convinced that not only the hope of the black man, but the hope of peace and the hope of the world rests in Africa."[42] Austin's enthusiasm invigorated the missions-minded at Pilgrim, who supported the establishment of new African hospitals and schools, as well as congregations.

As these Black Baptists continued to donate money to help Christianize but also improve the quality of life for people in Africa, the news at home was filled with reports of the May 1954 *Brown v. Board of Education* decision; the December 1955 arrest of Rosa Parks and the subsequent, yearlong Montgomery bus boycott; and the 1955 murder of Emmett Till in Mississippi. As the United States headed toward a more focused collision over institutionalized racism, the opening of US relations with Nigeria in 1960, the year of its independence from Great Britain, expedited Baptist religious and philanthropic work.

In August of 1962, Sallie Martin publicly threw her name, notoriety, and financial support behind Nigerian missions, a cause that by then had been adopted by several denominations. She presented a benefit "musical extravaganza" at Hyde Park Bible Church in Chicago, featuring the recently reconstituted Sallie Martin Singers, Mahalia Jackson, and a youth choir from Detroit.[43] Martin was similarly involved when the Baptist Foreign Mission Bureau held a fundraiser for a new general hospital in Issele-Uku on August 28, 1964. Coordinator of the rally, Margaret Smith, began her appeal for funds with a caveat that would soon change for herself and Martin: "Since we can't go there, we can attend this meeting, give our financial support, and tell the story of the great work being done for the Nigerians."[44] About a late 1964 fundraiser, the *Defender* reported that Austin's goal for the hospital complex, a ten-building block and medical equipment, was $450,000. Issele-Uku champion Rev. S. W. Martin attended the fundraiser. Eventually, the hoped-for medical buildings and five schools, each with a chapel, were built and named for generous Chicago benefactors: Progressive Baptist Church, Shiloh Baptist Church, and Mrs. Sallie Martin.[45]

To boost giving, Margaret Smith and Sallie Martin traveled to Issele-Uku in November of 1965.[46] Though the gravesite of her son, Joel, is located in Tunisia, some 1,700 miles from Nigeria, the trip to the continent where Martin's son died in battle must have taken on double significance. A *Defender* photo of November 27, 1965, shows a beaming Margaret Smith, labeled a fieldworker for the Progressive National Baptist Convention, and Sallie Martin, "gospel singer and missionary," on their return from Issele-Uku.[47] Twenty or so years later, Martin reflected, "I wanted to go to Africa, where I been sending my money, 'cause I wanted to see what they'd been doing. Thank the Lord I found everything well, with good buildings, as nice as any you have here, and I thank the Lord for that."[48]

The First Church of Deliverance intensified its efforts to bring the message of Metropolitan Spiritual Churches into Africa at a national congress in 1970. Sallie Martin was named by that organization to spearhead the Africa missionary enterprise into Nigeria, collaborating with Foreign Mission Secretary of the MSC, Logan Kearsey.[49] Martin also accompanied Rev. Cobbs to missionary churches in Montego Bay, Jamaica, probably around that time. Martin's life of travel had expanded in step with her passion for foreign missions.

Martin's Fading Star, the NBC, and Civil Rights

Coalescing around Black Baptists in the mid-1950s, the Civil Rights Movement coincided with the election of another powerful Chicago orator as the NBC president, J. H. Jackson. He pastored Olivet Baptist Church (founded 1850), a stop on the Underground Railroad and mother church to Ebenezer Baptist and Pilgrim Baptist congregations. In contrast to J. C. Austin of Pilgrim Baptist, Jackson aligned more closely with white Democrats who wielded power on the South Side.[50]

During the first decade of Jackson's five consecutive presidential terms (1953–1982), the mighty NBC arrived at a crossroads. While Jackson had supported the 1956 Montgomery bus boycott, by 1960 he was admonishing his massive congregation not to support civil rights activism. His politics naturally infused the NBC and posed a dilemma. Would that organization, the parent of the NCGCC and foundational network for the proliferation of early gospel music, continue its conservatism in the face of 1960s civil engagement, or would it centralize equal rights in its mission and embrace the nonviolent protest movement of Martin Luther King Jr.? As such controversies often resolve in religious societies, there soon was an organizational divide: the pro–civil rights wing split away from the NBC in 1961, forming the Progressive National Baptist Convention (PNBC).[51] A modern PNBC writer frames the situation:

> From a religious perspective, churches from across the United States were suffering from an identity crisis fostered by racism, and conservative political policies and practices that supported segregation and U.S. apartheid. Theologians, seminary students and religious leaders were now openly questioning theological constructs and historical assumptions that were the basis for doctrinal practices that supported two societies in America: one White and the other Black.[52]

In 1961, T. M. Chambers was named as the first president of the PNBC, which considered the freedom of Africans, as well as diasporic Africans, as central to its mission. PNBC members took particular pride in serving as the denominational home of Martin Luther King Jr., who spoke at each annual meeting until his death.

The child of one of Sallie Martin's familiars, Martin Luther King Jr. was only fifteen years old when he first met Sallie in the senior Rev. King's Atlanta church. She must have watched the younger King's progress carefully, as well as the more violent and destructive rallies and demonstrations that occurred in most major cities in the 1960s and '70s. Interviewed eight years after King's assassination, Martin conveyed something a young adult had said to her: "we can't get anywhere by just being nice." Martin reminisced as if responding to the spirit of that complaint.

> You came this far on [being nice] . . . [Before . . .] you couldn't go in a hotel . . . [being nice is] . . . what made it possible for you. . . . Martin Luther King brought you this far by the help of God, not what you all are teaching. . . . But [for] about ten years or more . . . [there has been] a lot of burning and tearing up and the thing about it, you're even down doing it to your own people. . . . You all need to stop going around talking about 'you don't like him and you don't this and you don't that'; you just might as well make up your mind we've got to live together. . . . I don't see why people teach that kind of thing, you take Elijah Muhammad? He's a wonderful man when it comes down to making a way of doing things that will help his people, but right behind it, he kills it with that little bit of hate that he teaches.[53]

Despite this accommodationist position, Sallie Martin's self-worth was a nonnegotiable, especially in business relationships. In her profession, some white business owners may have been relatively easy to avoid; others, such as Specialty Records founder Art Rupe, were crucial to her career development. Success came first in her mind, which placed her at odds with the younger generations who demanded resistance.

In contrast to her humble beginnings, Martin was also wealthy and privileged by the 1960s, and saw political demonstrations, violence, and looting as very real threats to the monetary fruits of her labor. The 1965 Watts riots affected businesses to within 1.5 miles from the space she had once rented for the Gospel Music Mart. Disturbances in Chicago's West Side were uncomfortably close to the Martin and Morris storefront in 1966; after the murder of King in 1968, they moved even closer.

Further, as the soul-infused gospel of James Cleveland and others caught hold, Dorsey's gospel blues came to be considered roots music, and Sallie Martin a culture bearer for an earlier time. She was booked for a blues concert at Chicago's Orchestra Hall in May of 1966 alongside Big Joe Williams and others.[54] Mention of her in a (Baltimore) *Afro-American* review of Charles Hobson's monograph, *The Gospel Truth*, was entitled "The Root of All Soul."[55] Thus, Sallie Martin was simultaneously revered and her sound considered a distant ancestor of the day's music.

The Black-proud soul genre had evolved from its gospel parent via rhythm and blues, and its songs increasingly expressed the values of civil engagement. The Civil Rights Movement was a singing movement in which gospel music, spirituals, hymns, and Top 40 tunes were pressed into service as freedom songs, what Bernice Johnson Reagon calls a "natural outpouring, evidencing the life force of the fight for freedom."[56] The spiritual "This Little Light of Mine," writes Reagon, was sung even more often than "We Shall Overcome." Freedom songs were regionally specific; protestors in Montgomery favored the battle song "Onward, Christian Soldiers." Eventually, regional chapters would meet and share their music at the annual Newport Folk Festivals. Repertoire for SNCC (Student Nonviolent Coordinating Committee) protests were not only regional, but also topical; in the face of danger, "Leaning on the Everlasting Arms" was a likely choice. Songs were also adapted from contemporary radio playlists. Little Willie John's "You Better Leave My Kitten Alone" (1959) became "You Better Leave Segregation Alone." Songs of James Brown—"Keep on Pushing" and "Say It Loud: I'm Black and I'm Proud" (1968)—were ready-made for the movement, as were "People Get Ready" (1965) by Curtis Mayfield and the Impressions and Aretha Franklin's cut of Otis Redding's "Respect" (1967). When asked about Franklin's combination of soul music with gospel in 1981, Martin replied, "Well, you see, I don't appreciate that. . . . you trying to do them both. . . . you just can't be on both sides of the fence at one time."[57] Nursing her own rigidity, Martin was left to watch from the sidelines as Franklin's generation developed and monetized a new public discourse.

A scant four years after the release of Cleveland's "Peace Be Still," Edwin Hawkins's use of a Latin groove, synthesizers, and a soul-influenced lead vocal by Dorothy Coombs Morrison created a successful crossover hit with "Oh Happy Day." Recorded in 1967 at Ephesians Church of God in Christ in Los Angeles, that song marks both the merger of soul and gospel and success of some of the first gospel stars—Edwin Hawkins from the Bay Area, as well as Andraé and Sandra Crouch from L.A.—who were not transplants to California. Kenneth Woods Jr. remembered that

> gospel music . . . began to change in 1968 [with] "Oh Happy Day." Edwin Hawkins. And then all the progeny after that, the younger [people], they wanted to get on board with that similar sound. And it has really changed since 1968. There was a convention in 1976, Dorsey's convention. I wasn't there. . . . But sometimes I would see Miss Martin and ask "How was the convention?" I remember she said, "Oh, the music was horrible!" Because it had changed. "Oh, I didn't like it, I couldn't stand it" [Martin would say]. I could hear her now, because of the young folk, and their styles changing. And after 1976, then you had more praise and worship . . . only thing about praise and worship, even though the beat is good, and I could play it all, the message is saying the same thing over and over again. I remember Miss Martin, and this during the time when

> James Cleveland was still popular, Miss Martin would say, "Oh, we need some new words!"[58]

Sallie Martin had become the victim of a closed mind.

Enduring Beyond

Endowed with good health and unflagging energy, Martin mourned the passing of many longtime friends and associates in the 1960s and '70s: Earle Hines (died 1960), Lucie Campbell (1963), Dorothy Simmons (1966), Lillian Bowles Pannell (1967), Rev. Junius Austin (1968), Roberta Martin (1969), Mahalia Jackson and Joe May (1972), Rev. Thurston Frazier and Rev. Earl Pleasant (1974), Rev. Arthur Atlas Peters (1975), and Rev. Clarence Cobbs (1979). She was frequently called upon to lend her voice to memorial services, for example in a Chicago event for James Cleveland's mother, Rosie Lee, in August of 1965. A few years later, the Chicago television program *Jubilee Showcase* presented a memorial tribute to Roberta Martin which featured the Sallie Martin Singers and the Barrett Sisters.[59]

This pattern was broken for the memorial service of Martin's longtime friend Mahalia Jackson, who died in January of 1972. On the day before the February 2, 1972 event, Martin was invited to speak for about two minutes. Stung by what she must have considered a demeaning, last-minute offer, Martin recalled responding, "Now listen, darling, I'm not a speaker, I'm a singer." In her own passive resistance against funeral organizers Willa Saunders Jones (Jackson's close friend) and Polly (Cylestine) Fletcher (Jackson's longtime assistant), Martin relinquished her place on the roster so that Delois Barrett Campbell could sing.[60] Nevertheless, Martin's name remains second in the "Remarks" section of the day's lineup, after Judge Ben Hooks of Memphis, and before Studs Terkel, Benjamin Mays (past president of Morehouse College), Hollywood business manager Lou Mindling, and Sammy Davis Jr. (sent to represent President Richard M. Nixon).[61]

Adored by a grieving nation, Aretha Franklin was given the honor of singing the closing number for the event, which drew eight thousand mourners to the Arie Crown Theater at McCormick Place in Chicago. Other performers included Robert Anderson, Willie Webb, and Mildred Falls; a choir of the Greater Salem Baptist Church conducted by Dorsey; and Robert Bradley. Coretta Scott King was a featured speaker. Martin's conversation with Laurraine Goreau several months later shows that she still resented the fact that Mahalia Jackson's service had closed with a crossover singer performing a highly decorated version of Dorsey's "Pre-

FIGURE 6.1. From left, Etta Moten Barnett, Duke Ellington, Sallie Martin. 1972 National Association of Negro Musicians ceremony, Chicago. Archives, Center for Black Music Research, Columbia College, Chicago. Photograph by Austin Hansen. Used with permission from Estate of Austin Hansen.

cious Lord, Take My Hand," and that Martin, herself, had not been honored with an opportunity to sing.[62] Aretha would have been the nation's resounding choice, however. Her selections were so moving and her power so great that two teenagers reportedly had to be restrained during her closing solo. In retrospect, any surviving remark made by Martin about Franklin's career encompassing R&B and gospel ("it ain't worth a dime"), must have been colored by this remembrance.

Sallie Martin was also featured in tributes to the lengthening careers of second-generation gospel leaders such as Gwendolyn Cooper Lightner, but the signal event of these last years before retirement was her acknowledgement by the Chicago-based National Association of Negro Musicians. She is captured in a photograph alongside two of the other honorees that year, actress and contralto Etta Moten Barnett and Duke Ellington (see figure 6.1).

Blessed with long life, Sallie Martin lived on to thrive in her retirement, adapting to the extent she was able, despite changes in public perception of her, the evolution of gospel music, and changes wrought in the lives of Black Americans by the Civil Rights Movement.

CHAPTER 7

Retirement, Legacy, and Conclusions

As a pioneer in gospel music's founding years and a celebrity in its Golden Age (1945–1965), Sallie Martin relished the final fifteen years of her life. She sold her interests in the Martin and Morris Music Studio (MMMS) to Kenneth Morris in 1973, together with the catalog she had bought from Lillian Bowles, some holdings of which she had rereleased under Martin's House of Music. Beyond simplifying her finances, her retirement from the publishing world also relieved her of the responsibility of touring; in her words, "I came home because it's too tough out there."[1] Still, Martin performed, appeared at social functions, and gave time and money to support missionary projects. This final chapter begins with an account of her most notable retirement activities, then briefly looks at the distribution of her wealth. The synopsis that closes this monograph is organized around Martin's watershed accomplishments and those of selected mentees, as well as her legacy in gospel music.

Retirement Performances, Appearances, and Honors

An artist as well-established as Sallie Martin maintained many personal and professional relationships which helped keep her name before the public in her retirement years. Likely as not, she sang whenever she appeared at public functions. Gospel consumers had developed very different tastes by the 1970s, but Martin wasn't concerned with innovation. Her remark at one performance was sincere: "Ain't got nothing new for you this evening. None of this modern music. Same old Sallie Martin, same old Jesus."[2] If her singing occasionally drew a lukewarm response, she responded with clever metaphors, for example, "If Mahalia is a Cadillac and Roberta [Martin] is a Buick, I'm just a Model T Ford, but I make it over the hill without shifting gears, and that's what counts, church, I make it over the hill."[3] Martin was a born storyteller and had a repertoire of quips that appear often in writings about her. "Some people said, 'You move too much, it looks like you are trying to get rock and roll into the church,' . . . I said, 'I don't move, something moves me.'"[4] When asked if her principles had changed during her career, she replied, "No, I've tried to be just as I was when I started."[5] She remained strong in her convictions, proud of her accomplishments, and unapologetic about her shortcomings.

Some years were especially memorable. In 1975, she sang on the first episode of *I'm So Happy*, the Cleveland, Ohio, television show of an NCGCC colleague, Rev. Earl Preston.[6] Newer associates also opened doors; Anthony Heilbut, record producer and author of *The Gospel Sound: Good News and Bad Times* (1972), organized a concert at the 1975 Newport Jazz Festival to honor the late Mahalia Jackson. Having given Sallie Martin pride of place in chapter one of his monograph, Heilbut engaged her, along with Dorsey, Marion Williams, Dorothy Love Coates, Claude Jeter, the Sensational Nightingales, and the J. C. White Singers for the Newport Festival performance. Martin apparently charmed the audience at a June 28 event at Carnegie Hall. The *Variety* critic wrote, "Dorsey at piano . . . accompanied a fine short set by the veteran Sallie Martin."[7] Earl Calloway of the *Chicago Defender* was also impressed; "most significant of the day," he wrote, was Sallie Martin's performance.[8]

At the close of that year, Martin was honored at a large-scale benefit in Los Angeles, the site of her expansion efforts on behalf of the Martin and Morris Music Studio beginning in 1940. The event was sponsored by the Los Angeles Council of Churches and took place at L.A.'s Forum on December 18, 1975.[9] Joe Westmoreland's Interdenominational Choir Foundation, comprising three hundred singers representing forty-seven churches, sang several numbers, accompanied by the L.A. Philharmonic under the baton of Zubin Mehta. Martin, the Caravans, Albertina Walker, Shirley Caesar, and others entertained the audience of three thousand children and older adults who were invited as special guests of the Council of Churches.

A few years later, Sallie Martin and Marion Williams traveled abroad to headline performances of a retrospective revue entitled *Gospel Caravan* at the Théâtre de Paris. Williams's features ("Didn't It Rain?", "Battle Hymn of the Republic," "Precious Lord," and "Oh Happy Day") and Martin's solo renditions of "Nobody Knows" and "God Put a Rainbow in the Clouds" anchored the show. The musical played in Paris from January 1 through March 18, 1979. Martin remembered,

> I sang every night except Monday night when I was off. Sunday we gave a matinee, and then Sunday nights. But now, you see, I didn't try to . . . be the main spokesman or something . . . I sang two solo numbers and then with the group . . . if [a song] had a background, I would sing in the background.[10]

Liner notes for an opening-night recording of the revue mentioned Martin's contributions to the genealogy of gospel; her style was "endowed with an astounding vitality so pure that one detects the first sounds of the American black church."[11] That comment comes close to capturing the essence of her sound.

While she was able, Sallie Martin greeted visitors in her apartment at 6719 South Crandon in Chicago, half a block from Lake Michigan and overlooking Jackson Park. In 1981, University of Michigan professor James Standifer interviewed her at length in that home. He persuaded her to describe the many awards that decorated table tops and walls. She received an award from the National Association of Negro Musicians 1972 (see chapter 6), was given the keys to the city of Cincinnati at some point, and was recognized as a leader at Howard University's Fine Arts Festival on March 28, 1980. Also in Washington, DC, she received formal thanks from Civil Rights activist and founder of the Bible Way Church, Bishop Smallwood E. Williams (1907–1991).[12] Martin received an award from Broadcast Music, Inc., in 1987.

In 1984, Martin hired a young gospel pianist to serve as her driver, assistant, and perhaps caregiver. Gregory Scott Cooper (1958–1993) noted without details that Martin had been awarded an honorary doctorate during her career (see below). That may have occurred prior to 1984, when Edwin Hawkins, of "Oh Happy Day" fame (1967), cut an LP featuring his Music and Arts Seminar Mass Choir in 1984. The dedication of that recording, on which Martin sings "No Not One," reads, "to the Mother of Gospel Music, Dr. Sallie Martin."[13] She was also awarded one square inch of historic land at 102 Lombard Street, Society Hill, Philadelphia, at the site of Hawkins's seminar. In February of 1985, Martin was honored alongside James Baldwin at the Los Angeles Public Library's sixth annual African American Living Legends Program (see figure 7.1). In that photo, taken three years before her death, Martin appears vital and fashionable as ever in her black-and-white houndstooth print ensemble and white orchid corsage.

She would soon begin to experience failing health; Heilbut observed changes that indicate she suffered a form of dementia.[14] She still had people in her corner, however. Kathryn Dorsey, the second wife of the Father of

FIGURE 7.1. James Baldwin and Sallie Martin at the African American Living Legends Program, A. C. Bilbrew Library, Los Angeles County Library, February 24, 1985.

Gospel Music, offered financial support during Martin's decline. Gregory Cooper also advocated for Sallie Martin when she was no longer able to do so herself. Most notable of Cooper's accomplishments was an impressive ninetieth birthday salute to Sallie Martin on November 22, 1985. A cast of all-stars who had agreed to appear, including Thomas A. Dorsey, James Cleveland, Doris Akers, Delois Barrett Campbell and the Barrett Sisters, Jessy Dixon, Albertina Walker, and the combined choirs of several Chicago churches, are listed on a beautifully lettered flyer (see figure 7.2). The event took place at the Fellowship Baptist Church in Chicago, with a reception that followed the next afternoon at McCormick Place Hotel. In the invitation, Cooper recounted her work as a humanitarian: "Throughout the years, she has developed a number of private scholarships, still giving stipends to less fortunate singers. One beneficiary of which she is most proud is a Baptist Missionary School in Nigeria" (see chapter 6).

★ Special Guest to appear:

DR. THOMAS A. DORSEY
"Father of Gospel Music"
REV. JAMES CLEVELAND – LOS ANGELES, CALIFORNIA
MIN. KEITH PRINGLE – WASHINGTON D.C.
VANESSA BELL ARMSTRONG – DETROIT, MICH.
DR. J. ROBERT BRADLEY – NASHVILLE, TENN.
DORIS AKERS – COLUMBUS, OHIO
DELORIS BARRETT CAMPBELL & THE BARRETT SISTERS
MOTHER WILLA MAE FORD SMITH – ST. LOUIS, MO.
RAYMOND RASBERRY – LOS ANGELES, CALIFORNIA
REV. DONALD VAILS – WASHINGTON D.C.
DOUGLAS MILLER – DALLAS, TEXAS
DR. PEARL WILLIAMS JONES – WASHINGTON, D.C.
COMBINED CHIORS OF FELLOWSHIP BAPTIST CHURCH
REV. MILTON BRUNSON & CHRIST TABERNACLE COMB. CHIORS
INEZ ANDREWS • FIRST CHURCH OF LOVE & FAITH
COMBINED CHIORS OF PILGRIM BAPTIST CHURCH
PROPHET L.K. JOHNSON & FIRST HOUSE OF PRAYER
JESSIE DIXON & SINGERS • ARTHUR SCALES
ALBERTINA WALKER • ELDER JAMES LENOX
CLEO RANDLE • JERRY BRATTON ...
... and many more.

REV. CLAY EVANS
Host Pastor
GREGORY COOPER
Chairperson
ETHEL BROWN
MARIAN CLARK
ALBERT MEDDERS
Co-Chairpersons

FRIDAY, NOVEMBER 22, 1985 – 7:30

Fellowship Baptist Church / Fellowship Square
45th Place and Princeston

FIGURE 7.2. Flyer, 90th Birthday Celebration. Archives, Center for Black Music Research, Columbia College, Chicago. Courtesy Fellowship Baptist Church, Chicago.

> Wes Smith of the *Chicago Tribune* described the ninetieth birthday affair.
>
> On Friday night, nearly 1,300 folks assembled . . . to celebrate Martin's birthday by singing her praises.
>
> And sing they did, and sing, and sing. A congregation that included the country's top gospel singers—Willie Mae Ford Smith, the Barrett Sisters, Vanessa Bell Armstrong, Albertina Walker and others—joined two rocking gospel choirs in raising holy hallelujah for more than five hours.
>
> . . . Martin was showered, as well, with proclamations from the mayors of Los Angeles and Chicago and gifts—including a solid silver slipper stuffed with cash.
>
> "Not only is she a remarkable person, she is really a troubadour for the Lord and an angel of Mercy," said Rev. George Riddick, vice-president of Operation PUSH.[15]

This coverage in the *Chicago Tribune*, together with the fact that the *Defender* did not cover the event, broke tradition in Sallie Martin's long relationship with the latter newspaper. An inaccurate birth year for Martin and incorrect use of "Queen" as her moniker suggest that Cooper may have supplied details as best he could, without input. The businesswoman and performer who had managed her brand so meticulously for so long was clearly failing. Longtime fan and music contributor to the *Los Angeles Sentinel* Virgie Murray set the record straight in her account of the celebration, however. Martin was named as "the Mother of Gospel Music," her actual soubriquet, rather "the Queen," an accolade reserved for Mahalia Jackson.[16]

Alongside the much younger white minister, gospel songwriter, and singer, Joel Hemphill (b. 1939), Sallie Martin was honored at BMI's 1987 Gospel Music Week. Gregory Cooper stands behind her in a *Billboard* photo taken at the event—to my knowledge the first publicity photo in which the spark is missing from her visage.[17] She passed away on June 18, 1988, in Chicago's Hyde Park Community Hospital. A two-day memorial event, featuring performances by Albertina Walker, J. Robert Bradley, the Barrett Sisters, and James Cleveland, among others, was held on June 24 and 25 at First Church of Deliverance. *Los Angeles Sentinel* writer F. Finley McRae, a fan who had covered Martin's career for more than a decade, peppered his announcement of her death and funeral with accolades. She was "a change-agent and the driving force behind gospel's world-wide acceptance and popularity," "gospel's one-person diplomatic corps," and "a humanitarian who established numerous scholarships and regularly contributed stipends to hundreds of singers."[18] Her remains are interred in Lincoln Cemetery, Blue Island, Chicago under the name Rev. Dr. Sallie Martin.

Three years after her death in 1988, Sallie Martin and daughter Cora Martin-Moore, a gospel star in her own right, were inducted into the Gospel Music Hall of Fame. Also posthumously, a couple of small-scale theater works celebrated Sallie Martin's life and personality. Jackie Taylor's *Great Women of Gospel* depicts Mahalia Jackson, Clara Ward, Rosetta Tharpe, Roberta Martin, and a "rambunctious" Sallie Martin, "who combined faith with finance."[19] Three years later, a play by Lori Reed entitled *Glory Sounds through Me: The Women of Gospel* was performed at the Missouri Historical Society's theater-in-residence in 1999. In this celebration of 1930s and '40s gospel women leaders, Monica Parks sang the role of Sallie Martin. Judith Newmark, theater critic for the *St. Louis Post-Dispatch,* writes as if she were a gospel insider.

> Sallie Martin, the gospel singer who became a successful music publisher, seems to offer more intriguing possibilities [than the] "saintlike Willie Mae Ford Smith." Were others jealous of her talent as a businesswoman? Was Martin's pride in her success diminished because it seemed too worldly? But Reed just hints at those questions, then backs off fast with powerhouse numbers that drown out unsettling questions.[20]

Martin's accomplishments have remained before the public in these new plays and in the hundreds of recordings, printed octavos, and press releases that she left behind.

A Word about Martin's Estate

Sallie Martin accumulated a great deal of wealth during her career; according to Boyer, she was the first woman made wealthy by gospel music.[21] Though the sums she dispensed for missions, travel, scholarships, Convention activities, and lifestyle will remain unknown, one digital trail illuminates her Chicago real estate holdings. Martin was listed as mortgagee in a trust deed executed by Drexel Bank in October of 1970 for a property at 6455 South Ellis Street in Chicago.[22] Martin and ex-husband Joe Langham dissolved co-ownership of two properties on October 18 and 25, 1972; the one at 500 East 81st Street in Chicago was transferred to Langham's sole ownership via quitclaim deed. Langham, in turn, released his claim on a property at 646 East Oakwood Boulevard, making Martin the sole owner. These transactions mark the end of their marriage.

A Sheriff's Deed, indicating the end stages of foreclosure, shows evidence of Martin's financial troubles about five years later. It was filed on

February 7, 1977, by the city of Chicago, against Sallie Martin et al., for an apartment block which extended from 1020 to 1032, where East 65th Street intersected with 6455 South Ellis Avenue. The property sold in a public auction two months later for $6,532.22, approximately $35,000 in 2024 dollars.

Martin appears to have sold her property at 626 East Oakwood to Thomas E. Williams, "a bachelor," in November of 1982, for $2,400. She remained a signatory on the mortgage, because three years later, an official notice to the public (*lis pendens*) indicated that the City of Chicago had filed suit against Sallie Martin et al.—a group including Williams, two banks, a title company, and a mortgage company. At that point, Martin resided in the 6719 South Crandon apartment.

Coincidentally, three days after her death on June 18, 1988, a notice of a Federal Tax Lien following up on unpaid taxes owed by the Sallie Martin Charitable Remainder Annuity Trust was reissued. Christian Communications of Chicagoland, Inc., was the trustee. That entity was founded in 1971 as a Christian television station for the Chicago area. Leading the effort was Pastor Owen C. Carr of the Stone Church. Call letters were established as WCFC ("Winning Chicagoland for Christ") in May of 1976. Television programming included Pat Robertson's *The 700 Club* and the *PTL (Praise the Lord) Club*, as well as well-known evangelists such as Jimmy Swaggart, Kenneth Copeland, and Oral Roberts. In her September 1981 conversation with Standifer, Martin mentioned seeing a singer associated with Edwin Hawkins on the *PTL Club*.[23]

The most that can be surmised from these records is, first, that Martin continued to own property into the early 1970s, and starting in 1977 she had trouble making her payments. A second finding confirms Heilbut's guess; at some point, Martin appears to have set up a major donation to televangelists. Both Heilbut and Kenneth Woods Jr. remarked on her straitened circumstances in the final years of her life; Woods confirmed that she spent her last weeks in the nursing facility run by First Church of Deliverance at 4316 South Wabash Avenue. The 199-bed establishment, Cobbs's response to poor conditions he observed in other Chicago facilities, opened on November 29, 1970.[24]

Heilbut mentioned that, toward the end of her life, Martin's beautiful, sequined gowns lay on the floor for lack of hanging space to store them.[25] It's impossible to ascertain the initial cash value of the Trust with Christian Communications of Chicagoland, Inc; $34,690 in late assessments was owed on the amount in 1987. Perhaps Martin or her financial consultant misunderstood her responsibility to pay taxes on the sum and the late fees had accrued over several years. Alternately, she may have committed a sizable fortune to the trust and the late assessments represented one year only. In any case, a release of lien on the Trust was issued by the Internal Revenue Service on June 1, 1989. A final document from the Cook County Recorder releases Talman Home Federal Savings and Loan from its claim as successor trustee of Sallie Martin's property at 646 East Oakwood Boulevard on May 10, 1989. The first woman made wealthy in Black gospel music appears to have died largely penniless, but surrounded by reminders of her former influence and considerable accomplishments.

Legacy through Selected Mentees

Sallie Martin mentored young gospel musicians in two primary ways that remain visible across the decades. First, selection for the Sallie Martin Singers provided no less than instant entrée into the gospel field. Julia Smith Whitfield (1918–1998), Cora (Brewer) Martin-Moore (1927–2005), and Dorothy Simmons (1910–1966) were the first long-term members. Cora received the most lasting benefits from her association with Sallie: touring the nation and making recordings, associating with gospel royalty from the age of thirteen, and being placed in charge of a sheet music store and teaching studio by the age of twenty-six. Soon, Cora was a religious disc jockey (1954–1955) with her own gospel radio program, a youth choir director (1952–1958) at Saint Paul Baptist Church, and ultimately, director of Saint Paul's influential Echoes of Eden choir from 1958 until her death in 2005. Cora Martin-Moore composed many important gospel songs, including "Heaven Sweet Heaven" (1953), "Do You Know the Lord Jesus for Yourself?" (1955), "What a Wonderful Savior I've Found" (1957), "He Is a Friend Of Mine" (1965), and "He'll Wash You Whiter than Snow," (1954), the latter of which was featured in Quincy Jones's 1969 film, *The Lost Man*. Several dedications on Cora's published compositions acknowledge Sallie Martin, the woman who so influenced her life.

Julia Smith Whitfield played piano on the earliest extant recordings of the Sallie Martin Singers, and when the group moved their home base to Los Angeles, Smith returned to Chicago (see Selected Discography). In demand first as accompanist for the gospel choir at Metropolitan Community Church and, later, for Dorsey at Pilgrim Baptist, she sang with Dorsey's traveling group and founded her own Choralaires in the 1940s. Also in that decade, Whitfield's group performed with the Sallie Martin Singers several times in Martin's former home of Atlanta.

Dorothy Simmons relocated to Los Angeles along with Martin's Singers in 1947 and soon founded a group with composer and vocalist Doris Akers. Their recordings, for example, "Meet in the Glory Land" (1953, Imperial

5271), were vehicles for Simmons's virtuosic soprano stylings and Akers's progressive text-setting and harmonizations.

Doris Akers (1923–1995), composer of the perennial song, "Sweet, Sweet Spirit," performed with the Sallie Martin Singers for a short while in 1946, then left to organize her own group and direct the choir at Eugene Smallwood's Opportunity Baptist Church. She and Dorothy Simmons founded the Simmons-Akers Singers in 1948.[26] By 1950, they had opened the Simmons and Akers Gospel Music Room, a studio, on 4268 South Central Avenue in Los Angeles. They toured and recorded together for about a decade, after which time Akers lent her substantial soloist, conducting, composing, and arranging talents to the Sky Pilot Choir of Los Angeles. About Akers's musicianship, Sallie Martin said, "I picked her up in California. She [didn't] read a single note, but she [could] hear every tone that's supposed to be there. . . . tenor, the bass, first soprano, second soprano, first and second alto."[27]

Playing piano in later iterations of the Sallie Martin Singers also boosted the career of Gwendolyn Cooper Lightner (1925–1999). Lightner's remarkable musical gifts landed her at the heart of the L.A. gospel scene, Saint Paul Baptist Church, in 1946. She managed the Los Angeles branch of the Martin and Morris Music Studio between 1948 and 1953 and taught singing, piano, and music theory in several Southern California cities as an MMMS employee. With Thurston Frazier, Lightner organized L.A.'s Voices of Hope Choir in 1947 for a March of Dimes fundraiser. It became a community choir in 1957 and made two recordings for Capitol Records. Later, Lightner was director of music at Mount Moriah Baptist Church. Attesting to her creativity, flexibility, and technical prowess, she was accompanist to the most powerful gospel singer in the world, Mahalia Jackson, from 1968 to 1972. The list of other singers and musicians who performed, toured, and recorded with Sallie is long (see chapters 5 and 6 and the selected discography).

The second way Sallie Martin mentored gospel musicians was by introducing or presenting young artists from outside the ranks of her Singers. Alex Bradford stated that Martin could be extremely kind and generous. He felt diminished by Mahalia Jackson's and Roberta Martin's persistent use of the nickname "little" Alex Bradford.

> Sallie wasn't like this. She'd take you from place to place, she'd stake you, she'd loan you some money. I'm not only speaking of me—Raymond Rasberry, Robert Anderson, James Cleveland, any other singers who needed a break, Miss Martin knew you couldn't afford it, she'd lock arms with you. . . . She's an astute, disciplinarian woman—and I love her.[28]

Bradford is credited with establishing the first Black gospel male choir in 1947 and contributed substantially to the mass choir movement of the 1950s. Martin and the Alex Bradford Singers appeared on the inaugural episode of Chicago's *TV Gospel Time* in the mid-1960s.

Heilbut points out that Bradford, Raymond Rasberry, Robert Anderson, and James Cleveland, among others, were almost certainly living as closeted gay men within a professional milieu that regarded homosexuality with ambivalence, if not phobia.[29] That perspective has persisted in many quarters. Rhonda Graham of the Wilmington, Delaware, *Sunday News Journal* wrote about Black gospel and the AIDS crisis, at one point using the 1994 funeral of Sallie Martin's personal attendant and AIDS victim, Gregory Cooper, as a case in point.[30] Prior to the 1980s, Broadway, opera, and gospel provided many queer people safe spaces in which to cultivate their musicianship, while masking their gender identity in flamboyant performativity. In such environments, relationships between gay male performers and renowned maternal females were typically accepting and supportive. As Bradford remembered, Sallie Martin locked arms with more than a handful of singers, many of whom were assumed to be gay.

Sallie Martin provided Kenneth Woods Jr. the chance to expand on an already established career performing with Beatrice Brown's Singers and as Brother Joe May's pianist. When Woods onboarded with Martin as curator, conductor, and arranger for a 1960s version of the Sallie Martin Singers, he was set free to exercise his many gifts. Their partnership allowed Woods the opportunity to publicize and monetize his impressive songs and arrangements in publications from the Bowles Company, which Martin owned, and in 1961 and 1963, Vee Jay recordings featuring the SMS.

A Long Life in Gospel Music

Having endured deep personal losses as a youngster growing up amid the racism of the Jim Crow South, Sallie Martin remained a courageous person. The orphaned fifteen-year-old, who announced to her cousins that she didn't like picking cotton and would therefore go alone to Atlanta, fully believed she would find her destiny in that city. It appears that even single motherhood at age nineteen did not dampen Martin's drive. When she married Wallace Martin at age twenty, her migrations within Georgia—from Penfield to Athens to Atlanta—seemed at an end. Then, in a single day, the Great Atlanta Fire of 1917 destroyed her home, one of nearly two thousand buildings leveled in seventy-three city blocks in the Old Fourth Ward. With no worldly goods remaining, she and Wallace, also a rural Georgian, uprooted again and migrated with Sallie's church family to a destination so far north—Cleveland, Ohio—that only Lake Erie separated it from Canada. There, the urban diversions of gambling and liquor consumption bore an unfamiliar northern accent. That strangeness, plus a strapped post–World War I economy, aggravated points of contention in the marriage that would bring about Martin's next major transition. Holding fast to the principles of a Sanctified faith that brooked no drinking and betting, she separated from Wallace soon after the 1930 census was taken. Even this latest restart seemed not to discourage Martin in her quest for stability and renown. She had learned about self-sufficiency at the age of fifteen, so being on her own was familiar. Her life experiences had not beaten Sallie Martin yet.

What they had done was reinforce her defensive side. Her self-sufficiency, imagination, and persistence cohabited with a hardened exterior and impenetrable cloak of respectability (neither uncommon among Black women in the 1930s). Her intractable nature was well known among members of the Sallie Martin Singers, who could expect no time for socializing after concerts on the road. Martin kept hold of all the train tickets and anyone who failed to follow her rules would be sent home. She repeated often that in her touring enterprise, being free to return to any location was uppermost in her mind. She took definitive steps to ensure that no scandal ever followed the Sallie Martin Singers.

For that and countless other strengths of personality and musicianship, Martin was respected, but her prickly exterior made her an easy target of gossip in the competitive and often petty gospel world. Singers, too, have placed Martin's fractious side foremost in their comments. Clara Ward described Rosetta Tharpe as "A nut. Fun! Fun! Fun!" Ward's pithy note about Sallie Martin was "Mean and sassy."[31] Dorsey, the primary benefactor of Martin's early drive and persistence, came to see her primarily as a caricature.

The twentieth century saw no measurable increase of Black women in the US labor force, as it did for white women. The unbroken participation of Black women in the labor market—a legacy of the slave system—never flagged after the Civil War. Sallie Martin was like the majority of her Black female peers who were born in relative anonymity and became successful in the mid-twentieth century. It's likely that she inherited her expectation of working outside the home from the women who surrounded her in childhood. Martin's strength of personality was nurtured in the small town of Penfield, Georgia, where her mother, grandparents, and extended family members made sure she took advantage of the educational opportunities available to her. Also, significantly, they watched her carefully during her formative experiences within a violently racist world. A final advantage

Penfield provided Sallie Martin was the opportunity to get away on a train (see chapter 1). On her own, Martin decided to join the Great Migration away from the old way of life to a succession of three large cities: Atlanta, where the Holiness faith captured her heart; Cleveland, where she began to realize that her marriage was unsustainable; and Chicago, where she achieved her destiny through gospel music.

After 1939, Martin continued to work consistently and creatively to establish a performance career and maintain a spotless reputation, goals well within her reach because of her business intuition and strong sense of self-worth. Always on display, Martin's unique vocalism was the sturdy vehicle that allowed her to testify and sermonize about her faith as she advertised the inventory of her businesses. Yet, even when teamed with her adopted daughter Cora, Sallie Martin never had a hit record. Such a concept, in retrospect, is beside the point in Martin's case. Vocally, Sallie would never have competed favorably with Mahalia Jackson, Willie Mae Ford Smith, or Marion Williams. A practical thinker, her late-in-life philosophy was that she had been everywhere she had wanted to go in her life, so her voice must have been sufficient to her purposes. Indeed, when considered in tandem with her own goals, Martin's vocal signature is laden with value. Her singing was powerful, flexible, and resilient enough to propel her through her chosen career, not as one of a crowd, but as a singular and successful pioneer in the shaping and proliferation of Black gospel music. Dorsey's unchivalrous remark, that she couldn't "sing a lick," was moderated by the second half of his statement, "but she can get over anywhere in the world." Indeed, she "got over" far more often than not.[32]

In gospel music of the late 1920s and early 1930s, double consciousness for Martin included rejection by the more staid Black congregations in Chicago and the Midwest. Sometimes, she and Dorsey received permission to perform in an early-1930s church service, only to be told that they had been forgotten as the congregation left the sanctuary.[33] Under Dorsey's coaching, Martin confronted her native ways of expression and proved flexible enough to tone down her Holiness shouting. Her more reserved performance practice substituted broad hand claps with "patting," and in place of more embodied shouting, she recalled "nobody was shaking but me."[34] As the public began to embrace freer expressions of religious zeal in gospel performance, Sallie Martin simply added back some of her old habits.

Along with a handful of others who worked diligently to found the NCGCC in 1933, Martin broke down barriers for Black sacred music across the nation. In 1936, at Dorsey's instigation, Martin first sang gospel blues songs in Los Angeles. Inevitably, however, Dorsey's tastes evolved with those of his market. Enthusiasm for Sallie Martin's shout-style vocality gave way to the magnetism of Mahalia Jackson's warmer, more agile lyricism. Rejected after making an immeasurable investment in Dorsey's company, Martin simply struck out on her own. With funding from the powerful Rev. Clarence H. Cobbs, she cofounded and built a tremendously successful publishing company with Kenneth Morris. Remaining open from 1940 to 1993, the Martin and Morris Music Studio remains the longest continuously operating Black music publishing company to date.

Unlike the situation for Dorsey, Theodore Frye, Kenneth Morris, and other male pioneers, the path to success for women in gospel did not build upon years of apprenticeship in blues and jazz. Women in early gospel were no less driven, but they held the tremendous responsibility of defining Black female religious professionalism, which they accomplished from within institutions. Lucie Campbell powered her way to the top of the National Baptist Convention's hierarchy on intellectual, musical, and organizational muscle. Even as they nurtured the National Convention of Gospel Choirs and Choruses, having first installed Dorsey as its president, Magnolia Lewis-Butts, Beatrice Brown, Willie Mae Ford Smith, Roberta Martin, and Sallie Martin and others engineered an infrastructure for the organization that foregrounded themselves in nationally visible roles. Importantly, these strong-willed, determined women collaborated biannually in conference and in board meetings to advance their mutually beneficial goals. They negotiated their differences and shared networks that would soon encompass the continental United States. In this way, women joined forces, challenging the sexist hierarchies of the mainstream Black churches.

Few women can be credited with the ordered transplantation of gospel to a completely new region to the extent that Sallie Martin can. In its first couple of years, the MMMS sold music to members of the Three Sons of Thunder in Los Angeles, the first ensemble to perform Dorsey-style music on the West Coast. Soon, Sallie Martin brought her intellect to the establishment of the Los Angeles branch of MMMS, collaborating with the Three Sons, all riding the wave of Sanctified religion prepared before them by Azusa Street Revivals of 1905–1915. Collaborations, performances, and entrepreneurship in L.A. further solidified Sallie Martin's power as co-owner of the Martin and Morris Music Studio. Looking back in 1991, Cora Martin-Moore remembered that in the 1940s and '50s, "L.A. gospel songwriters usually favored black-owned publishing firms like Martin and Morris."[35]

Interwoven among those highlights was Sallie's founding of the Los Angeles Gospel Choral Union, and Cora's and her collaboration with Rev.

John L. Branham and his crack musical team at Saint Paul Baptist in Los Angeles, James Earl Hines and Gwen C. Lightner, after 1943. Martin hired a booking agent in 1944 and began officially operating a West Coast branch of the MMMS, the Gospel Music Mart, in 1947. Lightner expanded the reach of the GMM through itinerantly teaching piano, voice, and music theory in San Diego, Long Beach, Riverside, San Francisco, and Bakersfield, as well as in Los Angeles.

In addition to continuing her public performances, notably on a six-week European tour with Rev. Cobbs and the First Church of Deliverance choir in 1966, Sallie Martin paid back Cobbs's initial investment of 1940 by captaining missions fundraising for him and for Rev. Austin of Pilgrim Baptist Church. The gifted musician she had first known as a child at that church, James Cleveland, became her late-in-life champion. Residing solely in Chicago in the final quarter of her life, Martin hired Kenneth Woods Jr. as accompanist of the new Sallie Martin Singers. Martin headlined a final album with the Gospel Choral Union of Chicago, temporarily named the Evangelical Choral Chapter in 1970, which featured her on one of her most favored barnburners, "God Put a Rainbow in the Clouds."

Sallie Martin was a phenomenon of nature, rarely motionless before the onset of her tenth decade. On the occasion of her death, Gregory Cooper likened Sallie Martin to Johnny Appleseed: "She planted a gospel seed wherever she went."[36] Both individually and through her labors for the NCGCC, Martin profoundly shaped the cultural work wrought by Black gospel. She had a hand in all of that organization's main tenets: youth education and monies to support it, preparation for excellence in ensemble and choir performance, musical accessibility, and proliferation of the Christian faith. Readers of this biography will recognize the power of one woman's belief that she deserved a place at the table of her dreams, and can now cite numerous instances in the life of Sallie Martin when hard work and single-mindedness underpinned her efforts to make those dreams a reality.

APPENDIX

Selected Discography

Recordings Featuring or Including Sallie Martin and/or Sallie Martin Singers, or a Group Led by Her, Excluding Rereleases

Personnel or Entities

Bibb, Leonard
Bell, Shirley
Black, Ruth
Bradford, Alex
Bradford, Bonnie
Bradford, Claudia
Bradley, Oscar Lee
Brewer, Cora
Brown, Charles
Bryant, David
Burke, Eugene
Childs, Theresa
CM Martin, Cora
Cooper, Gwendolyn
Dixon, Jessy
Dolphin's of Hollywood
Dorsey, Thomas A.
Folk, Bessie
Gary, Edith
Gladney, Eric
Goodson, Albert
Greene, Imogene
Hines, J. Earle
Lamare, Joseph Hilton "Nappy"
Lightner, Gwendolyn Cooper
Lomax, Charlie Mae
May, Joe
Miller, Fred
Neely, Lee Charles
Patrick, Berda Young
Polk, Lonnie
Powell, Sara Jordan
Reid, Jewel Williams
RSB Singers, Okeh label
Simmons, Dorothy
Singleton, Zutty
Smith, Julia
SMS, Sallie Martin Singers
Thompson, Terrance D.
Timmons, Claude O.
Weston, Dave/David
Whitfield, Julia Smith
Williams, Marion
Woods, Jr., Kenneth

Selected Discography by Year and Label (See Bibliography for Television and Video)

As general references, the author recommends Discogs, an online resource; and *The Gospel Discography 1943–2000*, revised third edition, by Cedric J. Hayes and Robert Laughton (West Vancouver, BC, Canada: Eyeball Productions, 2014).

BRONZE, RECORDED 1940, (RELEASED 1945)

Martin and Morris Singers, Smith, Brewer, Lomax, Simmons

I Know I Have Another Building, 108B
I'm Walking with My Jesus, 111A?
It Must Be Jesus' Love Divine, 111B?
On the Jericho Road, 108A

EARLY 1940S

Sallie Martin Singers of Joy, maybe Smith, Brewer, Lomax, Simmons

There Must Be a Heaven Somewhere

BRONZE, CA. 1944

Sallie Martin Singers

Jesus I Love You, 124A
Get Away Jordan, 124B

MARTIN AND MORRIS, CA. 1945

Sallie Martin Gospel Singers

I'm Going to Bury Myself in Jesus' Arms
Joy in My Soul

RADIO RECORDERS/ALADDIN, APRIL 21, 1947

Brewer, Simmons, others unknown

Even Me, Even Me, 155–2
Four and Twenty Elders (not released)
He's a Friend of Mine, 153–1
Jesus Steps Right In, 151–1
Just a Few Days to Labor, 154–1
You Know, Lord, 152–1

ST. PAUL BAPTIST CHURCH, LOS ANGELES, ECHOES OF EDEN CHOIR, FEBRUARY 27, 1948 (RADIO BROADCAST)

Black, CM, Gladney, Hines, Cooper

Didn't It Rain (CM and choir)

Dig a Little Deeper in God's Love (CM and choir)
Just a Closer Walk with Thee, Sallie Martin Singers

EXCELLOREC, DOLPHIN'S OF HOLLYWOOD, CA. 1949

Sallie Martin Nationally Famous Singers, CM, Weston, Smith
(I'm going to) Move On Up a Little Higher, EC 909A, Dolphin's 112
King Jesus Will Roll All Burdens Away, EC 909B, Dolphin's as above
Only a Look at Jesus, EC918
There Must Be a Heaven Somewhere, EC918

EXCLUSIVE, DOLPHIN'S SPECIALTY, LATE 1949

Sallie Martin and Her Nationally Famous Quintette, CM, Weston, Smith
Jesus, SA 518; Exclusive 136; Dolphin's 111
Thank You Jesus, SA 519, Exclusive and Dolphin's as above

CAPITOL, SEPTEMBER 1949

Smith, Lamare, Bibb, Singleton
In My Heart, 57–848
(Jesus Is the Answer) He's All I Need, 57–848
Jesus Is the Only One, 57–70048
The Little Wooden Church on the Hill, 57–70048

CAPITOL, MARCH 10, 1950

Cora and Sallie Martin, CS, Smith, Lamare, Bibb, Singleton
Do You Know Him, 967
I'm Going to Follow Jesus, 967
Love Like a River in My Soul, 1140 (promo)
Satisfied, 1140 (promo on live jazz album Capitol T-2137)

SPECIALTY/VENICE, APRIL 5, 1950

May, Patrick, CM, Childs, Weston
Oh Yes, He Set Me Free
Working on a Building

SPECIALTY/UNIVERSAL RECORDERS AUGUST 16, 1950

CM, Weston, Goodson
Ain't That Good News
God Is a Battle Axe
I'm Getting Nearer to My Lord (feat. CM)
There Is No Sorrow that Heaven Cannot Heal (feat. CM)

SPECIALTY, DECEMBER 15, 1950

Sallie Martin Singers, CM, Childs, Weston, feat. May
Didn't It Rain (feat. CM), take 2
Didn't It Rain (feat. CM), 391B
Every Day and Every Hour (feat. SM, May), 391A
God Is a Battle Axe (feat. SM), take 2
Oh What a Time, CM
Oh Yes, He Set Me Free CM JM, take 2

SPECIALTY, JUNE 20, 1951

Sallie Martin Singers and CM, Patrick, Polk, Weston, Goodson
The Good Old Way DW, take 2
Jesus Is Waiting (feat. Polk)
Eyes Hath Not Seen CM, take 1
Eyes Hath Not Seen CM, 808B
Throw Out the Lifeline CM, SM, 808A

OKEH, 1951

R. S. V. Singers, SM, TAD (composers)
Inside the Beautiful Gate

SPECIALTY, 1952

CM, JM
Until We Meet Again w/ He's Able to Carry You Through, 823

SPECIALTY/UNIVERSAL RECORDERS, MARCH 10, 1952

SM, CM, JM, Childs, Brown
Working on the Building
Working on the Building, 1953, 10-inch shellac, 841

SPECIALTY, MARCH 31, 1952

SM, CM, B Bradford, C Bradford, Patrick, Weston, Miller, Reid
Great day (feat. SM)
I Know It's Well with My Soul (feat. CM)
Jesus Said (feat. Miller)
I Called the Lord and Got an Answer (feat. CM)
There Is a Fountain Filled with Blood (feat. Miller)

SPECIALTY/VENICE/UNIVERSAL, JUNE 27, 1952, ELKS AUDITORIUM

SM, CM, Childs, Miller, Brown, May
It's a Long, Long Way
It's a Long, Long Way, 1953, 10-inch shellac, 841

SPECIALTY, MARCH 1953, 78 SHELLAC

Sallie Martin Singers, CM, Childs, Weston, feat. May
He's Able to Carry Me Through (feat. CM, JM), 823B
I'll Make It Somehow (feat. SM, JM)
I'll Make It Somehow (feat. SM, JM), 399
Oh Yes, He Set Me Free (feat. CM, JM), 399A
Until We Meet Again (feat. CM), 823A

SPECIALTY, 1953

Alex Bradford, Too Close (to Heaven) (Bradford Specials singers)
He'll Wash You Whiter than Snow (feat. SM and Alex Bradford)

SPECIALTY, JULY 1954

Martin Singers
In My Home Over There, RPM 413
Don't Wonder About Him, RPM 413

SPECIALTY, 1955, VINYL 45

May and the Pilgrim Travelers
Speak! Lord Jesus (composed by SM)
It Don't Cost Very Much (composed by TAD)

SPECIALTY, SEPTEMBER 24, 1955, NOT ISSUED

Gospel Train (Get On Board) SM, CM

SPECIALTY, SEPTEMBER 1955, NOT ISSUED

Introduction, Hold On to God's Unchanging Hand
Hold On to God's Unchanging Hand

SPECIALTY 1960, 78

SM and CM Singers, SP 808

VEE JAY, DECEMBER 1961 PRECIOUS LORD VJLP 5021, VEE JAY 908

Sallie Martin Singers, Gary, Bell, Powell, Dixon Woods Jr.
Come Thou Fount (feat. SM) 61–2277
God Is Moving (feat. Powell, Bell) 61–2278
I Need Him (feat. Gary, comp. Woods Jr.) 61–2271
Let Me Cross Over
No One Ever Cared (Cares) (feat. SM) VJ 61–2272
Old Ship of Zion (feat. SM and Gary) 61–2273
Own Me as a Child

Search My Heart (feat. SM, comp. SM) 61–2274
That's What He's Done for Me (feat. SM, comp. Woods Jr.)
There's Not a Friend (feat. SM)

VEE JAY, FEBRUARY 1963 GOD IS HERE VJ 5041

SM, Folk, Bell, Burke, Woods Jr., piano/organ, Dixon or Herndon, piano/organ

Is Your All on the Alter [Altar] (feat. SM) 63–3118
Jesus I Love You 63–3124
Keep Me Jesus (feat. SM) 63–2121
God Is Here (feat. Bell) 63–3113
He's in My Heart (feat. SM) 63–3115
Let Jesus Come Into Your Heart (feat. SM) 63–3117
Nothing but the Grace of God 63–3114
Seeking for Me (feat. Bell) 63–3116
When He Comes (feat. Folk) 63–3119
How Tedious and Tasteless 63–3120
Closer to Jesus (feat. Folk) 63–3122
I Was Glad When They Said unto Me (feat. SM) 63–3123

SAVOY, LATE 1969, 1970, MG-14242

Sallie Martin and the Evangelical Choral Chapter, Woods, Jr.

Amazing Grace
It Don't Cost Very Much
God Put a Rainbow in the Sky
I Heard the Voice
Lead Me to Calvary
Let Us Give Our Best in Service
The Little Wooden Church on the Hill (That Wooden Church on the Hill)
They Found No Fault in Him
Wonderful Is His Name
Yes, God Is Real

COLUMBIA, REISSUED CA. 1972, PRECIOUS LORD: GREAT SONGS OF THOMAS A. DORSEY KG 32151

I'll Tell It Wherever I Go, 5/164 SM, Dorsey piano, Thompson drums

MAHALIA JACKSON TRIBUTE, NEWPORT JAZZ FESTIVAL, FALL 1979; https://www.youtube.com/watch?v=KCG1DL0y7l0

I know Who Holds Tomorrow (feat. SM)

BIRTHRIGHT, EDWIN HAWKINS, 1984, ANGELS WILL BE SINGING, MUSIC AND ARTS SEMINAR MASS CHOIR, BRS-4045

No, Not One (feat. SM)

FRANCE: AUVIDIS TEMPO, 1988, *GOSPEL CARAVAN* (CD)

SM, Williams, choir

Nobody Knows (feat. SM), A6128
God Put a Rainbow in the Cloud (feat. SM)

SPECIALTY/VENICE, 1993, COMPILATION THROW OUT THE LIFELINE, PREVIOUSLY UNRELEASED SONGS

Lord, I Need You Every Day of My Life
On the Other Side
One of These Mornings
Thy Servant's Prayer, Amen

HOB RECORDS, 1960, THE GREAT JAMES CLEVELAND (237)

SM and The [Gospel] Chimes, Dixon, Imogene Greene, Claude O. Timmons, Lee Charles Neely all vocal

I Won't Let Nothin' Turn Me Around (feat. SM), 237
SM sings "One Step at a Time," (feat. SM) track 3, as presented at King Solomon Baptist Church, Detroit

PEWBURNER (EL CERRITO, CA), 2004, 2007 PEWBURNER RECORDS PRESENTS: THE GREAT GOSPEL GROUNDCREWS OF THE PAST (PREVIOUSLY UNISSUED ONLY), MULTIPLE TAKES

Sallie Martin Singers (tracks 1–16) and Cora Martin Singers (17–26)

I'll Tell It Wherever I Go, SMS
Jesus Is Real to Me, SMS
Old Ship of Zion, Live with Dorsey, The Best of Vee Jay
Let Us Go Back to God (feat. SM)
Never Will He Turn His Back on Me (1964?)
Our Father, with the original Blind Boys of Mississippi
Precious Lord, takes 1 and 3

Notes

Introduction

1. Leo Treitler, "Gender and Other Dualities in Music History," 23.

2. Anthony Heilbut, *The Gospel Sound*, 17.

3. Michael W. Harris, *The Rise of Gospel Blues*, 257, 262, 270, respectively.

4. Horace Clarence Boyer and Lloyd Yearwood, *The Golden Age of Gospel*, 63.

5. Roxanne Regina Reed, "Preaching and Piety," 306. Reed also pointed out, intuitively, that "Sallie Martin, unlike Dorsey, bore no title affirming her status as a major figure in the building of gospel" (30).

6. Harris, *Rise of Gospel Blues*, 257.

7. Robert M. Marovich, *A City Called Heaven*. In addition to answering dozens of questions and facilitating access to archival materials, Marovich created an opportunity for me to sit in conversation with Kenneth Woods Jr., Martin's final accompanist, on March 7, 2023.

Jacqueline Cogdell DjeDje, "A Historical Overview of Black Gospel Music in Los Angeles"; "Gospel Music in the Los Angeles Black Community"; and "Los Angeles Composers of African American Gospel Music."

8. Gerri Hirshey and Anthony Bozza, "Mothers of Invention," *Rolling Stone* 773 (November 13, 1997), 44–49.

9. Nina Sun Eidsheim, *The Race of Sound*, 11.

10. Sallie Martin quoted in Laurraine Goreau, "Interview with Sallie Martin," November 4, 1972.

11. That event inspired Dorsey's important gospel recreation: "Precious Lord, Take My Hand." Dorsey's rhythmicized and re-texted version of the preexisting "Must Jesus Bear the Cross Alone?" by Thomas Shepherd saw far greater popularity than the original ever did.

12. A restored scene featuring Martin and Dorsey in the 2019 rerelease of *Say Amen, Somebody!* contains one such reminder.

13. Heilbut, *The Gospel Sound*, 16.

14. Sallie Martin in Goreau, "Interview," 7; and Sallie Martin quoted in James Standifer, "Interview with Sallie Martin," September 19, 1981. I am grateful to Robert M. Marovich for providing me with a photocopy of Standifer's transcript. Prior to my work, Martin's hometown was reported as Pittsfield. Because no town of that name ever existed in Georgia and she stated that she grew up in Greene County, it was clear that the correct name is Penfield.

15. Thomas A. Dorsey, "Did It Happen to You like It Happened to Me" (1930s) and "I'm Just a Sinner Saved by Grace" (1937), respectively.

16. Edwin Hawkins and the Music and Arts Seminar Mass Choir, *Angels Will Be Singing*; also, *Gospel Caravan*, concept produced by Jerry Wilson and Maurice Dumay; and *Say Amen, Somebody!*, directed by George T. Nierenberg.

17. Thomas James O'Toole, "Shadows of the Cross."

18. Ashon Crawley, email to author, January 11, 2024. Prepublication writing used with permission.

19. Wallace D. Best, *Passionately Human, No Less Divine*, 158–60.

Chapter 1. Elusive Origins and the Power of Place

Epigraph: Sallie Martin, to James Standifer, "Interview with Sallie Martin," 1, September 19, 1981 (transcript, 1–33, formerly available at the African American Music Collection of the University of Michigan; transcript provided to present author courtesy Robert M. Marovich). All subsequent citations of Martin's words will be cited by the interviewer's surname (Standifer).

1. An Ancestry.com user who wishes to remain anonymous suggested to me that Martin was born out of wedlock. Martin told Standifer that she was raised by her mother and grandparents, all of whom had died by 1915 (Standifer, 1).

2. Standifer transcribed the town as Pittsfield, which may be what the 86-year-old Martin remembered, but since no town has ever existed in Georgia by that name, it's clear she meant Penfield in Greene County.

3. The vast majority of Black people in Greene County were enslaved; I have assumed at least some of Martin's ancestors were among that group.

4. Hernando DeSoto may have crossed the Oconee River and entered present-day Greene County during his exploration of 1540.

5. Scull Shoals [sic.] is so named for the human remains washed out of the mounds by flood waters of the Oconee River. The Oconee River was navigable all the way to Savannah before agriculture was widely practiced there.

6. Jonathan M. Bryant, *How Curious a Land*, 15; Miller Handley Karnes, "Law, Labor, and Land in the Postbellum Cotton South."

7. Details of the Creek War and the War of 1812, though fascinating, lie beyond the scope of this study. The superior hunting grounds that had for generations supported Indigenous communities on the Oconee River were acquired from the Creek Nation in 1783, in a sort of kangaroo land-cession hearing. Creeks were pushed into present-day Alabama in 1836; they joined the Cherokee Nation on the Trail of Tears in 1838.

8. For more on enslaved forces—including women—hired from their owners to work on the railroads in adjacent Wilkes County, see Daina Ramey Berry, *Swing the Sickle, for the Harvest is Ripe*, 114–15.

9. Related in Standifer, 1–2.

10. Bryant, *How Curious a Land*, 199, n21.

11. Ibid., 23.

12. The patrol laws Georgia passed in 1765 remained fundamentally unchanged before the War. All white men between the ages of sixteen and sixty were required to participate; plantations were examined every two weeks for runaways and those without passes to visit; *Slave Laws of Georgia*.

13. Sally E. Hadden, "Slave Patrols," *New Georgia Encyclopedia*, last edited Aug. 2, 2018, https://www.georgiaencyclopedia.org/articles/history-archaeology/slave-patrols.

14. Bryant, *How Curious a Land*, 27, quoting Georgia narratives in the Federal Writers' Project, *The American Slave: A Composite Autobiography*, edited by George P. Rawick, vols. 13–14 (Washington, DC: Smithsonian Libraries and Archives).

15. Anthony Heilbut, *The Gospel Sound*, 5.

16. For more on Mercer University, the life of its founder, and his watershed hymnals, see Kay Norton, *Baptist Offspring, Southern Midwife*.

17. Mercer University, so named in 1838, remained in Penfield until 1871, when it was relocated to Macon, Georgia, its current home. At that point, the Mercer Chapel was given to Penfield Baptist Church.

18. Thaddeus Brockett Rice, *History of Greene County, Georgia*, 257–61.

19. Heilbut, *The Gospel Sound*, 4–6.

20. Existence of churches is not the only measure of sacred gatherings. Brush arbor worship meetings, where Blacks clandestinely exercised their own spirituality prior to 1865, surely characterized much Black antebellum religious experience. The first Black Christian congregation in Georgia was allowed by whites in Savannah as early as 1773. It was given the name African Baptist Church in 1788.

21. In chapter 5 of the *History of Greene County*, "The Churches of Greene County," 104–27, Rice provides founding dates for the first Presbyterian (1786), Methodist (1786), and Baptist (1785) congregations in Greene County.

22. Jonathan M. Bryant, "My Soul An't Yours, Mas'r,'" 404.

23. Bryant, *How Curious a Land*, 147.

24. Ibid., 123–24.

25. Walter C. Rucker and Sabriya Kaleen Jubilee, "From Black Nadir to Brown v. Board."

26. In January of 1868, the student body comprised twenty-five male and five female students who came to school consistently and punctually. Only one of the students was over sixteen years old, indicating that education stopped at that age. In that first month, fifteen students studied spelling and reading and there were two advanced readers. Reportedly, no students had enough background to participate in other subjects, such as arithmetic.

27. Two of the children had been free before the war.

28. Thirteenth Census of the United States, 1910, statistics for Georgia.

29. Heilbut, *The Gospel Sound,* 6.

30. Standifer, 1.

31. All quoted material in this paragraph is from Heilbut, *The Gospel Sound,* 6.

32. Stanford University, "Williams, Adam Daniel (A. D.)," The Martin Luther King Jr., Research and Education Institute, accessed February 6, 2025, https://kinginstitute.stanford.edu/encyclopedia/williams-adam-daniel-d.

33. Clayborne Carson, Ralph E. Lucker, and Penny A. Russell, eds., *Called to Serve.*

34. Standifer, 2.

35. The Fire Baptized Holiness denomination was founded in Iowa in 1895. Its headquarters were moved to Royston, Georgia, just under a hundred miles from Atlanta, in 1902. An offshoot took the name Colored Fire-Baptized Holiness Church in 1908, and that group founded the church in Atlanta's Old Fourth Ward that Martin joined. Known by some simply as Hogue Street today, it is located on several parcels of land extending from the corner of 496 Old Wheat Street to 64 Hogue Street, about three blocks from historic Ebenezer Baptist Church. For more on sanctified religion, see chapter 2.

36. Heilbut, *The Gospel Sound,* 7.

37. Heilbut's words, *The Gospel Sound,* 6, with a parenthetical remark by Martin.

38. Clifford M. Kuhn, Harlon E. Joye, and E. Bernard West, *Living Atlanta,* 9.

39. Kuhn, Joye, and West, Living Atlanta, 10; and Tera W. Hunter, *To 'Joy My Freedom,* 147, 153–54.

40. Hunter, 156, relating data from the *Atlanta Independent,* May 16, 1914.

41. Hunter, 163, quoting Jim O'Neal and Amy O'Neal, "Living Blues Interview: Georgia Tom Dorsey," *Living Blues: A Journal of the Black American Blues Tradition* 20 (Mar.-Apr. 1975): 18.

42. Wallace Martin is listed as Joel's stepfather in the 1930 census, so it is clear he was not the biological father of the child.

43. Standifer, 5.

44. Ibid.

45. F. Finley McRae, "Sallie Martin Obituary," *Los Angeles Sentinel,* July 14, 1988, A10.

46. The 1920 census records that they rented a residence at 2333 East 39th Street.

47. Heilbut, *The Gospel Sound,* 6.

48. Wallace Martin registered for the draft in December of 1917 and February of 1942, but apparently never served.

49. Heilbut, *The Gospel Sound,* 7; Standifer, 5–6.

50. Standifer, 6. She may have referred to the post–World War I recession, which extended from August 1918 to March of 1919, or the more severe

recession beginning in January of 1920 and lasting until July of 1921. Employment and automobile production fell significantly, partly as a result of the reabsorption of 2.9 million members of the US Armed Forces into the civilian labor force.

51. Standifer, 6.

52. Wallace Martin and Sallie never divorced; he died in Chicago on March 12, 1950. Joel Martin may have continued to reside with his mother after 1923, or may have been sent back to Georgia to live with family members. His early life is even more mysterious than that of his mother.

Chapter 2. Chicago, 1923–1933

Epigraph: Standifer, 6; Anthony Heilbut, *The Gospel Sound*, 7

1. Heilbut, *The Gospel Sound*, 6. Emphasis in original. See chapter 1.

2. Martin's religious convictions must have precluded divorce; she and Wallace lived together briefly in Chicago, but later separated and remained so until his death in 1950.

3. Mark H. Haller, "Policy Gambling, Entertainment, and the Emergence of Black Politics," 726.

4. Undated *Chicago Tribune* of 1931; quoted in Ron Grossman, "'Big Bill' Thompson: Chicago's Unfiltered Mayor," *Chicago Tribune*, February 5, 2016, updated May 26, 2022, https://www.chicagotribune.com/2016/02/05/big-bill-thompson-chicagos-unfiltered-mayor.

5. Quoted in Heilbut, *The Gospel Sound*, 7. The brief and turbulent term of Chicago's next corrupt mayor, Anton Joseph Cermak (a.k.a. Antonín Josef Čermák, April 7, 1931-March 6, 1933), ended shortly after he was assassinated.

6. W. E. B. Du Bois, *The Souls of Black Folk*, 2–3.

7. Rae Linda Brown, ed., *The Heart of a Woman*, 3 and ff., and 85.

8. Robert G. Gardner, Charles O. Walker, J. R. Huddlestun, and Waldo P. Harris III, *A History of the Georgia Baptist Association, 1784–1984*, 16–17.

9. Evelyn Brooks Higginbotham, *Righteous Discontent*, 2. She clarifies that in the history of Black Baptists, "convention" has almost the same meaning as "denomination."

10. Paul Harvey, *Redeeming the South*, 228.

11. Bureau of the Census, Religious Bodies, 1906, vol. 1, 13739. Bureau of the Census, Religious Bodies, 1916, part 1, vol. 1, 12128. Harvey, 228 and 309 n. 8, quoting William E. Montgomery, *Under Their Own Vine and Fig Tree: The African-American Church in the South, 1865–1900*, 1058.

12. Significantly, the white Southern Baptist Convention was proslavery and did not vote to issue an apology for that position until 1995.

13. See Higginbotham, *Righteous Discontent*, 150 and ff.

14. Boyd also pioneered by urging black citizens of Nashville to buy their children Black dolls from the National Negro Doll Company (supported by Marcus Garvey and the United Negro Improvement Association). Harvey, 248.

15. Harvey, 245.

16. Pentecost, occurring roughly fifty days after Passover, is prioritized over Christ's resurrection in Pentecostal congregations.

17. Alain Locke, *The New Negro.*

18. Louis A. Dulaney, "Broadcasting Ignorance," *Chicago Defender*, September 1, 1934, 14; quoted in Robert M. Marovich, *A City Called Heaven*, 62.

19. Arthur E. Holt, from an article published in the *American Journal of Sociology* 34 (July 1928), 175; quoted in Wallace Best, *Passionately Human, No Less Divine*, 12–13.

20. Marovich, *A City Called Heaven*, 24.

21. Mark Burford, *Mahalia Jackson and the Black Gospel Field*, 79.

22. Michael W. Harris, *The Rise of Gospel Blues*, 196.

23. Ebenezer Missionary Baptist Church Archives, Chicago Public Library, accessed February 6, 2025, https://www.chipublib.org/fa-ebenezer-missionary-baptist-church-archives.

24. Robert Lee Sutherland, "An Analysis of Negro Churches in Chicago," (PhD diss., University of Chicago, 1930), 79, quoted in Marovich, *A City Called Heaven*, 24.

25. Ira De Augustine Reid, "Let Us Prey," *Opportunity* 4 (1926): 274–78; quoted in Susan Nance, "Mystery of the Moorish Science Temple," 123.

26. Haller, 730.

27. Laurraine Goreau, "Interview with Sallie Martin," side A, 3.

28. Ibid.

29. Ibid., 4. Jackson was known to her family and friends as Mahala (not Mahalia).

30. Ibid., 3–4.

31. Standifer, 5.

32. Ibid., 21.

33. Heilbut, *The Gospel Sound*, 4. In contrast to shaking, "shouting" allowed everyday norms of movement and song to blossom into more frenzied bodily and vocal expressions.

34. Spoken Introduction, *Professor Thomas Andrew Dorsey*. Martin is introduced in this way prior to a performance of Dorsey's "How About You," discussed below.

35. Kenny Ulmer, quoted in Gretchen Henkel, "The Gospel Truth," *Los Angeles Times*, September 4, 1979, 4.

36. Horace Clarence Boyer, in *This Far by Faith.*

37. Quoted in Goreau, "Interview," 1. Later, rehearsals moved to East 59th Street and South Wabash Avenue.

38. Harris, 125.

39. *Gospel Pearls*, hymn 48, verse 4.

40. Harris, 168–69.

41. Reproduced in Harris, 168.

42. Harris, 169.

43. Goreau, "Interview," 1–2.

44. Harris, 246. Harris considered these qualities to be inheritances from the slavery era. Then, "brush arbor" meetings—clandestine and spiritual, where shouts might have taken place—were facilitated by a caller whose improvised verses within the call-and-response framework spoke for the entire assemblage. "The caller . . . differed from the respondents only as the other component of an antiphonal ensemble."

45. Harris, 255–56.

46. Robert M. Marovich, interviews with Kenneth Woods Jr.

47. Goreau, "Interview," 2.

48. Marovich, *A City Called Heaven*, 82.

49. Roxanne Regina Reed, "Preaching and Piety," 30.

50. John G. Hunter, *Atlanta Daily World*, November 27, 1932. The ten best choirs were from Saint Paul AME, Mt. Moriah Baptist, Morning Star Baptist, Greater Saint John, Ebenezer Baptist, Bethlehem District, Mt. Moriah 2, Metropolitan Community Church, Walters AME Zion, and Pilgrim Baptist.

51. Standifer, 9. Marovich wrote that the address was near 40th Street and South Parkway (*A City Called Heaven*, 82).

52. Standifer, 10.

53. Ibid.

54. Maude Roberts George, "National Association of Musicians Meet Here Next Week: Musicians Start 12th Annual Meet Sunday," *Chicago Defender*, Aug. 23, 1930, 1.

55. Standifer, 7.

56. Harris, 211 and ff.

57. The NCGCC, "NCGCC—Our History," accessed April 16, 2025, https://www.ncgcc.org/about.html.

58. Where, exactly, the NCGCC held its first "official" meeting depends upon interpretation. *Chicago Defender* notices affirm that the concept of the organization had been formed by September of 1933, when a meeting of Chicago choirs occurred. As Willie Mae Ford Smith shows in *Say Amen, Somebody!* (see chapter 4), however, St. Louis members consider their city as the founding place.

59. *Chicago Defender,* "Gospel Singers Close National Meeting," September 9, 1933, 15.

60. *Chicago Defender*, July 8, 1933, 7.

61. Heilbut, *The Gospel Sound*, 8.

Chapter 3. Curating an Identity with Business Partners, 1933–1949

1. Among other cities, Martin founded GCUs in Chicago, Indianapolis, Terre Haute, and Los Angeles.

2. Descriptions such as these were printed on Thomas A. Dorsey's "Did It Happen to You Like It Happened to Me" (1930s).

3. She had hired a manager for her Los Angeles appearances by 1944. Her 1940s recorded music is given close attention in chapter 5.

4. *Chicago Defender*, January 28, 1933, 1.

5. *Chicago Defender*, April 8, 1933, 2.

6. "Gospel Singers Close National Meeting," *Chicago Defender*, September 9, 1933, 15. The "Professor" title may have originated with the NCGCC; it remained part of his public name, and Martin referred to him that way in the Goreau interview (Lorraine Goreau, "Interview with Sallie Martin"). Such honorific titles, like Dr., were at first reserved for males in gospel, and for Dorsey in particular.

7. Ibid.

8. Victor Hugo Green's self-published *The Negro Motorist Green Book* did not appear until 1936, prior to which time Black motorists relied on word of mouth.

9. *Chicago Defender*, July 21, 1934, 13. Again, whether this was the first or second full NCGCC meeting is open to interpretation. Hopefully, archives of the NCGCC will soon be available to outside researchers, and this question laid to rest.

10. *Chicago Defender*, "Gospel Singers Close Second Annual Meet," August 11, 1934, 13.

11. Thereafter, one day at each convention would be dedicated to raising scholarship funds to support Convention attendance for musically gifted youth. For more on Roberta Martin, see chapter 4.

12. *Chicago Defender*, July 11, 1936, 12.

13. *Chicago Defender*, March 2, 1935, 13.

14. "Gospel Leaders Hold Board Meet: Plan Erection of School for Race Music," *Chicago Defender*, February 29, 1936, 12. The "Gospel Singers College" opened at 4048 South Lake Park Avenue in Chicago. Mark Burford, *Mahalia Jackson and the Black Gospel Field*, 84.

15. *Chicago Defender*, March 23, 1934. A photo of the group may be seen in Michael W. Harris, "Dorsey's Female Gospel Quartette," in *The Rise of Gospel Blues*, between pages 150 and 151. Martin stands at far right. The Dorsey Quartette recorded four sides on the Vocalion label in March of 1932. Recordings will be examined in chapter 5. Traveling ensembles were also part and parcel of the preexisting white gospel industry, where all-male quartets marketed the James D. Vaughan company's music beginning in 1910. Emulating vaudeville and barbershop quartet vocalizations, the white quartets may have experienced less vocal fatigue.

16. Goreau, "Interview with Sallie Martin," 2.

17. Standifer, 19.

18. America Robinson, letter to James D. Burrus, April 18, 1877, Dordrecht, Holland, America Robinson Letters, Fisk University Library Special Collections; quoted in Sandra Graham, "On the Road to Freedom."

19. Marian Divers, "Maywood, IL News," *Chicago Defender*, February 29, 1934, 12.

20. Goreau, “Interview,” 6.

21. Roberta Martin and Theodore Frye organized the junior chorus at Ebenezer Baptist Church, and from that group selected a quartet of adolescent boys for a performance at the 1934 Chicago “Century of Progress” World’s Fair. The original group comprised Robert Anderson and Willie Webb (age 14), James Lawrence (13), Eugene Smith (12), and Norsalus McKissick (10). The group was renamed the Roberta Martin Singers in 1935. Robert M. Marovich, *A City Called Heaven*, 109.

22. The photo appears in Bernice Johnson Reagon, *We’ll Understand It Better By and By*, after page 180. Front row, left to right: Roberta Martin, Sallie Martin. Back row, left to right: Willie Webb, Robert Anderson, Eugene Smith.

23. Goreau, “Interview,” 1, and Standifer (paraphrased), 14.

24. Standifer, 13. Roberta Martin’s musical education clearly influenced her goals for the group and its sound.

25. Standifer, 22.

26. Martin did perform at least once during this period, with Dorsey at Bethel AME Church in Indianapolis on December 11, 1935. *Indianapolis Recorder*, December 14, 1935, 11.

27. If she hoped for a fulfilling experience as a grandmother, however, she would be disappointed. By the time of the 1940 census, Katherine Johnson Martin was a single head of household, and in February of 1941, when Joel enlisted in the US Army, his marital status indicated “divorced with dependents.” Joel Martin was killed in action in Carthage, Tunisia, on December 4, 1942. Katherine married Robert Marcellus Cutright (1904–1994) and their blended family—her three children, aged 15, 13, and 11; and his four, aged 8, 7, 3, and 1—resided in the same household as of the 1950 census. Sallie Martin appears not to have retained a strong connection with Joel and Katherine’s children (see chapter 7).

28. “Throng Hears Gospel Choir in Music Fest,” *Chicago Defender*, July 11, 1936, 12. She raised $155.80, the equivalent of $2,133 in today’s currency.

29. “Gospel Singer Is on Tour of West,” *Chicago Defender*, July 25, 1936, 12; and “Boost Rev. A. W. Womack for A. M. E. Z. [sic.] Bishop: Whole City Endorses Dr. Womack,” *Indianapolis Recorder*, March 31, 1934, 8. https://newspapers.library.in.gov/cgi-bin/indiana?a=d&d=INR19340331-01.1.8.

30. Womack was also president of the Indianapolis chapter of the NAACP. *Indianapolis Recorder*, July 27, 1935.

31. “Gospel Singer Is on Tour of West,” *Chicago Defender*, July 26, 1936, 12. Composer and arranger Hall Johnson (1888–1970) founded his Hall Johnson Negro Choir in 1925. Johnson’s arrangements, compositions, and his choir were featured often in Hollywood films and soundtracks in the 1930s and ’40s.

32. *Indianapolis Recorder*, September 26, 1936, 4, and October 2, 1936, 14.

33. “Chatting with Lue Swarz in St. Louis, MO,” *Pittsburgh Courier*, October 31, 1936, 10A.

34. “Gospel Choral Union Heads,” *Pittsburgh Courier*, March 20, 1937, 11. The event was also reported in the *Indianapolis Recorder* on the same day.

35. "Chicagoans Visit Eastern Churches," *New York Amsterdam News*, May 15, 1937, 10.

36. *Pittsburgh Courier*, December 10, 1938, 19, and the same issue, 23.

37. "Gospel Choruses Hold National Convention in Indianapolis," *Chicago Defender*, August 21, 1937, 3. The National Association for the Advancement of Colored People (NAACP) was founded on February 12, 1909. Womack was nominated to receive the CME church's highest honor for his "ability to represent the race," among other things, at that CME's national conference, planned for May 1938 in Indianapolis.

38. Louis P. Masur, "Why It Took a Century to Pass an Antilynching Law," *Washington Post*, December 28, 2018. https://www.washingtonpost.com/outlook/2018/12/28/why-it-took-century-pass-an-antilynching-law.

39. Standifer, 4–5.

40. *Online Athens*, "Lynching Report Recalls Grim History, Some of It in Athens Area," March 13, 2015, http://onlineathens.com/uga/2015/03/12/lynching-report-recalls-grim-history-some-it-athens-area.

41. Tuskegee University maintains a chronology of "Lynchings by State and Race," covering 1882 to 1968. "Lynching Stats Year Dates Causes," accessed February 6, 2025, https://archive.tuskegee.edu/repository/digital-collection/lynching-information/lynchings-stats-year-dates-causes/.

42. Goreau, "Interview," 8.

43. Standifer, 11.

44. Michael W. Harris relays Dorsey's account of how he groomed both Sallie Martin and Jackson as his ideal callers. *The Rise of Gospel Blues*, 256 and ff.

45. When he registered for the draft on October 16, 1940, Morris listed Clarence H. Cobbs (5139 S. Michigan Avenue) as next of kin. The 1940 census lists Morris's home as 4315 Indiana Avenue, perhaps indicating a residence on the second floor of the MMMS building.

46. "Kenneth Morris: I'll Be a Servant of the Lord," interview in *We'll Understand It Better By and By*, edited by Bernice Johnson Reagon, 330. "Manhattan Conservatory" probably referred to the New York College of Music, an institution whose alumni include Jerome Kern (1902) and Lil Hardin Armstrong (1929).

47. Quoted in Reagon, "Kenneth Morris: I'll Be a Servant," 331.

48. Brian Dolinar, *The Negro in Illinois: The WPA Papers* (Urbana: University of Illinois Press), 274, fn. 9–10.

49. Tristan Cabello, "Queer Bronzeville."

50. For a fuller discussion of Cobbs's alleged homosexuality, see Wallace Best, *Passionately Human, No Less Divine*, 188–89.

51. "Police Probe Scandal Rumor on Rev. Cobb," *Chicago Defender*, November 25, 1939, 1. The fulness of life as a homosexual is not in question here, but it was in 1939.

52. "Says 'Virtue and Integrity Were Injured,'" *Chicago Defender*, December 9, 1939, 9.

53. Several months later, Cobbs did eject a *Defender* reporter from the First Church of Deliverance before an advertised speech began. R. D. Griffith, a Coptic bishop from Ethiopia and close associate of Haile Selassie, had drawn the reporter to First Church on October 23, 1940. Cobbs reportedly told the newspaper's Diana Briggs that he would "cancel the whole program rather than allow the *Chicago Defender* to report the event"; "Rev. Cobbs Halts Service to Oust *Defender* Scribe," *Chicago Defender,* 26 October 1940, 7.

54. Cabello, "Queer Bronzeville." "In an article published on Jan. 13, 1949, by the *Defender*, the word 'homosexuality' was printed for the first time in that newspaper. A report on the existence of homosexual practices within the Black community, this mention of the word . . . is but the first of many, in which the *Defender*, and later African American magazines such as *Jet Magazine* and *Ebony Magazine* would try to define the limits of their community's sexual practices."

55. Best, *Passionately Human*, 188–90.

56. They were surrounded by cohorts in Black entrepreneurship in Bronzeville. In 1938, Chicago's 47th Street Black Business District (a few streets over from the MMMS) had a total of 320 businesses, 26 percent of which were owned by Black businesspeople; Juliet E. K. Walker, *The History of Black Business in America*, table 8.2, 227. Nothing similar to printing or publishing was listed among Walker's fourteen categories of businesses.

57. The building at 4312–4314 S. Indiana survives as of February 2023, but their first location across the street has been destroyed.

58. Horace Clarence Boyer, "Kenneth Morris," 314. Morris actively composed while employed by Lillian Bowles, but waited for publishing until after 1940, when he could claim all rights for himself.

59. Marovich, *A City Called Heaven*, 175.

60. Much has been made of the legend that Morris heard it from a Pullman porter; a staged photo of Morris and a porter is extant in the Martin and Morris Music Company Records. However, Morris related the true story about Hurse's choir to Reagon in 1987; "Kenneth Morris," 336.

61. Quoted in Reagon, "Kenneth Morris," 333, 336–37.

62. Gertrude Ward also lost control of some of her musical assets. See chapter 4.

63. Quoted in Reagon, *We'll Understand It Better By and By*, 333.

64. When customers submitted their own arrangements, prices were adjusted accordingly.

65. Kenneth Morris, *Improving the Music in the Church* (Chicago: MMMS, 1949), in Martin and Morris Music Company Records, series 4, 1.

66. Morris, *Improving the Music*, 64.

67. Martin and Morris Music Company Papers.

68. Anthony Griggs, "Gospel Music Is His Fortune," *Chicago Defender,* November 4, 1972, 32.

69. Quoted in Reagon, "Kenneth Morris," 333. In 1944, $100,000 amounted to nearly $1.8 million in 2024 dollars. $200,000 in 1964 is roughly equivalent

to $2.04 million in 2024 dollars. US Bureau of Labor Statistics, "CPI Inflation Calculator," accessed February 12, 2025, https://www.bls.gov/data/inflation_calculator.htm.

Chapter 4. Interconnected Spheres of Influence: Sallie Martin and Early Peers

1. This is by no means a complete account of important women in the early gospel era. Arizona Juanita Dranes (1891–1963), singer and pianist, introduced ragtime and barrelhouse styles in her Church of God in Christ (COGIC) piano accompaniments and laid a path for others in her generation. Sister Rosetta Tharpe (1915–1973) is celebrated as the first great recording artist in gospel. Her guitar stylings were foundational in the evolution of rhythm and blues and rock and roll. Beatrice Brown (ca. 1898–1967), of Indianapolis, toured with Martin in the 1930s and subsequently worked with her in the NCGCC. Like Martin, Brown ran a publishing business and a touring vocal group.

2. Episode 14 of NPR's *Wade in the Water* radio series addresses the broad impact of Campbell's creativity; Bernice Johnson Reagon, Pearl Williams-Jones, and Lisa Pertillar Brevard, "Lucie Campbell."

3. The latter was recorded by the Ward Singers in 1949; Original Five Blind Boys in 1950; the Pilgrim Travelers and Soul Stirrers in 1951; and B. B. King in 1959. It remains a favorite in Black and white gospel, evidenced in bluegrass renditions by Doyle Lawson and Quicksilver (1981) and John Cowan (2010).

4. Roxanne Regina Reed, "Preaching and Piety," 213 and ff.

5. Quoted in Luvenia A. George, "Lucie E. Campbell," 119. Emphasis in original.

6. Horace Clarence Boyer, "Lucie E. Campbell," 81–108; and Luvenia A. George, "Lucie E. Campbell," 109–19.

7. Quoted in Charles Walker, "Lucie E. Campbell Williams," 125.

8. Reed, 76 and 82.

9. She migrated through Memphis, Tennessee, but was born in Mississippi. See "Reader Asks about Gospel Music Publisher Lillian Bowles," My Auction Finds, accessed February 12, 2025, https://myauctionfinds.com/2014/03/14/reader-asks-about-gospel-music-publisher-lillian-bowles.

10. Standifer, 12.

11. *Chicago Defender*, May 21, 1938.

12. Ad copy from an August 25, 1962, *Chicago Defender* gave Bowles Music House, not the Martin and Morris Music Service, as an access point for tickets to Martin's Musical Extravaganza to benefit Nigerian missions (page 10).

13. Developed in the late nineteenth century by François Delsarte (1811–1871), this method trained girls and women to render graceful poses as a way to study the bodily expression of emotion. Such sculptural stances conjured images of classical figures like Ariadne and, prophetically for Butts, the biblical Esther. See Genevieve Stebbins, *Delsarte System of Dramatic Expression* (New York: Edgar S. Werner, 1886).

14. Portions of this section and the one below, about Roberta Martin, appeared in Kay Norton, "The Pedagogical Legacies of Three Black Gospel Pioneers," 97–114.

15. Despite Jones's penchant for classical repertoire, the *Chicago Defender* only listed the group's "spiritual" selections for a performance at Orchestra Hall in 1920: "Old Kentucky Home," "Steal Away," and "Go Long Mule." Quoted in Lynn Abbott and Doug Seroff, *To Do This, You Must Know How*, 225–26.

16. J. Wesley Jones, "West Side News," *Chicago Defender*, June 5, 1920, 13. Butts's assistance is cited in Robert M. Marovich, *A City Called Heaven*, 85.

17. *Chicago Defender*, August 24, 1935, 15.

18. Brian Halstoos, "Pageant and Passion," 85. Several mainline Chicago churches, such as the Met, upheld the superiority of Western European classicism in the early 1930s. Gospel flourished first in more demonstrative congregations. See Robert M. Marovich, "Sing a New Song," 26.

19. Marovich, "Sing a New Song," 39, n. 18. When minister W. D. Cook died in 1930, Butts renamed her group the Cook Singers.

20. Maude Roberts George, "News of the Music World," *Chicago Defender*, August 29, 1931, 15; noted in Robert M. Marovich, *A City Called Heaven*, 85.

21. Mark Burford, *Mahalia Jackson and the Black Gospel Field*, 79–80. Burford pointed out that the Ebenezer choir initiated the "purposeful institutionalizing of black gospel singing and the extension of this organization nationally," thus earning it the soubriquet, "birthplace of gospel music."

22. Thomas A. Dorsey, *The Thomas A. Dorsey Story: From Blues-Jazz to Gospel Song* (Chicago: Thomas A. Dorsey, 1961), related in Michael W. Harris, *The Rise of Gospel Blues*, 190.

23. Quoted in Harris, 223.

24. "Defender's Massed Chorus Takes Music Festival Honor: Thunderous Applause Greets Singing of Spirituals," *Chicago Defender*, August 30, 1930, 1. See also Mark Burford, "Black and White, Then 'Red' All Over," 1–6.

25. Dorsey, interviews with Harris on February 2, 1976, and January 26, 1977, quoted in Harris, *The Rise of Gospel Blues,* 214.

26. *Chicago Defender,* September 9, 1933, 15.

27. "Chicago Gospel Chorus Honor Founders in Lavish Anniversary Celebration," *Chicago Defender,* July 6, 1935, 22. Also honored were Dorsey, National President; Frye as National Treasurer; and Lewis, National First Vice President.

28. "Metropolitan S[unday] [School] to Present Older Girls Chorus," *Chicago Defender*, December 7, 1935, 10. The Bible School chorus was directed by Lewis-Butts and accompanied by Clyde Winkfield.

29. "Metropolitan Prize-Winning Choir to Sing at Festival" *Chicago Defender,* April 11, 1936, 15. The caption for this impressive photo reiterates that the Met choir was under the "personal" direction of Jones; it also names the soloists and notes that Lewis-Butts was narrator for Théodore DuBois's *Seven Last Words of Christ* (1867), the performance of which was a Good Friday annual tradition at the Met. Related in Marovich, "Sing a New Song," 27.

30. "1935 Metropolitan Community Church Annual Report," Save the Met Papers, Vivian Harsh Collection, Chicago Public Library, quoted in Marovich, *A City Called Heaven*, 85.

31. "California: Berkeley, Cal[ifornia]," *Chicago Defender*, September 25, 1937, 6.

32. Grace W. Tomkins, "Music News," *Chicago Defender*, March 16, 1940, 8.

33. Ward resided in Philadelphia by the time of the 1930 census.

34. "Clara Ward Is Ex-Child Star," *Los Angeles Sentinel*, October 15, 1959, C2.

35. Don Cusic, "How I Got Over," essay for the 2017 inclusion of "How I Got Over" (1950) into the National Recording Registry, Library of Congress.

36. Willa Ward-Royster, *How I Got Over*, 85.

37. Standifer, 24.

38. Brewster was pastor of East Trigg Avenue Baptist Church in Memphis, one of the places where Elvis Presley learned to love Black Baptist singing.

39. Ward-Royster, *How I Got Over*.

40. Waseda Minako, "Gospel Music in Japan."

41. Anthony Heilbut, *The Gospel Sound*, 106.

42. Ward-Royster, *How I Got Over*.

43. "Church Moves to New Site," *Los Angeles Sentinel*, August 17, 1976, C7.

44. Hugh Downs, Interview with Gertrude Ward.

45. Mark Coltrain, "Willie Mae Ford Smith," *Mississippi Encyclopedia*, accessed February 12, 2025, http://mississippiencyclopedia.org/entries/willa-mae-ford-smith/.

46. Harper Barnes, *St. Louis Post-Dispatch*, February 7, 1993, 3E. See also William Thomas Dargan and Kathy White Bullock, "Willie Mae Ford Smith of St. Louis."

47. *Say Amen, Somebody!*

48. Quoted in Marovich, *A City Called Heaven*, 123.

49. Heilbut, *The Gospel Sound*, 344.

50. Quoted in Irene V. Jackson, "Afro-American Gospel Music and Its Social Setting," 91.

51. Jackson, 92. Roberta married William Martin in 1928 or '29 and, though they stayed together for one year only, she retained his surname. They divorced in 1940 or '41, having had no children.

52. Marovich, *A City Called Heaven*, 109.

53. Jackson, 102.

54. Ibid., 93.

55. Quoted in Pearl Williams-Jones and Bernice Johnson Reagon (eds.), "Conversations: Roberta Martin Singers Roundtable," 298.

56. Idella Lulumae Johnson, "Development of African-American Gospel Piano Style (1926–1960)," 334.

57. Quoted in Williams-Jones and Reagon, 298.

58. Standifer, 13.

59. "Roberta Martin Musical Tribute at New Covenant," *Chicago Defender*, August 13, 1966, 16.

60. Emmett G. Price III, "Roberta Martin," in *Encyclopedia of American Gospel Music*, edited by W. K. McNeil (New York: Taylor and Francis, 2005), 272.

61. Horace Clarence Boyer, "Roberta Martin," 286.

62. According to the 1940 Census, Emma L. Jackson, a music teacher born in Louisiana and "working on her own account," lived in a large boarding house at an address that no longer exists in Chicago's 4th Ward. The Chicago-Cook County Deaths and Stillbirths Index records that one Emma L. Jackson Craig passed away on October 23, 1946. Given the custom of changing surnames after marriage, it is impossible to ascertain if this is the same Jackson, but I have ended my coverage of her life in 1946.

63. Horace Clarence Boyer, *The Golden Age of Gospel*, 76.

64. "Off to Dixie," *Chicago Defender*, January 22, 1944, 14.

65. Laurraine Goreau was insistent that the move occurred in 1927, a date she pressed in her interview with Sallie Martin (Nov. 4, 1972), but Mark Burford has constructed a solid case, based on oral history and the 1930 census, that Jackson still resided in New Orleans in 1930.

66. Burford, *Mahalia Jackson and the Gospel Field,* 65.

67. Ibid., 70.

68. Laurraine Goreau, "Interview with Sallie Martin," 4.

69. Burford, *Mahalia Jackson and the Gospel Field,* 87.

70. That recording sold 8 million copies.

71. Burford, *Mahalia Jackson and the Gospel Field,* 154.

72. Goreau, "Interview," 14.

73. Ted Ston's "Heard and Seen," column in the *Chicago Defender*, January 13, 1959, 21.

74. Burford, *Mahalia Jackson and the Gospel Field,* 82.

Chapter 5. Los Angeles, the Sallie Martin Singers, and Recordings, 1940–1956

1. Anthony Heilbut, *The Gospel Sound,* 9 and 57. McPherson was more of an attraction to white Angelenos than to Black, judging by more than 2,500 citations in an *L. A. Times* search. The same query in the *Los Angeles Sentinel* yielded only nine. Martin's "get "happy" described a highly vocal, embodied response typical of sanctified worship.

2. See the discussion of 1930s touring in chapter 3.

3. Don Lee White, quoted in Jacqueline Cogdell DjeDje and Eddie S. Meadows, *California Soul,* 129.

4. Birgitta J. Johnson's descriptors of sanctified singing include "hand

clapping, foot stomping, call-and-response performance, rhythmic complexities, persistent beat, improvisatory singing, and heterophonic textures . . . as well as speaking and singing in tongues, holy dancing, and the use of drums and other percussive instruments"; Birgitta J. Johnson, "Church of God in Christ, Inc."

5. DjeDje and Meadows, 125.

6. Jacqueline Cogdell DjeDje, "Gospel Music in the Los Angeles Black Community," 39.

7. Jacqueline Cogdell DjeDje, "Los Angeles Composers of African American Gospel Music," 430.

8. Arson was responsible for a blaze that burned Victory Baptist Church to the ground on the night of September 10, 2022.

9. Several L.A. churches eclipsed Victory Baptist in emulating Chicago churches' broadcast worship services. See discussion below. Tragically, Peters, purportedly a gay man, was found murdered and his body mutilated on September 25, 1975. Unsubstantiated though persistent accounts suggest that his death was more a lynching than a general homicide.

10. Southern Christian Leadership Conference (SCLC) leader Ralph David Abernathy preached at Peters's memorial service in 1975, and Rev. King Sr. also played a leading role. "Obsequies of Reverend Arthur Atlas Peters, Victory Baptist Church, Sept. 30, 1975," University of Southern California Digital Library, Gospel Music History Archive, accessed February 12, 2025, https://calisphere.org/item/c3c1ffe794b61da2d199b3edef8083b8/.

11. Nathan John Kirkpatrick of Long Beach, California, sometimes sang with the Three Sons of Thunder. He, too, became a minister.

12. Fruits of Frazier's friendship with James Cleveland include the Frazier-Cleveland Publishing Company and the Gospel Music Workshop of America (Cleveland's answer to Dorsey's NCGCC) in 1968.

13. Smithsonian Online Virtual Archives (NMAH) contains an album of gospel music scores collected or composed by Smallwood and nineteen additional loose copies of his own issues. Publication dates range from 1931 to 1945.

14. In the *Encyclopedia of American Gospel Music*, Sherry Sherrod DuPree dated his printing business from 1931 to 1945, but I suspect a typographical error. Even for the precocious Smallwood, opening a business at age eleven would have been a stretch. W. K. McNeil (ed.), *Encyclopedia of American Gospel Music*, 134.

15. Kenneth Morris was equally enthusiastic about the Hammond. Members of First Church of Deliverance in Chicago still proudly share that theirs was the first such organ in a church.

16. Robert M. Marovich, *City Called Heaven*, 187.

17. DjeDje and Meadows, *California Soul*, 135. Kenneth Morris tutored her on his famous "bounce" style of accompaniment, which traveled with her to L.A. She is also known as Gwendolyn Lightner, and is discussed later in this chapter.

18. Gwendolyn Cooper Lightner, quoted in DjeDje and Meadows, 133.

19. Capitol Records released a broadcast version of "I'm So Glad Jesus Lifted Me" (Capitol 40018) in April 1947, and an album, *Revival Day: The St. Paul Church Choir of Los Angeles* (Capitol T791) in 1957.

20. In an interview with Opal Louis Nations, Ruth Black-Castille remembered, "We toured throughout the South constantly, appearing mostly at school auditoriums. We always headlined, local groups opened for us. Hines was good to us and he got along well with everyone." The New Goodwill Singers stayed together for four years and recorded at least forty-five songs for Sacred Records in Los Angeles. Tony Cummings, "Prof. James Earle Hines & The St Paul Church Choir Of Los Angeles."

21. "Leaves for Boston," *Chicago Defender*, November 25, 1939, 2. At the time, Quarles was an artist's model and former singer in the First Church of Deliverance choir.

22. Smith was alternately known as Julia Smith and Julia Mae Whitfield. She married Alfred C. Smith early in life and later was wed to McHenry "Mac" Whitfield.

23. Clipping, courtesy Carlous Adams, Facebook, February 11, 2023. This is the only indication I have seen that Necie Morris sang in the group.

24. The Celestial Trio also included Marion Peeples and Willie Ruffin. Luvenia George Collection, Box 9, Folder 21, Dorsey's "Someway, Sometime, Somehow, Somewhere," "as sung by the Celestial Gospel Trio," Dorsey Publishing, 1951.

25. Personnel for Smith's group included Rosetta Howard, Lovie Bradford, Mary Gloster, Geraldine Moses, Ethel Clay, and "little" Junette Smith, the founder's daughter (1953–2022); *Chicago Defender*, October 20, 1962, 15—Martin appears as Sallie Martin Langham in this article.

26. See Linda M. Chatters, Robert Joseph Taylor, and Rukmalie Jayakodie, "Fictive Kinship Relations in Black Extended Families."

27. DjeDje, "Los Angeles Composers," 436. Cora married Henry A. Moore (1907–2004), a native of Alabama, on October 8, 1965.

28. Frederick Douglas Haynes Family Papers.

29. Heilbut, *The Gospel Sound,* 12; *Los Angeles Sentinel*, December 2, 1948. The first mention of their co-owned Simmons-Akers Gospel Music Room, where they offered coaching, records, and sheet music, occurred in the April 6, 1950, *Los Angeles Sentinel*. See below for more on Doris Akers.

30. Like that of the SMS, their personnel changed periodically. At their four-year anniversary celebration at Saint Paul Baptist on June 22, 1952, the group included Louise Byrd and Doris Jean Hayes. Helen Henderson also sang with them. Chris Fenner, "Doris Akers, 21 May 1921–26 July 1995," *Hymnology Archive*, February 12, 2021, revised April 30, 2021, https://www.hymnologyarchive.com/doris-akers.

31. Their recording of "It Must Be Jesus' Love Divine" is not readily available. The other three were remastered on *Sallie and Cora Martin: Just a Little*

Talk with Jesus, Gospel Friend Records, 2014. Robert M. Marovich's liner notes provide an important outline of Sallie Martin's discography.

32. By 1940, "On the Jericho Road" had appeared in at least nine hymnals, but its popularity surely owed more to radio broadcasts from places like WSM in Nashville (whose Barn Dance became the Grand Ole Opry in 1925) and WLSAM in Chicago. The latter's "National Barn Dance," beginning in 1924, established Chicago as the center of country music alongside the city's prowess in jazz. Catering to mostly white audiences, these "hillbilly" shows nonetheless marked the merger of urban and rural culture that would have appealed to transplanted Black audiences, as well.

33. Robert M. Marovich, interviews with Kenneth Woods Jr.

34. Also possible, as Woods suggested to Marovich, is that the pianist was Melva Williams.

35. Standifer, 16, 17, and 19, respectively.

36. DjeDje, "Los Angeles Composers," 430.

37. Laurraine Goreau, "Interview with Sallie Martin," 5.

38. Ibid., 9–10.

39. "But you can't do that anymore," she said in 1972. Goreau, "Interview," 7.

40. Her untimely death is credited to a lethal combination of dieting and insomnia drugs.

41. Goreau, "Interview," 7.

42. Standifer, 15.

43. Goreau, "Interview," 10.

44. *Cleveland Call and Post*, October 11, 1941, 3B.

45. Joel Martin's remains are interred in Tunisia.

46. Quoted in Bernice Johnson Reagon, "Kenneth Morris," 333, 336–37.

47. See chapter 3.

48. Eugene Smallwood, "Gospel in Los Angeles."

49. Martin and Morris Music Company Records, series 1. I believe Martin mistakenly wrote August instead of September, since it was sent from Dallas.

50. *Indianapolis Recorder*, May 1, 1948, 6.

51. *Los Angeles Sentinel*, January 17, 1946, 10. Among other things, "sponsoring" claimed the cachet associated with a well-known Angeleno. In turn, she sponsored or presented many gospel newcomers in her performances.

52. *Los Angeles Sentinel*, March 13, 1947, 6; Victor Hugo Green's *The Negro Travelers' Green Book* or *The Negro Motorist Green Book* (Victor Hugo Green, 1936) was available in most major cities in the United States by 1939.

53. Deborah Verdice Smith Barney, "The Gospel Announcer and the Black Gospel Music Tradition," 91.

54. Sallie Martin's Ledger 1942–43 (May 5, 1942 through Jan of 43), in Martin and Morris Music Company Records, series 2, 6. Used with permission.

55. Gwendolyn Cooper Lightner, Gospel in Los Angeles lecture series, interview by Jacqueline Cogdell DjeDje.

56. DjeDje, "Los Angeles Composers," 416.

57. Also featured in the recording were Cora, Dave Weston, and Julia Smith. John Dolphin (a.k.a. "Lovin' John," 1902–1958) opened Dolphin's of Hollywood, a record store open twenty-four hours a day, in 1948. The store featured live DJs and a radio show; the Penguins' "Earth Angel (Will You Be Mine") was released in 1954, during a live broadcast at Dolphin's. The proprietor founded his independent record label, Recorded in Hollywood (RIH), in 1950.

58. *Los Angeles Sentinel*, August 25, 1949, A7.

59. National Baptist Convention "Conventionites," *Pittsburgh Courier*, 17 September 1949, 3. The NCGCC met in Los Angeles from August 29 through October 2, 1949, and the NBC met two weeks later in that city.

60. *New York Amsterdam News*, September 4, 1948, 16.

61. Quoted in Anthony Heilbut, jacket notes, in *Women of Gospel's Golden Age: Volume I*, CD (n.p.: Specialty Records, 1994).

62. Robert M. Marovich, "Pseudonyms and Session Men."

63. Lee Hildebrand, liner notes, *The Sallie Martin Singers: Gospel Twofer*, "Precious Lord" & "God Is Here," CD, Vee-Jay reissue, 1993, NVG2–606.

64. *Los Angeles Sentinel*, January 5, 1950, 4.

65. Art Rupe, quoted in Lee Hildebrand and Opal Nations (reissue producers), liner notes, *Thunderbolt of the Middle West*.

66. He continued with Specialty until 1958, then recorded with a Nashville label and returned to the South.

67. *Billboard*, May 5, 1951, 82.

68. "God Is a Battle Axe," "Oh What a Time," and "Didn't It Rain," featuring Cora; "Every Day and Every Hour" and "I'll Make It Somehow," featuring Sallie and Joe May; "Oh Yes, He Set Me Free" and "He's Able to Carry Me Through," with Cora and May; and Cora Martin on "Until We Meet Again."

69. A Specialty reissue entitled *Brother Joe May Live 1952–1955: With Special Appearances by Annette May and the Sallie Martin Singers, and Prof. J. Earle Hines*, includes these recordings.

70. "Gospel Shouters Hit Trail: Lillian Cumber Sets Up Major Booking Operation," *Billboard*, December 20, 1952, 19.

71. Ted Merriman, "African American Actors, Los Angeles, 1940s," UCLA Library Digital Collections, accessed February 12, 2025, https://digital.library.ucla.edu/catalog/ark:/21198/zz0025pcgp.

72. *Los Angeles Sentinel*, April 29, 1954.

73. *Chicago Defender*, July 28, 1945, 18, and 16, emphasis mine.

74. "Stars Galore In Los Angeles Club's Show," *Chicago Defender*, April 11, 1953.

75. *Chicago Defender*, August 6, 1956, 17.

76. The 1910 census records that Joe was nearly a year old on April 22, 1910. Jo Marie Langham Cooper's Affidavit of Heirship of Langham's property states that he was eighty-six years old on May 28, 1996, the year of Joe's death, which would indicate a birth year of 1910.

77. Affidavit of Heirship, Jo Marie Langham Cooper; Recordings of the Cook

County Clerk's Office, document 97654945, accessed April 7, 2025, https://crs.cookcountyclerkil.gov/Search.

78. Kay Norton, interview with Kenneth Woods Jr.

79. *Chicago Defender*, January 20, 1968, 18. JoMarie was a senior at Chicago Teachers College, while the groom was a student at Roosevelt University.

80. Affidavit of Heirship, JoMarie Langham Cooper.

81. Standifer, 29.

82. DjeDje, "Los Angeles Composers," 432–33.

Chapter 6. Gospel Stardom, Missions, and Civil Rights, 1960–1973

1. Woods expressed that thought to me in his home on March 7, 2023.

2. The Colored Methodist Episcopal denomination adopted the name Christian Methodist Episcopal Church, CMEC, in 1954.

3. *Chicago Defender*, January 18, 1969, 25.

4. *Chicago Defender*, March 6, 1971, 22; and March 13, 1971, 23.

5. Fundraising for a place for gospel education and short-term living began alongside the founding of the NCGCC; a first milestone of fundraising occurred prior to the death of Magnolia Lewis-Butts in 1949 (see chapter 2). By the time the facility finally opened in 1971, the NCGCC may not have been financially sound enough for its upkeep. No mention of the building appears in the *Defender* after 1971; at the time of this writing, it was an apartment complex.

6. For a history of these efforts, see Robert E. Weems, *Desegregating the Dollar*.

7. Letter from Kenneth Morris to Ira E. Harris, January 13, 1961, Martin and Morris Music Company Records, series 1, 2.

8. Kenneth Morris to Henry Mlady, January 24, 1964, Martin and Morris Music Company Records, series 1, 2.

9. Sporadically, she released music under the imprint of "Martin's House of Music (formerly Bowles)."

10. The MMMS inventory still contained songs by all these publishers and many others at the time of its closing in 1993. Martin and Morris Music Company Records, series 2, 14–22.

11. Robert M. Marovich, *Peace Be Still*.

12. Horace Clarence Boyer and Lloyd Yearwood, *The Golden Age of Gospel*, 247.

13. Birgitta Joelisa Johnson, "Oh, for a Thousand Tongues to Sing," 127.

14. Ibid., 137.

15. Gospel had so pervasive an influence on R&B and the music that followed it that even today, one scarcely hears a major artist in Broadway, country, hip hop, or rock whose backup vocal ensemble doesn't evoke gospel timbres. The Hammond B3 is nearly as ubiquitous. So named in 1949 and ascendant

in the 1950s, rhythm and blues borrowed freely from gospel in its formative stages.

16. Mark Burford, "Sam Cooke as Pop Album Artist."

17. Cleveland formed his own version of the NCGCC, the Gospel Music Workshop of America, in 1968.

18. Marovich, *Peace Be Still*, 46, and chapter 8.

19. Standifer, 23.

20. Robert M. Marovich, interview with Kenneth Woods Jr., A 22.

21. Della Reese was also a sometime member of the Brown Singers.

22. Marovich interview with Woods, B 12. Sallie Martin filled the role of music director for an educational and evangelical tour with Rev. Carole B. Priester (1916–2007) in 1953. Their itinerary included Columbus, Albany, and Savannah, Georgia; Georgia State University in Atlanta; and Tuskegee Institute. Priester was the Charleston-based evangelist and leader of the revival Woods mentioned. *Norfolk Journal and Guide,* January 9, 1954, A4.

23. Marovich interview with Woods, B 22.

24. An arranging contract with the company followed in 1965, during which time Woods created lead sheets for the likes of Andraé Crouch.

25. Gaines was well known for these unique talents; he is pictured with his saw on a jacket illustration of the LP *The Living Legend: Miss Sallie Martin and the Evangelical Choral Chapter* (Savoy, 1970).

26. The journey ended at Southampton, England. One-way fares in tourist class were $255 ($2,401 in 2023 dollars), while first-class tickets were $465 ($4,378). See the footer to "The Last Ocean Liners: Cunard Line," accessed February 17, 2024, https://lastoceanliners.com/line/cunard-line?1 =CUN#Queen +Elizabeth.

27. "1st Church Choir Embarks on European Concert Tour: Hold 'Bon Voyage' Musical Monday," *Chicago Defender*, May 21, 1966, 12.

28. *The Living Legend: Miss Sallie Martin and the Evangelical Choral Chapter.*

29. Luke 4:18 (New King James Version): "The Spirit of the Lord is upon Me,/Because He has anointed Me/To preach the gospel to the poor;/He has sent Me to heal the brokenhearted,/To proclaim liberty to the captives/And recovery of sight to the blind,/To set at liberty those who are oppressed." For a timeline of earliest Black American missionaries to Native Americans, Jamaica, and Africa, see Yale Divinity School Library, *Treasures of the Day Missions Library: Early African American Missionaries*, https://web.library.yale.edu/sites/default/files/files/divinity/Special%20Collections/AfricanAmericanMissionaries.pdf/.

30. Sandy Dwayne Martin, *Black Baptists and African Missions*, 65.

31. Sylvia M. Jacobs, "The Historical Role of Afro-Americans in American Missionary Efforts in Africa," 6.

32. For more on the history of US Black missions, see C. C. Adams and A. Marshall, *Negro Baptists and Foreign Missions.* The first white Baptist missionary to be sent to the African continent was Alfred Saker (1814–1880),

who traveled to Cameroon in 1848, just ten years after Great Britain freed its enslaved colonial subjects.

33. Kai Perry Parker, "Faith Without Hope," 239-ff. A controversial figure in Ethiopia, Selassie reigned from 1930 to 1974 and only ended his own practice of slavery in 1942. Austin's support of Selassie violated President Roosevelt's policy of nonintervention.

34. Parker argues that gospel was perceived on these occasions as the music of war, a tool representing resistance to European domination of African Christianity; "Faith Without Hope," 240.

35. *Chicago Defender*, November 23, 1935, 18, related in Parker, 240.

36. Martin's other place of worship, First Church of Deliverance, hosted Selassie's representative in October of 1940.

37. Adams and Marshall, *Negro Baptists and Foreign Missions*, 47. Pilgrim Baptist's missions team, including Sallie Martin, upheld the truth, if not the mischaracterization of women volunteers in that description.

38. "Expands Church Holdings in Africa Missions," *Chicago Defender*, May 3, 1958, 4.

39. One account states that Rev. Dr. Martin "established 37 Pilgrim Baptist churches in Edo/Delta States, 38 primary schools, a hospital and 3 technical schools in Issele-uku, Ofagbe, Uromi, a teacher Training College, (presently housing the NYSC orientation camp) and gave scholarships to so many indigenes of Issele-uku and other towns during his time"; Ifeanyi Okowa, related in "Rev. Dr. Martin: 42 Years After," *The Truth Newspaper*, accessed February 17, 2025, https://thetruthnewspaperonline.wordpress.com/2018/06/13/rev-dr-martin-42-years-after/. See also Isaac Ese Oghene Ekpon, "Martin, Samuel Wadiei," accessed February 17, 2025, *Dictionary of African Christian Biography*, https://dacb.org/stories/nigeria/martin-samuel.

40. "Plans Completed for Baptist Convention: Seek to Raise $15,000 during Mission Meet," *New York Amsterdam News*, September 4, 1948.

41. This refers to the area identified as the southwestern Pacific Theatre during World War II.

42. Quoted in Randall K. Burkett, "The Baptist Church in Years of Crisis: J. C. Austin and Pilgrim Baptist Church, 1926–1950," in Timothy E. Fulop and Albert J. Raboteau, eds., *African-American Religion*.

43. *Chicago Defender*, August 25, 1962, 10.

44. *Chicago Defender*, August 27, 1964, 11. Margaret Smith was the onetime National President of the Women's Department of the Progressive National Baptist Convention; president of the Baptist State Convention of Illinois; and Midwest field representative of the Baptist Foreign Mission Bureau, USA. She helped raise monies to build churches and schools in Africa and Haiti; page 112, Illinois Blue Book, 1981–1982, (Illinois Digital Archives), accessed February 17, 2025, http://www.idaillinois.org/digital/collection/bb/id/35514.

45. *Chicago Defender*, January 2, 1965, 15.

46. Ibid.

47. *Chicago Defender*, November 27, 1965, 12. On that day, Sallie Martin's church affiliation was listed as the First Church of Deliverance.

48. "Sallie Martin, rough cut number 1," interview with Bernice Johnson Reagon.

49. *Chicago Defender*, July 25, 1970, 24.

50. Because US firms were the Italian military's major oil supplier, whites at first sided with Mussolini, whose air force put on a thrilling display for the 1933 Century of Progress Exhibition in Chicago; Parker, *Faith Without Hope*, 240. See also "Italian Pavilion," Chicagology, accessed February 17, 2025, https://chicagology.com/centuryprogress/1933fair51; and this volume, chapter 2.

51. The controversial rupture of the NBC involved a lawsuit brought by, among others, Martin Luther King Jr. and Ralph David Abernathy Sr. At least one fatality occurred as factions fought to gain the podium at the 1961 annual Convention.

52. PBNC, "History of PNBC."

53. Laurraine Goreau, "Interview with Sallie Martin," B 2.

54. *Chicago Defender*, May 2, 1966, 8.

55. Al Rutledge, "The Root of All Soul," (Baltimore) *Afro-American*, July 20, 1968.

56. Bernice Johnson Reagon, "Music in the Civil Rights Movement," in *Eyes on the Prize*.

57. Standifer, 25.

58. Marovich, interview with Woods, B 8.

59. *Chicago Defender*, January 18, 1969.

60. Lucille Younger, "8,000 Bid Mahalia Farwell," *Chicago Defender*, February 2, 1972. Campbell's name does not appear on the program.

61. Order of Service, courtesy Tobias Green; in answer to my query, he uploaded it to Facebook through The Gospel Music History Group. Goreau, "Interview," 15–16.

62. Ibid., 16.

Chapter 7. Retirement, Legacy, and Conclusions

1. Laurraine Goreau, "Interview with Sallie Martin," 9.

2. Anthony Heilbut, *The Gospel Sound*, 4.

3. Standifer, 18.

4. Wes Smith, "Friends Sing Praises of Gospel 'Queen' at 90," *Chicago Tribune*, November 25, 1985, 1.

5. Standifer, 30.

6. *Cleveland Post and Call*, September 6, 1975. Martin also sang at the Prestonians' 32-year anniversary; *Post and Call*, August 5, 1981, 6A.

7. *Variety*, July 2, 1975, 61.

8. *Chicago Defender*, July 12, 1975.

9. Virgie W. Murray, "Gospel Tribute Slated at Forum," *Los Angeles Sentinel*,

Dec. 11, 1975, C8, with photo of Sallie Martin. The event took place on December 18, 1975.

10. Standifer, 30.

11. Quoted in liner notes, page 6, of *Gospel Caravan*, CD, Auvidis A 6128 (1988). This was a live recording of opening night at Théatre de Paris, Feb. 22–23, 1979. Concept produced by Jerry Wilson and Maurice Dumay.

12. Standifer, 31.

13. Edwin Hawkins and the Music & Arts Seminar Mass Choir, *Angels Will Be Singing*, LP, Birthright BRS 4045 (1984).

14. Kay Norton, interview with Anthony Heilbut, December 14, 2015.

15. Smith, "Friends Sing Praises of Gospel 'Queen' at 90." Operation PUSH (People United to Serve Humanity) replaced Operation Breadbasket when Jesse Jackson broke with the Southern Christian Leadership Conference in 1971. Operation PUSH flourished in the Hyde Park neighborhood of Chicago until about 1980.

16. Virgie M. Murray, editor, "Sallie Martin Feted on 90th," *Los Angeles Sentinel*, November 28, 1985, C8.

17. *Billboard*, March 21, 1987, 54. Reportedly, Gregory Scott Cooper was among the many closeted gay men in the gospel industry to fall victim to AIDS. His mentee relationship with James Cleveland is mentioned in Rhonda Graham, "And the Choir Sings On," *Sunday News Journal* (Wilmington, DE), October 23, 1994, reprinted at Blackstripe, May 25, 1995, http://www.qrd.org/qrd/www/culture/black/articles/gospel.html.

18. F. Finley McRae, "Sallie Martin, 2-Day Funeral Rites Held for Gospel Great," *Los Angeles Sentinel*, July 14, 1988, A1 and A10.

19. Lawrence Bommer, special to the *Chicago Tribune*, January 16, 1996, "Grande Dames Black Ensemble Salutes Gospel's Stalwart Women." Bommer wrote, "Most memorable is deep-voiced Shirley Wahls, whose Sallie Martin seems a reincarnation" (that is, Wahls's performance as Sallie Martin was exceptionally persuasive).

20. Judith Newmark, Theatre Critic, "Strong Cast Enhances Play about Gospel Greats," *St. Louis Post-Dispatch*, February 23, 1999, D3.

21. Horace Clarence Boyer, *The Golden Age of Gospel*, 63.

22. Martin paid off that loan on May 5, 1973. These and all other real estate records mentioned here were obtained from the Cook County Recorder on July 10, 2023. The Los Angeles County Recorder found no real estate listed in her name; the residence at 4134 Degnan Boulevard, from which she wrote Kenneth Morris in 1956, must either have been a rental or belonged to Joe Langham, whom she had recently married (see chapter 5).

23. Standifer, 28.

24. "Church History," *First Church of Deliverance*, accessed February 19, 2025, https://fcdchicago.org/church-history.

25. Norton, interview with Heilbut.

26. The Simmons-Akers trio toured extensively and was invited to perform

at the National Baptist Convention when it convened in Los Angeles in 1949. Around 1950, Hawkins left the group. Personnel in late 1954 included Christine Kittrell and Ruth Black, making a quartet. One iteration of the group included Helen Henderson.

27. Standifer, 22.

28. Alex Bradford, quoted in Heilbut, *The Gospel Sound*, 152–53.

29. Heilbut's thesis is more broadly discussed in his book *The Fan Who Knew Too Much*.

30. Graham, "And the Choir Sings On."

31. Quoted in Willa Ward-Royster, *How I Got Over*, 191.

32. Dorsey, quoted in Michael W. Harris, *The Rise of Gospel Blues*, 257.

33. Standifer, 21.

34. Ibid.

35. Martin-Moore, quoted in an interview, in Jacqueline Cogdell DjeDje, "Los Angeles Composers of African American Gospel Music," 427.

36. David Silverman, "Singer's Legacy Glitters at City Gospel Festival: Sallie Martin Still Reigns as Queen," obituary, *Chicago Tribune*, June 20, 1988, 7.

Bibliography

Archival Newspapers

Alabama Tribune (Montgomery)
Atlanta Daily World
California Eagle
Chicago Defender
Chicago Tribune
Cleveland Call and Post
Indianapolis Recorder
Kansas City Star
Lexington (KY) Herald-Leader
Los Angeles Sentinel
Los Angeles Times
New York Age
New York Amsterdam News
Norfolk Journal and Guide
Northwest Enterprise (Seattle, WA)
Pittsburgh Courier
Shreveport (LA) Journal
St. Louis Argus
St. Louis Post-Dispatch
St. Paul (MN) Recorder
Washington Afro American

Other Archival or Historical Sources

Adams, C. C., and A. Marshall. *Negro Baptists and Foreign Missions*. Foreign Mission Board of the NBC—USA, Inc., 1944.

African American Living Legends Program Photos. A. C. Bilbrew Library, Los Angeles County Library.

Archives, Center for Black Music Research, Columbia College, Chicago.

Bureau of the Census. *Religious Bodies: 1906 (Part I)*. Washington, DC: Government Printing Office, 1910. Documenting the American South. https://docsouth.unc.edu/church/census/census.html.

——. *Religious Bodies: 1916 (Part I)*. Washington, DC: Government Printing Office, 1919. https://catalog.hathitrust.org/Record/001408065.

Cook County Recorder, Chicago. https://www.cookcountyclerkil.gov/recordings.

Dolinar, Brian (ed.). *The Negro in Illinois: The WPA Papers*. Urbana: University of Illinois Press, 2013.

Ebenezer Missionary Baptist Church Archives. Chicago Public Library.

Estate of Austin Hansen.

Frederick Douglas Haynes Family Papers. Online Archive of California. California Historical Society.

Goreau, Laurraine. "Interview with Sallie Martin." November 4, 1972. Laurraine Goreau Collection, audio files and transcription (LG001), side A (1–19), and side B (1–4). Tulane University Special Collections. Tulane University, New Orleans, LA.

Gospel Pearls. Edited by Willa A. Townsend. Sunday School Publishing Board, National Baptist Convention of America, 1921.

Illinois Writers' Project. "Negro in Illinois. Carter G. Woodson, Chicago, IL."

Lightner, Gwendolyn Cooper. Gospel in Los Angeles Lecture Series. Jacqueline Cogdell DjeDje, creator. March 2, 1989. The Internet Archive, University of California-Los Angeles Ethnomusicology Archive. https://archive.org/details/calauem_000060.

Los Angeles County Recorder. https://www.lavote.gov/home/recorder.

Luvenia George Collection. Archives of African American Music and Culture. Indiana University Archives Online.

Marovich, Robert M. Interviews with Kenneth Woods Jr. Robert M. Marovich Collection. Archives of African American Music and Culture. Indiana University, Bloomington.

Martin and Morris Music Company Papers. Chicago Public Library. Accessed February 12, 2025. https://www.chipublib.org/fa-martin-and-morris-music-company-papers/.

Martin and Morris Music Company Records. Archives Center, National Museum of American History, Smithsonian Institution. https://americanhistory.si.edu/collections/ac-collection/sova-nmah-ac-0492.

Norton, Kay. Phone interview with Anthony Heilbut. December 14, 2015.

——. Interview with Kenneth Woods Jr., March 7, 2023.

Rice, Thaddeus Brockett. *History of Greene County Georgia, 1786–1886,* edited by Carolyn White Williams. Macon, GA: J. W. Burke Company, 1961.

Rutledge, Al. "The Root of All Soul." *Afro-American* (Baltimore, MD), July

20, 1968. https://www.proquest.com/historical-newspapers/root-all-soul/docview/532195708/se-2.

Slave Laws of Georgia, 1755–1860. A slideshow by the Board of Regents of the University System of Georgia. Georgia Archives. https://www.georgiaarchives.org/assets/documents/Slave_Laws_of_Georgia_1755-1860.pdf.

Smallwood, Eugene. "Gospel in Los Angeles." October 24, 1991. Part of a lecture series organized by Jacqueline Cogdell DjeDje, University of California—Los Angeles Ethnomusicology Archive. California Revealed. https://californiarevealed.org/do/62ab47f6-6f01-4035-9928-46eb62c34f94.

Smithsonian Online Virtual Archives. Archives Center, National Museum of American History. Access through https://sova.si.edu/.

Standifer, James. "Interview with Sallie Martin," September 19, 1981. Transcript, 1–33, formerly available at the African American Music Collection of the University of Michigan. Courtesy Robert M. Marovich.

Treasures of the Day Missions Library: Early African American Missionaries. Yale University Library online. https://web.library.yale.edu/sites/default/files/files/divinity/Special%20Collections/AfricanAmericanMissionaries.pdf.

University of Southern California Digital Library, Gospel Music History Archive.

Weston, Dave. "Gospel in Los Angeles." Guest lecture on Music of African-Americans, organized by Jacqueline Cogdell DjeDje. November 21, 1991. Internet Archive. University of California—Los Angeles Ethnomusicology Archive. https://archive.org/details/calauem_000086 .

Magazines, Non-Archival News Sources, and Websites

Billboard.

Cabello, Tristan. "Queer Bronzeville, 1900–1985: The History of African American Gays and Lesbians on Chicago's South Side." Accessed February 4, 2025. https://outhistory.org/exhibits/show/queer-bronzeville.

Cummings, Tony. "Prof. James Earle Hines & The St Paul Church Choir Of Los Angeles: Gospel Roots." *Cross Rhythms*, April 24, 2009. https://www.crossrhythms.co.uk/articles/music/Prof_James_Earle_Hines__The_St_Paul_Church_Choir_Of_Los_Angeles_Gospel_Roots_/35703/p1/.

Progressive National Baptist Convention (PNBC). "History of PNBC." Accessed February 4, 2025. https://pnbc.org/content/history-of-the-pnbc/.

"Rev. Dr. [S. W.] Martin: 42 Years After." *The Truth Newspaper*. Accessed February 4, 2025. https://thetruthnewspaperonline.wordpress.com/2018/06/13/rev-dr-martin-42-years-after/.

Rolling Stone.

Shearer, Lee. "Lynching Report Recalls Grim History, Some of It in Athens Area." *Online Athens* (Georgia). March 11, 2015. https://www.onlineathens

.com/story/news/local/2015/03/12/lynching-report-recalls-grim-history-some-it-athens-area/15500475007/.
Sunday News Journal (Wilmington, DE).
Variety.
Washington Post.

Books, Articles, Dissertations, and Papers

Abbott, Lynn, and Doug Seroff. *To Do This, You Must Know How: Music Pedagogy in the Black Gospel Quartet Tradition*. Jackson: University Press of Mississippi, 2013.

Barney, Deborah Verdice Smith. "The Gospel Announcer and the Black Gospel Music Tradition." PhD diss., Michigan State University, 1994.

Berry, Daina Ramey. *Swing the Sickle, for the Harvest is Ripe: Gender and Slavery in Antebellum Georgia*. Urbana: University of Illinois Press, 2007.

Best, Wallace. *Passionately Human, No Less Divine: Religion and Culture in Black Chicago, 1915–1952*. Princeton, NJ: Princeton University Press, 2005.

Boyer, Horace Clarence. "Kenneth Morris: Composer and Dean of Black Gospel Music Publishers." In *We'll Understand It Better By and By: Pioneering African American Gospel Composers,* edited by Bernice Johnson Reagon. Washington, DC: Smithsonian Press, 1992.

——. "Lucie E. Campbell: Composer for the National Baptist Convention." In *We'll Understand It By and By*.

——. "Roberta Martin: Innovator of Modern Gospel Music." In *We'll Understand It By and By*.

Boyer, Horace Clarence, and Lloyd Yearwood. *The Golden Age of Gospel*. Urbana: University of Illinois Press, 2000.

Brown, Rae Linda. *The Heart of a Woman: The Life and Music of Florence B. Price,* edited by Guthrie P. Ramsey Jr. Urbana: University of Illinois Press, 2020.

Bryant, Jonathan M. *How Curious a Land: Conflict and Change in Greene County, Georgia, 1850–1885*. Chapel Hill: University of North Carolina Press, 1996.

——. "'My Soul An't Yours, Mas'r': The Records of the African Church at Penfield, 1848–1863." *Georgia Historical Quarterly* 75, no. 2 (Summer 1991): 401–12.

Burford, Mark. "Black and White, then 'Red' All Over: Chicago's American Negro Music Festival." *American Music Review* 44, no. 2 (Spring 2015): 1–6.

——. *Mahalia Jackson and the Black Gospel Field*. New York: Oxford University Press, 2019.

——. "Sam Cooke as Pop Album Artist—A Reinvention in Three Songs." *Journal of the American Musicological Society* 65, no. 1 (Spring 2012): 113–78, 298.

Carson, Clayborne, Ralph E. Lucker, and Penny A. Russell, eds. *Called to Serve*. Volume 1 in the Papers of Martin Luther King, Jr., January 1929–September 1951. University of California Press, 1992.

Chatters, Linda M., Robert Joseph Taylor, and Rukmalie Jayakodie. "Fictive Kinship Relations in Black Extended Families." *Journal of Comparative Family Studies* 25, no. 3 (1994): 297–312. https://www.jstor.org/stable/41602341.

Collins, Patricia Hill. "What's in a Name? Womanism, Black Feminism, and Beyond." *Black Scholar* 26, no. 1 (1996): 9–17.

Cusic, Don. "How I Got Over: Clara Ward and the Ward Singers, 1950." Library of Congress. https://www.loc.gov/static/programs/national-recording-preservation-board/documents/HowIGotOver.pdf.

Dargan, William Thomas, and Kathy White Bullock. "Willie Mae Ford Smith of St. Louis: A Shaping Influence upon Black Gospel Singing Style." *Black Music Research Journal* 9, no. 2 (Autumn 1989): 249–70. https://doi.org/10.2307/779426.

DjeDje, Jacqueline Cogdell. "A Historical Overview of Black Gospel Music in Los Angeles." *Black Music Research Bulletin* 10, no. 1 (Spring 1988): 1–5.

———. "Gospel Music in the Los Angeles Black Community: A Historical Overview." *Black Music Research Journal* (1989): 35–79.

———. "Los Angeles Composers of African American Gospel Music: The First Generations." *American Music* (1993): 412–57.

———, and Eddie S. Meadows. *California Soul: Music of African Americans in the West*. Berkeley: University of California Press, 1998. https://doi.org/10.1525/9780520918146.

Du Bois, W. E. B. *The Souls of Black Folk*. Reprinted from the version published by A. C. McClurg & Co. (Chicago), 1903. N.p.: Dover Publications, 1994.

Eidsheim, Nina Sun. *The Race of Sound: Listening, Timbre, & Vocality in African American Music*. Durham, NC: Duke University Press, 2019.

Floyd, Samuel A., Jr. "Ring Shout! Literary Studies, Historical Studies, and Black Music Inquiry." *Black Music Research Journal* 11, no. 2 (1991; repr. Supplement 2002): 49–70.

Fulop, Timothy E., and Albert J. Raboteau, eds. *African-American Religion: Interpretive Essays in History and Culture*. New York: Routledge, 1997.

Gardner, Robert G., Charles O. Walker, J. R. Huddlestun, and Waldo P. Harris III. *A History of the Georgia Baptist Association, 1784–1984*. Atlanta: Georgia Baptist Historical Society, 1988.

George, Luvenia A. "Lucie E. Campbell: Her Nurturing and Expansion of Gospel Music in the National Baptist Convention, USA, Inc." In *We'll Understand It Better By and By: Pioneering African American Gospel Composers*, edited by Bernice Johnson Reagon. Washington, DC: Smithsonian Press, 1992.

Goreau, Laurraine. *Just Mahalia, Baby*. Waco, TX: Word Books, 1975.

Graham, Rhonda. "Special Report: And the Choir Sings On." Reprint of an article that first appeared Oct. 23, 1994, in the *Sunday News Journal* (Wilmington, DE). The Blackstripe. Accessed February 5, 2025. http://www.qrd.org/qrd/www/culture/black/articles/gospel.html.

Graham, Sandra. "On the Road to Freedom: The Contracts of the Fisk Jubilee Singers." *American Music* 24, no. 1 (Spring 2006): 1–29. https://doi.org/10.2307/25046002.

Haller, Mark H. "Policy Gambling, Entertainment, and the Emergence of Black Politics: Chicago from 1900 to 1940." *Journal of Social History* 24, no. 4 (Summer 1991): 719–39.

Halstoos, Brian. "Pageant and Passion: Willa Saunders Jones and Early Black Sacred Drama in Chicago." *Journal of American Drama and Theatre* 19, no. 2 (Spring 2007): 77–97.

Harris, Michael W. *The Rise of Gospel Blues: The Music of Thomas Andrew Dorsey in the Urban Church*. New York: Oxford University Press, 1992.

Harvey, Paul. *Redeeming the South: Religious Cultures and Racial Identities among Southern Baptists, 1865–1925*. Chapel Hill: University of North Carolina Press, 1997.

Heilbut, Anthony. *The Fan Who Knew Too Much: Aretha Franklin, the Rise of the Soap Opera, Children of the Gospel Church, and Other Meditations*. New York: Alfred A. Knopf, 2012.

——. *The Gospel Sound: Good News and Bad Times*. Updated and revised edition. New York: Limelight Editions, 1997.

Higginbotham, Evelyn Brooks. *Righteous Discontent: The Women's Movement in the Black Baptist Church, 1880–1920*. Cambridge, MA: Harvard University Press, 1993.

Hunter, Tera W. *To 'Joy My Freedom: Southern Black Women's Lives and Labors after the Civil War*. Cambridge, MA: Harvard University Press, 1997.

Jackson, Irene V. "Afro-American Gospel Music and Its Social Setting: With Special Attention to Roberta Martin." PhD diss., Wesleyan University, 1974.

Jackson, Jerma A. *Singing in My Soul: Black Gospel Music in a Secular Age*. Chapel Hill: University of North Carolina Press, 2004.

——. "Testifying at the Cross: Thomas Andrew Dorsey, Sister Rosetta Tharpe, and the Politics of African-American Sacred and Secular Music." PhD diss., Rutgers University, 1995.

Jacobs, Sylvia M. "The Historical Role of Afro-Americans in American Missionary Efforts in Africa." In *Black Americans and the Missionary Movement in Africa*, edited by Sylvia M. Jacobs. Westport, CT: Greenwood Press, 1982.

Johnson, Birgitta J. "Church of God in Christ, Inc." (COGIC). *Grove Music Online*. Published October 16, 2013. Accessed February 5, 2025. https://www.oxfordmusiconline.com/grovemusic/view/10.1093/gmo/9781561592630.001.0001/omo-9781561592630-e-1002248894.

Johnson, Birgitta Joelisa. "'Oh, for a Thousand Tongues to Sing': Music and Worship in African American Megachurches of Los Angeles, California." PhD diss., University of California-Los Angeles, 2008.

Johnson, Idella Lulamae. "Development of African American Gospel Piano Style (1926–1960): A Socio-Musical Analysis of Arizona Dranes and Thomas A. Dorsey." PhD diss., University of Pittsburgh, 2009.

Karnes, Miller Handley. "Law, Labor, and Land in the Postbellum Cotton South: The Peonage Cases in Oglethorpe County, Georgia, 1865–1940." PhD diss., University of Ilinois at Urbana-Champaign, 2000.

Kernodle, Tammy L. "Black Women Working Together: Jazz, Gender, and the Politics of Validation." *Black Music Research Journal* 34, no. 1 (Spring 2014): 27–55.

———. "Work the Works: The Role of African-American Women in the Development of Contemporary Gospel." *Black Music Research Journal* 26, no. 1 (Spring 2006): 89–109.

Kuhn, Clifford M., Harlon E. Joye, and E. Bernard West. *Living Atlanta: An Oral History of the City, 1914–1948*. Atlanta Historical Society and University of Georgia Press, 1990.

Locke, Alain, and Winold Reiss. *The New Negro*. New York: Albert and Charles Boni, 1925.

Marovich, Robert M. *A City Called Heaven: Chicago and the Birth of Gospel Music*. Urbana: University of Illinois Press, 2015.

———. *Peace Be Still: How James Cleveland and the Angelic Choir Created a Gospel Classic*. Urbana: University of Illinois Press, 2021.

———. "Pseudonyms and Session Men: Blurring the Boundaries between Sacred and Secular." *Gospel Roots of Rock and Roll*, July 23, 2018. http://xpngospelroots.org/pseudonyms-and-session-men-blurring-the-boundaries-between-sacred-and-secular-by-robert-m-marovich/.

———. "Sing a New Song," *Chicago History* (Winter 2017): 24–39.

Martin, Sandy Dwayne. *Black Baptists and African Missions: The Origins of a Movement, 1880–1915*. Macon, GA: Mercer University Press, 1989.

McNeil, W. K., ed. *Encyclopedia of American Gospel Music*. New York: Taylor and Francis, 2010.

Minako, Waseda. "Gospel Music in Japan: Transplantation and Localization of African American Religious Singing." *Yearbook for Traditional Music* 45 (2013): 187–213.

Nance, Susan. "Mystery of the Moorish Science Temple: Southern Blacks and American Alternative Spirituality in 1920s Chicago." *Religion and American Culture: A Journal of Interpretation* 12, no. 2 (2002): 123–66.

Norton, Kay. *Baptist Offspring, Southern Midwife: Jesse Mercer's Cluster of Spiritual Songs, 1810*. Warren, MI: Harmonie Park Press, 2002.

———. "The Pedagogical Legacies of Three Black Gospel Pioneers: Magnolia Lewis-Butts, Sallie Martin, and Roberta Martin." In *Legacies of Power in American Music: Essays in Honor of Michael J. Budds*, edited by Judith A. Mabary. New York: Routledge, 2023.

———. "Yes, Gospel Is Real: Half a Century with Chicago's Martin and Morris Company." *Journal of the Society for American Music* 11, no. 4 (2017): 420–51.

O'Toole, Thomas James. "Shadows of the Cross: Barack Obama, Clerical Politics, and Gay Rights Compartmentalization in the Black Church." PhD diss., Cornell University, 2016.

Parker, Kai Perry. "Faith Without Hope: Black Protestants, Chicago, and the Critique of Progress, 1914–1968." PhD Diss., University of Chicago, 2019.

Pollard, Deborah Smith. "That Text, That Timbre: Introducing Gospel

Announcer Edna Tatum." In *Black Women and Music: More Than the Blues*, edited by Eileen M. Hayes and Linda F. Williams. Urbana: University of Illinois Press, 2007.

Reagon, Bernice Johnson. "Kenneth Morris: 'I'll Be a Servant for the Lord.'" In *We'll Understand It Better By and By: Pioneering African American Gospel Composers*, edited by Bernice Johnson Reagon. Washington, DC: Smithsonian Press, 1992.

——. "Music in the Civil Rights Movement." From an interview by Maria Daniel, July 2006, WGBH-Boston. In *Eyes on the Prize: America's Civil Rights Movement*. Accessed February 5, 2025. https://www.pbs.org/wgbh/americanexperience/features/eyesontheprize-music-civil-rights-movement.

——, ed. *We'll Understand It Better By and By: Pioneering African American Gospel Composers*. Washington, DC: Smithsonian Press, 1992.

Reed, Roxanne Regina. "Preaching and Piety: The Politics of Women's Voice in African-American Gospel Music with Special Attention to Gospel Music Pioneer Lucie E. Campbell." PhD diss., University of Wisconsin-Madison, 2003.

Rucker, Walter C., and Sabriya Kaleen Jubilee. "From Black Nadir to Brown v. Board: Education and Empowerment in Black Georgian Communities, 1865 to 1954." *Negro Educational Review* 58, no. 3–4 (Jan. 2007): 1–18.

Thomas, Jesse O. *Negro Participation in the Texas Centennial Exposition*. Boston: Christopher Publishing House, 1938.

Treitler, Leo. "Gender and Other Dualities in Music History." In *Musicology and Difference: Gender and Sexuality in Music Scholarship*, edited by Ruth A. Solie. Berkeley: University of California Press, 1993.

Walker, Charles. "Lucie E. Campbell Williams: A Cultural Biography." In *We'll Understand It Better By and By: Pioneering African American Gospel Composers*, edited by Bernice Johnson Reagon. Washington, DC: Smithsonian Press, 1992.

Walker, Juliet E. K. *The History of Black Business in America*. New York: Macmillan, 1998.

Ward-Royster, Willa, as told to Toni Rose, with a foreword by Horace Clarence Boyer. *How I Got Over: Clara Ward and the World Famous Ward Singers*. Philadelphia: Temple University Press, 1997.

Weems, Robert E. *Desegregating the Dollar: African American Consumerism in the Twentieth Century*. New York: New York University Press, 1998.

Williams-Jones, Pearl, and Bernice Johnson Reagon, eds. "Conversations: Roberta Martin Singers Roundtable." In *We'll Understand It Better By and By: Pioneering African American Gospel Composers*, edited by Bernice Johnson Reagon. Washington, DC: Smithsonian Press, 1992.

Audio and Video Recordings (see Discography for music recordings)

Boyer, Horace Clarence. Interviewed and appeared in *This Far by Faith: African-American Spiritual Journeys*, Episode 3, "Guide My Feet." Produced, directed, and written by Lulie Haddad. Video. Aired on PBS, 2003. Transcript for download at https://www.pbs.org/thisfarbyfaith/about/episode_3.html.

Downs, Hugh. Interview with Gertrude Ward. "Over Easy," 1977. Video. https://www.youtube.com/watch?v=9sEHVFSDiDE. No longer available online.

Gospel Caravan (revue). Live recording of opening night at Théatre de Paris, February 22–23, 1979. Concept Jerry Wilson and Maurice Dumay. Audio recording. Paris: Auvidis, 1979 (LP); 1988 (CD).

Hawkins, Edwin, and the Music and Arts Seminar Mass Choir. *Angels Will Be Singing*. Birthright BRS-4045, 1984. Audio. Los Angeles: Word, 1984.

Hildebrand, Lee. Liner notes. *The Sallie Martin Singers: Gospel Twofer, "Precious Lord" & "God Is Here."* Vee-Jay reissue, 1993, NVG2-606.

——, and Opal Nations (reissue prod.). Liner notes. *Thunderbolt of the Middle West* (Brother Joe May), Specialty reissue, 1992.

Jubilee Showcase. Directed by George Paul, producer Sid Ordower. With Sallie Martin and Her Singers of Joy. Recorded April 26, 1964 and March 1, 1964. "Keep in Touch with Jesus," "There's No Friend Like the Lonely Jesus." WLS/ABC Television show, Chicago. 13-JS-64 and 13-JS-64 revised.

The Living Legend: Miss Sallie Martin and the Evangelical Choral Chapter. LP. Savoy Records, 1970.

NGCGG Convention. Philadelphia. "God Put a Rainbow in the Sky," "There's Not a Friend Like the Lowly Jesus." 1985. Private video on YouTube.

Reagon, Bernice Johnson, Pearl Williams-Jones, and Lisa Pertillar Brevard. "Lucie Campbell: Gospel's First African American Woman Composer." *Wade in the Water: African American Sacred Music Traditions*, episode 14. Radio series produced by National Public Radio and the Smithsonian Institution, 1994. https://www.npr.org/series/726103231/wade-in-the-water/.

Sallie and Cora Martin: Just a Little Talk with Jesus. Stockholm: Gospel Friend Records, 2014. Audio CD. Liner Notes by Robert Marovich. Audio.

"Sallie Martin, rough cut number 1." With Bernice Johnson Reagon. Undated video. Box 308, Video 4, Program in African American Culture Collection. Archives Center, National Museum of American History, Smithsonian Institution. Transcription by Kay Norton.

Say Amen, Somebody! Directed by George T. Nierenberg; photography by Ed Lachman and Don Lenzer; edited by Paul Barnes; produced by Mr. Nierenberg and Karen Nierenberg; a GTN Production. 1981, remastered 1982. Video.

Spoken Introduction. *Professor Thomas Andrew Dorsey: The Maestro Sings His Masterpieces*. Detroit: The Sound of Gospel Records, 1980. Audio LP.

Time for Religion. Directed by Thomas A. Dorsey. "The Little Wooden Church on the Hill," July 20 and 27, 1960. Video. WTTWTV series, Chicago.

TV Gospel Time. "Wonderful Jesus," Sallie Martin with youth choir, 1962. Video. NBC's variety program, Washington, DC.

Index

Index of Song Titles

KAY NORTON is a Professor of Musicology in the School of Music, Dance and Theatre at Arizona State University.

The University of Illinois Press
is a founding member of the
Association of University Presses.

Composed in 10.5/13 Mercury Text
with Caecilia display
by Jim Proefrock
at the University of Illinois Press
Manufactured by Sheridan Books, Inc.

University of Illinois Press
1325 South Oak Street
Champaign, IL 61820-6903
www.press.uillinois.edu